Learning Through Writing

Learning Through Writing:
Stages of Growth in English

Bernard T. Harrison

NFER-Nelson

Published by The NFER-Nelson Publishing Company Ltd.,
Darville House, 2 Oxford Road East,
Windsor, Berks. SL4 1DF.

First Published 1983
© Bernard T. Harrison, 1983
ISBN 0-7005-0532-6
Code No. 8138 02 1

Typeset by Cambrian Typesetters,
Farnborough, Hants

Distributed in the USA by Humanities Press Inc.,
Atlantic Highlands, New Jersey 07716 USA

Contents

Acknowledgements

Chapter One
  English as Encounter: efforts towards meaning   1

Chapter Two
  The School, the Group and the Teaching   26

Chapter Three
  Stages in Writing Growth and a Case Study   39

Chapter Four
  Telling   59

Chapter Five
  Reflecting   84

Chapter Six
  Identifying   107

Chapter Seven
  Organizing   128

Chapter Eight
  Integrating   150

Bibliography   170

To Sandie, for Lawrence and his fellow inheritors

In a sense, I have been writing this all my life. The roots go a long way down; growth has at times been retarded by frosts and storms of circumstance. But in an unobtrusive corner of the mind, the idea has been growing very slowly and steadily . . .

Ian Suttie, *The Origins of Love and Hate*, 1935

Acknowledgements

Acknowledgement is offered with gratitude to my students and my teachers, past and present, for their good co-labour. In particular, I thank my brother Peter, who first enabled the self-belief to write these chapters; Paddy Creber, who gave me both space and guidance in their telling; and all the students whose writings have provided the foundations for this book.

Acknowledgements

CHAPTER ONE

English as Encounter: efforts towards meaning

the being of language;
the language of being

(Martin Heidegger)

This book is about English studies in schools; in particular it is concerned with the exacting task of writing, that pupils face from day to day in English lessons. Its chapters are based on the written work of a group of older secondary school students, aged from fourteen to seventeen, who were members of the same 'mixed ability' group for three years in an urban comprehensive school.

Any teacher who wishes to convey some sense of the truth of 'the way it was' in an actual classroom is faced with a number of sharp choices about what to include, how to order, how to present and so on, from the abundance of events of just one classroom lesson. This book has elected to dwell largely, but not exclusively, on the writing of older pupils; yet in choosing to look in particular at the writing of learners, it would be wrong to suppress the interdependence of learning with teaching; or of writing with talking, listening, reading and dramatic activity. It is promised, then, that the writing examples will not be split off from other important aspects of English work.

The chapters of this book constitute, in essence, an educational report. As such, the reader will reasonably expect to find some clarity in its planning and argument; yet if it aims to win genuine, full attention from its readers, it cannot afford to be a narrowly, 'transactionally' specialist report. It must have something at least of the novelist's desire to show, to generate personal recognition from the reader. Just as important as the teacher's disposition to organize, project and make an impact is the learner's capacity to wonder, to move and feel around, internalize, and then to narrate, to tell 'how it was'. As far as this aspect of the book is concerned, a good test for it would be to ascertain whether it might be read with enjoyment and profit by someone who has nothing to do with professional teaching, yet who finds that it has something to say about *all* human learning and teaching activities. For any eventual 'uses' that these chapters may have will depend a good deal on whether the accounts given of learning and teaching are felt, in terms of the reader's ordinary human experience, to be authentic. The work is offered, then, in this spirit: 'let us see if visualizing like this — which you may recognize as the way I have truly seen and understood it — helps towards a clearer vision of what happens typically to someone who is engaged in an act of learning'. The reader is invited to engage in critical (and, at times, literary-critical) discussion on experiences that concern us all, specialist and non-specialist alike. No better response than this can be imagined or expected, for there are no certain statements that can be made about the mind's processes, about the nature of learning and meaning. Acknowledging this truth, Peter Lomas has said of his own recent work that 'The reader who is looking for certainty should put this book down now. The dangers of uncertainty are many . . . It may encourage a smug and naive reliance on ones spontaneous intuitive reactions . . . But that is a risk we have to take unless we deny the enigma of life'. (*The Case for a Personal Psychotherapy*, 1981)

The study of pupils' writing on which this book is based came to identify what might be regarded as five broadly familiar, normal stages of growth in writing response among the individuals concerned. Each of these stages is explored and illustrated in successive chapters (Four to Eight). The stages (which are introduced and outlined in Chapter Three) depict a pattern of development, as revealed through the writing of the pupils involved, given an approach to teaching which kept close ties with poetry, fiction and drama in English studies; and given a correspondingly active interest in the learners' own experience of their world and themselves. These stages are offered as a kind of distillation of processes observed in the writings of one classroom over three years, with the invitation urged on the reader, to check them for whatever general truth they may hold, against his or her own experience of the 'way it is', in human learning.

Each chapter illustrates, then, stages of being and becoming through the writing-art of learners. As such, the book does not claim to offer a direct contribution to English teaching method. On the other hand, it is hoped that the attention given to the writing of pupils in the most vulnerable and difficult years of adolescence will offer some kind of contribution to the debate which has begun on the radical changes of attitude and provision that are needed for this critical phase of schooling. The stages of development through writing that will be described are seen as stages in growth to *meaning* — stages which are served, ideally, by all the acts of language and learning in good English work.

Teachers, inspectors, teacher-trainers and advisers are agreed that such a debate is long overdue. The existing sixteen-plus external examination system has much to answer for here; but if there are to be changes they will be brought about in the main by a shift of imaginative vision among teachers and parents, concerning the possibilities of learning and teaching at this level. The pressures in the fourth and fifth years against creative work throughout the curriculum have been described in the survey of secondary schools in the late seventies by H.M. Inspectors (*Aspects of Secondary Education in England,* 1979); as for English Studies in particular, it is notable that the Schools Council's English Committee proposed in its policy statement *English in the 1980's* (1979) to turn its attention to what is happening in the 13–16 age range. More substantially, the Report by the Calouste Gulbenkian Foundation, *The Arts in Schools* (1982) has presented the case for a thorough revision of the curriculum at this level, with more ample provision of arts learning and activity. The impetus begun here by national bodies will need all the support that is possible from schools and local authorities, in order to restore a respect for personal and creative learning at this level. It was clear, for instance, on the evidence of the ten per cent sample survey by H.M. Inspectors of all maintained secondary schools in England and Wales, that the quality of teaching in the fourth and fifth years of the secondary school is adversely affected by the drive towards examination success. The same pattern occurs in English Studies as elsewhere in the curriculum: too many long monologues from the teachers; too much reliance on dictated or duplicated notes; more opportunity needed for exploration or enquiry by the learner; more provision of critical and constructive comment on written work, and so on. In short, reforms will involve more time and resources for teaching, and a greater respect shown for the personal presence and creative capacity of the learner.

Understandably the survey by the HMI's stopped short of specific political challenge; but it has to be faced that our adolescents cannot be well educated on the cheap, any more than any other group in our schools. They need a plentiful supply and range of good books, whereas English Departments throughout the country complain about the serious shortage of this most basic commodity for good English work. For the books to be well employed, they need well-qualified, well-trained specialist teachers of English, who have ample time for both adequate planning and marking, and also opportunities for personal and professional refreshment – for example, with appropriate in-service training and study-leave (there has grown a tendency for heads to revert to recruiting non-specialists at increasingly senior stages of secondary school teaching, 'because of the cuts'). Especially, they need – and this is not so directly an economic issue as one of 'climate' in the school – some essential time and space for recognition, given with the curriculum, for their needs as individual learners. But at the time of writing, most of these proposals are Utopian – except for the last.

Here, given the vision and the will, it is possible, even within the constraints of present examination systems and cuts, to improve the 'climate' of our classrooms. What kind of vision, then, do we need?

The possibilities of play and the qualities of relationship in learning

Now that the 'eleven-plus' examination has disappeared it is likely that nowhere is the notion of 'play' more suppresssed in learning than in the years around the sixteen-plus and eighteen-plus examinations. To plead for more sense of 'play' is not, as might be thought, to opt for indulgence in 'self-expression', at the expense of disciplined modes of enquiry; it is, rather, to draw attention to the possibility of involving the learner's personal volition, in the act of learning. When this is ignored, the all-too familiar classroom reactions of boredom and rebellion begin to grow. To take an instance from the class on whom this study of writing is based: when working in their lower-sixth year on a Dickens novel, the class was asked to take part in a simple game of observation, where they had to parody certain gestures and habits that had been noticed among people that they knew. The game led to a flow of discussion on the uses of caricature, which helped to illuminate the text at the point reached by the class. This miming interlude also had a healing influence, in lifting the group from an uncommunicative, constrained mood that had seemed to settle on them around that time. On the following day, this written reflection on the lesson was handed in:

> Lessons this term were terrible — perhaps English has been so hopeless because we're all trying like hell to resist it — I mean refusing to allow ourselves to be taken in by it — I certainly saw you as a teacher, one of 'them' — I really think that the only way our English lessons can proceed is through games which you *must* join in to be part of us — like we should all go out together — the whole class should embrace — but of course we won't. I see the only future for mankind is playing the type of game we played today — that is superb — it breaks down barriers, breaks down all the restricting bonds — especially I think the present bond of being opposed to anything to do with school including English. English is emotion. Emotion is touch. We must touch. We must touch . . . The trouble with English in the upper school is that you don't think or have forgotten that we still need sensation through sight, feel, smell, and you know the lot. The trouble is that we're only given the sensation of the written work and that's a killer. I really enjoyed that English lesson today. Suddenly it meant everything and brought me into existence inside the dark stuffy confines of the school —
>
> No thoughts
> No thoughts
> Just the rushing wind

Combing back my hair
just the vastness of an ocean echoed in trees
silvery glittery waving of the light and dark grasses
The sun rushing, streaming pouring down — and the power of life.

We need to play roles in order to survive — but we over-play, I suppose.
I shouldn't have to play roles — the outsider in all of us should be
allowed to function so long as we don't physically assault another
person.

(Robert, aged sixteen)

Robert's piece is written in a mood of turbulent lyricism; he exaggerates
the importance of a single, modest enough, classroom event. But he offers
too an important judgement on the nature of the discipline of English
studies: that when feeling is not quickened by fresh experience, then our
thought and our language are clichéd: our play is reduced to enacting
stereotyped roles. Without the quickening, the free engaging of the feelings,
there can be no intelligent discourse, no discipline.

The quality of learning is bound up with all our language acts — talking,
listening, writing, reading and non-verbal. And as Robert's writing informs
us, there has always to be a feeling-engagement if there is to be any true
quickening of new thought. This *poetic* mode of expressing and communicating reveals the essentially poetic nature of all language, when used
creatively. Robert's reflections also remind us of a further fundamental
principle about the nature of language, which is that we cannot discourse
usefully on 'language development' without seeking to look again at — to
respect — the realm of the growing, learning individual. For the teacher
cannot evade relationship in learning — with the learner, with what is to
be learned. And Robert's point about the need for 'play' among teacher
and learners in literary studies helps to lift the dust from an insight
reached long enough ago by John Dover Wilson:

Not instruction but recreation, re-creation in the fullest meaning of the
word, is here the teacher's function ... Above all, the teacher must
never forget that most poetry is play, divine play if you will, play that
sometimes needs an effort and strict observance of rules before the
game is fully mastered, yet when all is said, in spirit and purpose, aim
and method, nothing but play.

(John Dover Wilson, *Poetry and the Child*, 1916)

The kind of relationship needed involves both careful support and
tactful non-interference. Consider, for instance, this poem by another
member of Robert's group:

Youth is a Gardener

"You are young".
This is said in the tone
as one would say:
"You are an alcoholic, you are insane".

And then:
"When I was your age . . ."
"You are too young to know your own mind."
People forget so easily.

Youth is a gardener
Turning,
Pondering on newly mown soil.
He seeks the branch
to be grafted on a great tree.
Always
There are new things to be discovered in the soil.
New budding leaves
Waiting to bloom.

He turns the clods of earth
slowly, thoughtfully,
sometimes impetuously,
damaging a poor worm.

These are his mistakes
And more earth must be turned
Before his day's work is done.

(Margaret, aged sixteen)

Like Robert's piece, this poem protests, then wonders on the processes of growth and discovery, dwelling on their delicacy. After the harsh opening, the rhythm is more gentle. A need for quiet acceptance and for leisure is revealed — time for the writer to be vague and ruminating, as her personal choices and directions gradually emerge. Implicit, too, is the need for protection during these stages of growth, expressed through the imagery of the tender plants of experience, on which youth can inflict even self-hurt by acting 'impetuously'. While new versions of existence are being sought and considered the emergent adult needs such a protecting 'garden' to explore, in which to rehearse a life's effort towards meaning.

Margaret's plea for a space where she may learn in safety from mistakes has to be seen as a natural stage in her encounters with new forms of learning. As her own 'gardener' metaphor implies, learning is, or should be, absorbing work, demanding her personal whole-hearted involvement. She will need the support, advice, encouragement, criticism of her teachers and peer-group and others; but only through her own freely-engaged practice will she come to work with full skill, sensitivity and commitment at the learning task. And in shaping her garden, the learner herself will be changed; for learning involves her in a giving of herself and a receiving of the new world, through which the learner becomes identified with what she has learned. Nowhere is this likely to be more true than in the relation between the learner and the mother-tongue, where the complex inter-acting of expression of self and communication to others *is* the speaker speaking, *is* the language itself. In the very process of inheriting a living language through listening and reading, we learn how to make our own unique contribution to it through our talking and writing.

In *Attachment and Loss* (Vol. 3) (1980) John Bowlby argues that our health and our growth depend on our success in forming and maintaining affectional bonds, first between child and parent and later between adult and adult. Nor do we grow out of such attachment needs when we reach adulthood; rather, it is when we are older that we become most vulnerable, through bereavement or other loss, to the grief which must be experienced when attachment bonds are broken. Our living involves us in a continuous making and breaking of such bonds. We cannot live without these interpersonal ties, even though they must eventually involve the one in mourning for the other's loss. Similarly the teacher-learner relationship must end, for the sake of the learner; but this need not impair its quality while it lasts.

If we are to gain new forms of knowing, we have to move forward; we are required, even at great cost, to renounce old forms, old clichés, worn-out patterns of knowledge in seeking renewal. It is harder to learn as we grow older, since by then we have more of our old selves to lose — though it is not impossible, so long as we choose to live rather than merely survive. As in personal relations, the quality of learning depends on the spirit in which it is enacted — that is, on the quality of love. This guiding principle has long been known, if only recently formulated as a 'scientific' proposition. The principle is embedded in Shakespeare's metaphor of the c(h)ords of love with which Cordelia freely ties herself again to her father. Cordelia's act of renewed commitment as an adult to her father was made possible by her earlier choice against his possessive claims on her. In exercising her volition, her capacity for choice, she discovers the strength of her own identity. It is such acts of volition that need to be rehearsed in the learning 'play' of the young adults in our classrooms, so that their capacity to confront life's difficulties with resilience and skill can grow.

In good teaching and learning, the play will motivate the discipline; and the discipline will serve, shape and justify the play. In the realms of language play, this will become an essentially poetic activity of creative interplay between individual and world, aimed at the shaping and revealing of meaning. For it is the natural task of learners to discover and express their being through their inherited language(s); and it is the teacher's task to give space and provision for this process, allowing — and even, when needed, coercing — the learners to take full responsibility for their own experience. But any 'coercing' needs to remain in healthy tension with that spirit of play, as defined by Dover Wilson.

Learning Through Encounter

Having dwelled on the kinds of play and relationships in learning which encourage a capacity for personal choice, the notion of learning through encounter has now to be considered. For it is only through confronting their own experience that learners can truly change and grow; this cannot be achieved wholly by mimesis, nor by rational argument on its own, nor by mere obedience to another's will. If learning and teaching are best rooted in personal encounter, why should adults ever impose harmful divisions on learning-teaching relations, and deny the other's personal presence as a potentially creative being? This problem haunts William Blake's *Songs of Innocence and Experience*, as in his depiction of the perfect self-trust of the Little Boy Lost (*Experience* version) who talks with candour about the love he feels for his parents — 'nought loves another as itself', he claims. He 'sets reason up for judge' of the Priest's 'most holy Mystery' — a mystery which houses anti-human doctrines, of fear, possessive 'love' and self-subjection, on which the priest's power system depends. So the body of the little boy, who offers reason, which itself emerges from his body's experience, is burned

in a holy place
Where many had been burned before.
The weeping parents wept in vain.
Are such things done on Albion's shore?

The priest — and, it follows, the priest in ourselves — cannot be changed simply by reasoning; we can only be liberated by the appeal for personal recognition by the Little Boy Lost, who represents also our own spontaneous, naive capacity to speak what we truly feel. It requires an act of sympathetic imagination to understand the 'otherness' of the learner — and thereby the 'other' within ourselves.

Blake's poetry and poetic prose compels so often a 'shock of recognition' when we read it; it can no longer be dismissed facilely as the work of an eccentric visionary. T.S. Eliot himself warned against the danger of Blake's being kept as a 'wild pet for the super-cultivated'; yet it has to be admitted that as far as educational thought on language and learning has been concerned he has remained a cult figure, useful for the odd quotation, but without mainstream influence. We could make better use of Blake's insights, and of much of our literary legacy, to refresh educational thought – to nurture qualities of wit, curiosity, subtlety, courage to hold to a vision, intelligence and irony in discourse on language and learning. We could learn how to admit our own feelings better, our own presence in our learning and teaching – in short, to learn through encounter.

Contact in Learning

Margaret's poem _Youth is a Gardener_ (quoted earlier) dwells on the learner's need for both adult support and personal space in the exacting task of encountering new learning. The apparent paradox of this view deserves further examination, if we wish to be clear about the nature of learning.

Writing itself is a peculiarly individual, private act, yet we write out of a personal – a bodily – response to the world. Where there is no give-and-take between a person and the world, then the one becomes overwhelmed by the other. There _must_ be interaction, or else both I and the world are denied. Even the private act of writing is in reality an act, the spoken word, and therefore dialogue. Thus the special conditions of writing are subject to the larger laws of learning and teaching, as far as contact between person and world are concerned.

Now if learning involves the body, then it involves the needs and risks to which the body is subject. These needs seem at times to be contradictory. On the one hand, we strive for contact with the world; we seek to commune with its 'otherness', in order to become fully human ourselves – indeed, in order to grow and learn at all. On the other hand, we require respect for our own distinct singleness of being, for our own separate space in the order of things. These are indeed contrary motives; yet one must never cancel out the other. As well as requiring the closest bonds possible with the teacher and with the world, the learner needs to choose a space for private retreat and self-reflection, in order to restore a sense of being in personal touch with both self and world.

The learner's personal presence demands recognition; teaching cannot be directed only to the disembodied mind of the learner as though the body could be safely left in a parking-lot, having transported its ghostly occupant, the mind, to the market-place of learning. The first stages and all subsequent stages of the search for meaning in the world are affectionally based, bound in our primary human ties. To be in touch in this primary sense is to be reassured of our reality. Coventry Patmore gently discloses such as experience of his son's efforts to regain a sense of being and place, in his poem _The Toys_:

My little Son, who look'd from thoughtful eyes
And moved and spoke in quiet grown-up wise,
Having my law the seventh time disobey'd,
I struck him and dismiss'd
With hard words and unkiss'd,
His Mother, who was patient, being dead.
Then, fearing lest his grief should hinder sleep,
I visited his bed,
But found him slumbering deep,
With darken'd eyelids, and their lashes yet
From his late sobbing wet.
And I, with moan,
Kissing away his tears, left others of my own;
For, on a table drawn beside his head,
He had put within his reach,
A box of counters and a red-vein'd stone,
A piece of glass abraded by the beach
And six or seven shells,
A bottle with bluebells
And two French copper coins, ranged there with careful art,
To comfort his sad heart . . .

Patmore's insight into his child's distress — gained through confessing his clumsy act against him — enables him to comprehend the little world that the boy has constructed, to endow pattern and meaning on his neighbouring objects. We see here the simple beginnings of magic, of metaphor, of religion, of culture (and indeed, Patmore later ends his poem by relating the intentions of the child's patterns specifically to adult versions of efforts to make meaning).

Patmore's lines show the redemptive power of affectional ties and of contact, and of the distress suffered when these are lacking. Yet in ordinary living, it may still prove difficult to be whole and balanced in our different kinds of human contacts. Thus sexual attitudes tend to veer between the prurient at one extreme, and the clinical at another; or adult relations with children may similarly veer confusingly between undue closeness and undue distance. That this fear of being simply in touch with children still lingers on in our schools was evidenced in an incident from my recent past, during my work as a chief examiner in English Studies, for an Examinations Board which examined the work of many thousands of children at the age of sixteen-plus. For part of the poetry section to an English paper, I had recommended the following poem, by Hugh Lewin, which he had written out of his experiences as a political prisoner in a South African gaol:

Touch

When I get out
I'm going to ask someone
to touch me
very gently please
and slowly,
touch me
I want
to learn again
how life feels.

I've not been touched
for seven years
for seven years
I've been untouched
out of touch
and I've learnt
to know now
the meaning of
untouchable

Untouched — not quite
I can count the things
that have touched me
One: fists
At the beginning
fierce mad fists
beating, beating
till I remember
screaming
Don't touch me
please don't touch me

Two: paws
The first four years of paws
every day
patting paws, searching
— arms up, shows off
legs apart —
prodding paws, systematic
heavy, indifferent
probing away
all privacy.

I don't want fists and paws
I want
to want to be touched
again
and to touch,
I want to feel alive
again
I want to say
when I get out
Here I am
please touch me.

(Hugh Lewin, from *Poets to the People*, ed.,
Barry Feinberg, 1974)

The poem was acknowledged by the English Committee of the Board (all of them practising and experienced teachers of English) as an appropriate choice for the paper; and although there was a tentative view expressed that it might be construed as 'political', the poem was unanimously adopted — with the description 'South African' deleted from the explanatory note that introduced the poem, in order to 'neutralize' the nature of the poet's political offence. Three days before the candidates were to have written their answers to this paper, they were allowed to read through the chosen poems with their teachers in class; and it was at this stage that one, or two, or more teachers found the poem too 'offensive' and 'embarrassing' to be read out to their fifth year students. Within hours, an emergency meeting of the examinations committee (not the English committee) of the Board met, and agreed to cancel the whole of the poetry section of the paper — for by this time, all the other chosen poems had become suspect too. Inevitably, a noisily unpleasant quarrel broke out over the affair, while the offending, inoffensive poem remained banned. A public figure connected with the Board was reported to have declared at a meeting where the issue was raised, that 'the chief examiner must have been very naive not to have known that to many local people 'touch' could mean only one thing — sexual intercourse . . .'. The English committee, together with a vast majority of schools involved could see no evidence of corrupting influences in the poem, and many of these protested vigorously at the sudden, intolerant action against it. But the damage done by the act of censorship could not now be easily put right; the students that year were examined on a Literature paper without poetry, and the affair was left for journalists to pick over the bones of the dispute in the columns of their newspapers.

The difficulties encountered in the 'Touch' poem by those readers who find it distasteful are, one supposes, real ones. This poem is 'innocent' in the sense of being inherently unharmful, but inasmuch as it expresses physical presence, a sexual interpretation is not impossible. More worrying, however, was the unwillingness of the poem's critics to accept that its central plea is for a far more ordinary form of human contact; 'touch' becomes in fact a metaphor for tenderness of relations, as well as operating literally in the poem. In this sense the poem offers a specific challenge to the teaching-learning relationship; it is the same challenge which Dr. Johnson offered, in claiming that 'want of tenderness is want of parts, and no less a proof of stupidity than depravity.' (quoted by Q.D. Leavis in 'The Englishness of the English Novel', 1981). The prude and censor seek to transcend or imprison sexuality; while the voyeur and pornographer seek detachment in order to be confined in its cell, with the rest of human experience barred out. Both extremes may eventually be seen to join ranks in their common denial of full bodily access and expression. Similarly both frigidity and ingratiation in ordinary relations conspire to deny genuine intimacy of contact. The taboo against touch, indeed, is a daily visible form of hostility to felt, personal modes of contact. As far as the teaching-learning relationship is concerned, the taboo lingers on as a complicating, damaging influence in our schools. Much patience and tact, as well as strength of purpose, will be needed, to foster the wider, more alert consciousness and sense of essential trust that are needed to allay irrational fears; and this effort may, again, have to be continuously made, repaired and renewed. Meanwhile, we may acknowledge with Lawrence that

> Education can never become a serious science until the human psyche is properly understood. And the human psyche cannot begin to be understood until we enter the dark continent of the unconscious.
> (D.H. Lawrence, *Psychology and the Unconscious*, 1923)

What Kind of Thought?
This chapter has dwelled so far on aspects of the learner's needs and of the nature of learning. Before moving on to the specific activity of writing, we need to look, if only briefly, at the learner's modes of thought — those acts of strange, symbiotic relationship between our individual subjectivity, and the surrounding human and beyond-human world, in which we operate, learn, grow, and become more than we were, before re-merging through death.

Through experience we both derive meaning from, and endow it on, our world. Our bodies contain the warp and weft of passive and active, perceived and perceiving states: and from these are woven the fabric of a 'third realm' of realized truth. But where, it might be urged, is the place of reason in such a view of man? Or (to use the more awkward-sounding modern terms), where are the 'cognitive' aspects to match the 'affective' aspects of growth? However the question is put, it cannot decently be avoided; for if a refreshed emphasis on the 'encounter' of learning would seem to exclude important modes of response and thought, it might allow the obverse, or 'shadow' of a new rationalism to loom, which would deny new-found freedoms.

Let us not assume facilely that our reasoning-generalizing activities have an autonomous 'half-life' of their own; they can only be a subsidiary activity of our thinking which involves our personal presence in whole attendance. Much teaching and learning by-passes personal presence in not calling for first-hand response; and because of this, the delusion grows that rational-generalizing processes should have their own separate realm. Such a view is more easily held in the sciences, where the teacher who would wish to guide the learner into personal encounter faces real problems of having to work within strict paradigms of what has already been judged as 'focally' known. Few writers have elucidated this problem better than John Macmurray, who showed in his essay on 'Reason in the Emotional Life' (in *Reason and Emotion*, 1935) how 'a conception of reason which is applicable to science, but not to religion or art must be a false conception, or at least an inadequate one'. In this essay, he works from the notion that reason is our capacity to 'behave in terms of the nature of the object, that is to say, to behave objectively. Reason is thus our capacity for objectivity.' But far from seeing this capacity for objectivity as a separate, split-off half of the psyche, he sees it, rather as the instrument by which we develop 'rational', as opposed to 'irrational feelings'.

It is the emotional life which is the 'core and essence' of our living. Rational thought must effectively serve that life, but it can only act negatively when dominant (by paralysing the positive emotions), and never creatively. The intellect draws its life from the body's life, but it is 'essentially instrumental. Thinking is not living. At its worst it is a substitute for living, at its best a means of living better'. We have to live with the whole of our bodies — emotional, rational and physical — and have to reconcile the curious confusions we experience as rational animals. The learner ought indeed to be capable of exercising essential logic; but if the emotional life is the 'core and essence of living', then essential logic will be part of a more comprehensive view of thinking and learning, of intelligent being and action.

Thus the instrument of reason may only find its perfect freedom in the service of the body's emotional life. While I am writing this chapter, I try to work towards offering something that stands as a 'true' statement about my experiences of teaching and learning. As I shape my version I am reminded, uncomfortably, that my 'total awareness' of those experiences is too complex and diffuse to be conveyed in neat formulations and summaries. At times I am tempted to abandon the enterprise, perhaps to attempt a novel instead — just as I might invite a student to 'tell it as a story', as a way of attempting to distil the essence of an experience. But I know, too, that an attempt to illuminate through fiction would be even more difficult; it would certainly be no escape from requirements for rigorous selection, continuity, and some essential logic.

In seeking to write about my response to my own response I shift between an open, wondering kind of thinking, and deliberate decisions about selecting, ordering, organizing my thoughts; between imaginative/ felt and critical/reasoning modes of emphasis; between attention to the pressure of 'need to tell', and attention to the need for a clear form that may win an audience's recognition. One mode can sometimes seem to be working very closely with, and even guiding the other; it is as though I were endowed with two 'thought-hands'. These might be compared with the way Barbara Hepworth has described the different functions of her two actual hands, when sculpting:

> My left hand is my thinking hand. The right is only a motor hand. This holds the hammer. The left hand, the thinking hand, must be relaxed, sensitive. The rhythms of thought pass through the fingers and grip of this hand into the stone. It is also a listening hand. It listens for weaknesses of flaws in the stone; for the possibility or immanence of fractures.
>
> (*Pictorial Autobiography*, 1976)

The complementary nature of the sculptor's two hands at work offers a good analogy for the way that our two modes of thought work together. A similar pattern can be discerned in all art activity, of course; consider, for instance, the quality of Bach's Fugues, where new feeling is achieved through intensity of technical effort, which was itself motivated by feeling. But, it may be urged, there may be occasions when the two 'hands' do not work best together. If we are required to be 'objective' – say, as a witness in a court of Law – is it not best if we confine ourselves strictly to undisputed 'facts', and give as clear an account of these as possible? Yet we know, again from ordinary experience, that it is impossible to convey the 'truth, the *whole* truth' of an event impartially, without emotion; the truth is, that we are emotionally, bodily involved in the very *act* of seeing. And even from judges it would be unrealistic to expect a purely objective 'justice'; for when they have made their decisions about the evidence, they must still consider an appropriate course of action. A complex of thought-modes will then come into play – interpreting, discriminating, evaluating, intuiting, exercising tact, self-criticism, a capacity to imagine the consequences of their decisions, awareness of all the parties involved and how they are likely to be affected, and so on. These are inevitably *value* judgements, whatever the letter of the Law. Judges may find it impossible to say *exactly* how and why a particular decision was reached; intuitive operations are elusive, and are not easily defined without distorting them in the process. Even though judges act on what looks like hard evidence and clear facts, they have to make a *personal* evaluation of those facts. They are entrusted not just as memory banks for their ability to retrieve and handle all the dust-laden information of past law, but for their *wisdom*. This wisdom will need the delicately complementary action of both thinking 'hands'.

Implications for the Learner-as-Writer

The notion of a split between what we feel and what we think has lingered since the Renaissance; it is viewed critically by Shakespeare, for instance, through Iago's cynical comment that without a 'scale of reason to poise another of sensuality, the blood and baseness of our nature would lead us to preposterous conclusions'. This notion of divided modes of awareness has affected even modern literary-critical thought, such as the influential work of I.A. Richards. Richard's work contains puzzling contradictions on the issue. In *Principles of Literary Criticism* (1924) he stated unequivocally that the

> world of poetry has in no sense any different reality from the rest of the world and has no special laws and no other worldly peculiarities. It is made up of experiences of exactly the same kinds as those that come to us in other ways.
>
> (Chapter 10)

He then qualified this, in Wordsworthian spirit, by declaring that poetry 'is more highly and delicately organised than other experiences'. This seems to be well in keeping with Richards' well-known view that all writing embraces sense, feeling, tone and intention, though in different proportions. But it is obliterated by a later chapter, when he argued for a distinction 'which needs to be kept clear' between 'referential' and 'emotive' language:

> A statement may be used for the sake of the reference, true or false, which it causes. This is the scientific use of language. But it may also be used for the sake of effects in emotion and attitude produced by the reference it occasions. This is the emotive use of language. The distinction once clearly grasped is simple. We may either use words for the sake of the references they promote, or we may use them for the sake of the attitudes and emotions which ensue.
>
> (I.A. Richards, *Principles of Literary Criticism*, Chapter 34)

The 'may also be used for' phrase has slid almost imperceptibly into a quite rigid 'either-or' distinction; with the result that Richards contradicts his earlier statement. It is an error that has since been echoed, with varying degrees of enthusiasm, by many writers on language and learning, so that by the end of the sixties members of the London Writing Research Unit felt justified in claiming that there was a theoretical fabric composed of insights from Sapir, Cassirer, Langer, Harding and Britton to support a 'duality' theory of language. Such a claim gave support to their transactional ← expressive → poetic model, as presented in their influential report on secondary school writing, *The Development of Writing Abilities, 11–18* (1975). Their view seems in some ways to correspond closely enough to Polanyi's version of subsidiary and focal forms of knowing; indeed Polanyi's work (along with insights from other phenomenological thinkers) is quoted with unreserved approval by the Unit. But on inspection it seems to refute Polanyi's position, in echoing the old dualism, rather than the new phenomenology. The apparent confusion here needs further scrutiny, since the proposals about the writing process that will be made in the chapters that follow are based on the notion of thinking and learning as a unifying, not dichotomous process.

Edward Sapir's distinction between 'patterns of reference and patterns of expression' would seem to support the Unit's model; but this distinction is born uneasily, from a sense that the two poles cannot be really distinguished. In *Language* (1921) Sapir dwells on the constant intermingling of particular patterns of experience with the 'quasi-mathematical form' of language. Even in scientific discourse, 'it may be seriously doubted whether the ideal of pure reference is ever attained by language'. Ordinary speech is directly expressive of these patterns, and is 'compounded by intended and unintended symbolism of expression.' Yet he concludes that within the highly complex patterns of language, there are 'isolable patterns of two distinct orders. These may roughly be defined as patterns of reference and patterns of expression.' Sapir conveys well the elusive, esoteric nature of expression; but his conclusion does not convince, since he has already laid a more powerful stress on the unattainability of purely 'referential' language, than on the positive existence of a referential-expressive polarity. A similarly unresolved problem seemed to affect Ernst Cassirer too, when he declared in *The Philosophy of Symbolic Forms* (1923) that emotional language, the language of poetic imagination went 'side by side' with conceptual, logical or scientific language; but he then added that '*primarily* man does not express thoughts and ideas, but feelings and affections.'

Do feelings 'share' thinking with rational processes, then, or is thinking essentially generated by the body's emotional life? The problem is raised, but not clarified here; yet Cassirer recognized that language depended entirely on poetic life for constant regeneration, since it is only through symbol-making and the poetic effort of language that reality and truth may be freshly embodied. Despite his own acknowledging of a split, the undercurrent of Cassirer's work moves us to recognize, with Macmurray, that the emotional life, which seeks expression and truth through our imaginative, symbol-making powers — powers that are served by our reasoning faculty — is our only life.

My argument is that our poetic intentions and our life-transactions should always be essentially in the same direction, not towards opposite poles. But it has to be conceded that, while no meaningful language is divorced from emotional content, by no means all the language we use is endowed with the cliché-breaking powers of fresh encounter. Countless daily communications take the form of repeated friendly exchanges, routine messages of information, instruction and so on, or 'encapsulated' wisdom like proverbs, theorems and formulae. But while such acts of language provide all the essential maintenance and repair of cells in the body of language and culture, they are not *learning*-transactions, in the meaning intended here. And inasmuch as this 'routine' language maintains the operations of a healthy language and culture, it is best seen as supporting a (poetic) quest-to-meaning, rather than taking a separate direction. For if we are not eventually engaged in creating new possibilities we are not, in any worthwhile sense, living.

As well as drawing on 'duality' notions of language, a rather different kind of support for the 'transactional' and 'poetic' poles of his writing model was sought by James Britton in 'What's the Use?' (1972), where he invoked Denis Harding's essay 'The Role of the Onlooker' (1937) to show how Harding's notion of 'participant' and 'spectator' roles in learning matched the transactional-poetic duality. But going back to Harding's essay after reading Britton, it is clear that Harding did not advance a straight dichotomy between 'participating' and 'spectating'. Harding offered *four* modes of response in his essay: activity, or motor response; comprehension, experiencing; and evaluating. He claimed that these 'aspects . . . possess no value implications', and furthermore that

it would be absurd to suggest that any one kind of relationship to events was likely to occur in isolation . . . in most activity, we must expect a continuous fusion of operative response, intellectual comprehension, perceptual enjoyment, and the fourth — the evaluative response.

He recognized that one of these modes, as 'aspects or phrases of a complex whole', might be dominant at any given time; but he wrote nothing that might support a positivist view of language such as Bertrand Russell's, who believed in the possibility of a 'universal' language, and who confidently distinguished between 'firmly factual language' on one side, and 'poetic' on the other.

Observing is, after all, an enacting in itself — and while Harding did not stress this, neither did he contradict such a view of response. The best thing to draw from Harding's article is the notion of a whole, inclusive response in our thinking and learning, not of splintered-off activities. Only when who we are and what we know are bound together in what we do, can our intentions and our acts be in harmony. Thus, bearing in mind the doubtfulness of 'poetic transactional' and participant-spectator' dualities — whatever the good intentions in the work of the London Writing Unit — it has to be recognized that our ideas about writing development now need to be revised, on lines of enquiry which hold to a unifying principle of thinking and learning. Carl Bereiter's claim, for instance (in 'Development in Writing', 1979) that 'with the conclusion of the definitive studies of Britton *et al* it is likely that research of this kind has yielded about all that it can concerning the normal course of writing development' must be questioned.

Even language that seems most 'transactional' — such as in the specifications for building a public hall; or laying down routines for a surgical operation; or planning a secondary school curriculum — should have strong roots in, and never be cut off or unduly distanced from the language of feelings and values, of art-discourse. In this way our social arrangements remain on behalf of *people*; the dangers, say, of modern business enterprise, or micro-chips, or educational theory assuming an inimical autonomy of their own, divorced from living contact, may be checked. Language is a 'criss-cross of utterance', an interrelating of human concerns. It can become an evil force if it becomes so exclusively 'firmly factual' that it fails to heed the other's living presence, as is powerfully evidenced in Tolstoy's short story, *The Death of Ivan Ilyich*. Ilyich, the successful lawyer and family man, full of self-esteem, and highly reputed for his good style as a prosecutor, learns that he is suffering from a fatal illness. Suddenly, the logical truism, 'All men must die. Caius is a man. Therefore Caius must die' confronts him as being true for *him*; he feels it now as a frightening reality, a truth about himself. But in his new vulnerability, brought on by suffering and fear, he has to endure the same callous professional disregard of his real needs from his own doctor that he has inflicted without thought on his own clients. Full of self-pity, cut off from his distressed but uncomprehending family, he struggles against the inescapable fact of existence that his whole way of living has conspired against his recognizing; until eventually, only moments before his death, he realizes that the journey down the horrifying blackness of a tunnel really *is* a journey — away from previous lies and towards an as yet undisclosed truth. He dies, released from the orderly lies of his previous existence, and therefore restored.

Writing to Express and Communicate Understanding

'Write O.E. *writan*, connected with Icel. *rita*, to tear, cut, scratch out, etc'. — *Brewer's Dictionary of Phrase and Fable*

Writing grows, with reading, from speaking and listening, which are the first arts of language; and while the vitality of writing depends intimately on living speech, it demands a more conscious sifting of expression. For one thing, writing is a much more gradual process, and because we cannot rely so much on sheer verbal fluency we may find it less easy to rely on clichéd expression. This prompted Denis Harding to suggest (in *Experience into Words*, 1963) that 'some people . . . speak so fluently that thought processes apart from words scarcely seem to occur . . . A subtler use of language often consists in breaking and re-shaping the more familiar verbal moulds.' At best, writing gives us opportunities of time and space that are less readily available in talking. The learner can explore emerging representations of experience, as perhaps only the most intimately delicate conversations allow. Because writing is such a private activity (even though its intention is to communicate, as with all language) we can meet with our own responses more purely according to the rhythm and pace of our own feeling-thought than is usually possible in speech. Writing, then, can be a uniquely valuable medium for encounter in learning.

Yet the very opportunities given by writing to 'think it out' more carefully make it an often much more daunting task than 'talking it through' — even when exploratory talk as a preliminary activity to writing has been encouraged. The Britton Report underlines the exactingly personal, inward, nature of writing — at least, of any writing which goes at all beyond perfunctory or closely directed repetition of the teacher's (or text-book's) phrases and sentences. An important insight of the Report (one which carries good weight against the depressing bulk of advice on 'How to write an essay' that is endemic in the text-book and correspondence college market) refuted the notion that writing is 'simply' a matter of establishing your ideas, or plan, and then setting it down:

> Now 'understanding' and 'expressing' are not necessarily influenced by making and following detailed plans. An essential part of the writing process is explaining the matter to oneself, and that is a highly idiosyncratic affair.

It is because we *are* learning that our writing is sometimes confused, repetitive, or meandering, since the writing down can itself provide a thread to trust to and follow, as we negotiate unfamiliar woods. The first phases of writing, as concepts begin shadowily to emerge, can involve all kinds of loose ends and jottings around that ought to be included, since they are felt to be potentially part of the pattern, yet they seem irreducible to any kind of order. This experience may be the more bewildering and frustrating in the face of new learning. And even when, perhaps after several abortive attempts a guiding idea or main approach has been conceived, some considerable time may still be needed for gestation before the writer can express and communicate, in writing. The kind of help that the learner is likely to require in this difficult business of 'getting it right' with both self and world needs to be offered with subtlety and tact. An example of such support at its best was given by Robert Witkin in a passage when he describes the 'creative partnership' offered by a teacher who has achieved a fine balance of uninterfering support, and respect for the freedom of the pupil to express his 'feeling-impulse' through his chosen medium of writing. He identifies one of the 'very few' English teachers he observed giving this kind of help effectively:

> As I watched her teach, I formed an entirely personal impression of the motive behind it which I would express as follows: 'Your idea, your feeling is important. It is a worthwhile and precious thing. It will live and take form if you can shape it in words — if you can work it through the medium and communicate it — not half of it or bits of it all mixed up with other things but the whole of it, your idea, your feeling — It isn't easy. Words are powerful things. They can deceive you or take you by surprise. They can hide or reveal you. Your idea can grow through the medium of words but *your idea* must control them. If your idea moves and grows in dance or alarm or sorrow then you must build your statements to move in the same way, in dance or alarm or sorrow.'
> (Robert Witkin, *The Intelligence of Feeling*, 1974)

This concentration of respect for the learner's experience and feeling is, perhaps, still rare in the classroom, although many teachers have acknowledged its power. Such a concern to nurture feeling is vividly illustrated by Tolstoy, for instance, who writes of his decision to read Gogol's 'Elf-King' to his classes at his free school of Yasnaya Polyana, and then take them in the dark of a winter's night through a wolf-inhabited forest. Tolstoy writes of how he wished to share an experience, to share fresh feelings with his pupils — so that 'greater liberty, greater simplicity and greater confidence' would grow among them. And in the middle of the forest, when one of the pupils had asked, 'What is drawing for?', it had led to such a good discussion on 'What a linden tree is for' and 'What singing is for' that Tolstoy concluded:

> It feels strange to me to repeat what we spoke that evening, but I remember we said everything, I think, that there was to be said on utility and on plastic and moral beauty.
> (Tolstoy, *The School at Yasnaya Polyana*, 1862)

Writing as Authentic Expression
Whatever the doubts aired about the 'transactional-poetic' split, it is clear that the findings of the London Writing Research Team proved valuable in

teacher-training and in-service work. The evidence, for instance, that the overwhelming majority of scripts examined by them (92 per cent) fell into the two least human-looking categories for sense of audience ('pupil to examiner' and 'pupil to teacher general') prompts many questions about the state of relationships in secondary school classrooms. Also, the evidence for the overwhelming amount of 'transactional' writing, as compared to that along the expressive-poetic line (only 5.5 per cent of the scripts were judged 'expressive') offered substance for a radical argument for change in schools' approaches to writing, once it is accepted that there *is* an expressive source (and, I should argue, a 'poetic' intention) to all writing that lives as a vehicle toward truth.

Having argued for a healing of the transactional-poetic split, it remains now to illustrate better what is meant by 'poetic' intention in writing. It has been suggested that poetic intention involves a desire to tell the truth about experience. We may, then, discern writing that is authentic, expressive of the real self; obversely, there may be writing that lacks such truthful intention, that is inauthentic, or even expressive — deliberately or inadvertently — of a false self. As an example of such contrasting modes, two pieces of writing are offered below. They are both passages from self-chosen topics, written as part of a longer English project (on 'Growing Up, Growing Strong'). The students — both girls — were aged twelve, in the same second year mixed-ability class of a comprehensive school:

(1) Caroline:

> The sun had reached the zenith in the sky. The sun beat down and nothing moved on the sandy beach except for the ripples in the calm sea. The sea was a deep blue and there was no land in sight. Samantha lay on her back watching the gulls turn and glide on the island of Grayne. How beautiful it all looked she thought, no holiday makers crowding the beach. Samantha was twelve and her father was probably the richest man in England. She lay her sun tanned head towards the sand and let the sand run through her fingers. She lay there for a few minutes and finally she decided to get up and go back to the house, where her mother, father, brothers Richard and Peter and sister Marion were living. She reached the steps of the 'White House' and just collapsed in a heap, the temperature being almost 86°F. Her mother, father and sister were on the terrace drinking 'Grayne Specials'. They were talking about going to the beach as Samantha approached. Her two brothers had gone to the neighbouring island to buy souvenirs so she could do what she liked. Her parents got up and went into the house. Marion stayed out with Samantha getting brown. Marion lay back and thought how she could show off to her friends and tell them that her father owned a house (the only one) and two four star hotels

on the island. How when her grandfather dies she would own Grayne with her brothers and sisters. 'If only I had it all,' she thought as Samantha drifted . . .

(2) Juliet:

The Two Me's (or Me and My Shell)

> I don't think 'The Two Me's is a very good title because there are lots of me's. Basically perhaps there are only two me's but there are tons of branches from those two. For instance I am an entirely different me with you than with Mr. Mason. I feel that I have to be very right and proper with him. I have to be very careful what I say. With you it dosn't matter so much (no offence of course). I can say and write what I feel. Even with Mum & Dad I have to be different me's. I think that is because they are very different people. Being two me's is often deceitful; it means that you arn't always your tru self. you put a barrier up in front of you which is the same as a shell (see second title). But sometimes it is because we don't want to hurt people. If I behaved as I do in the Youth Club at Guide's I don't know what 'Leftie' and Captain' would do. People grow a shell round themselfes when they have something to hide. or they are very shy, or they have very little self confidence. Desprite criminals build a shell round themselves. They have to, for fear of letting any secrets out. Shy people build a shell around themselves for different reasons. Some think that if they build a barrier round them they canot say anthing wrong or they won't be laughed at. Others try to hide themselves behind their shell I think everybody builds a shell round him (or her) self, but some shells are easier to break than others.

Taking the London Writing Unit's function-category model for a start, both these pieces would seem to be on their 'expressive-poetic line', and neither could be classed as 'perfunctory' writing. But to class Caroline's piece as 'poetic' ('a verbal construct, patterned verbalization of the writer's feelings and ideas . . . would include items such as a short story . . .', Britton *et al*, 1975) would imply a meagre evaluation of 'poetic' writing. More urgently, we need to discern the *differences* between these two pieces. The audience-categories model is more helpfully revealing; we realize that Juliet's piece is quite distinctly addressed to the teacher as a trusted adult, while Caroline's can only be said to be an 'unknown' audience. But the more worrying aspect of Caroline's piece is its seeming failure to address anyone (including herself) in particular, for it is clearly not healthily 'impersonal'. She seems to be caught up in a particularly sterile kind of fantasizing, at the expense of reaching out, of relating, and of growth. Caroline's piece suggests that her thinking is taking an unhappy direction, away from reality. 'Look how our partner's rapt', says Banquo of his friend Macbeth, who has withdrawn from intimacy and openness to brood on acquisition of the 'imperial theme'. Caroline, too, is 'rapt'. We are made aware of some barrier or — to borrow the image developed by Juliet in her piece — 'shell' around her, which removes her from creative contact with her world. She uses the clichés of advertisers and pulp writers with good technical skills, but nothing that is redolent of the individual Caroline comes through — only evidence of correctness, formality and a compliant acceptance of others' fantasies. Of course, *something* has happened: there has been some kind of response to and involvement with the kind of pulp-stories that we have all dissipated our attention on, from time to time. But it is as though the commercial fantasies have only been inertly stored by her; there has been no creative or reflective play on her part, no free engagement of her subjective being — but, rather, a kind of numbness and distance, disguised by acquisitive fantasies. It is not unusual for children, or adults, to 'lose' themselves in such 'compensatory' — though in this case, essentially sterile — dreams; it can be caused by, and can cause breaks in normal relationships. In fact, Caroline's fairly brief phase of 'unreal' writing was, not surprisingly, coinciding with a phase when she was out of harmony with her group of friends in the class. She was enduring a period of rather hard teasing from them, which had brought unwelcome attention from the rest of her peers. As a quiet, hard-working but rather tense girl she had got into the habit of offering 'sweets for friendship'; and while many were inclined to exploit her, it was evident that some of her tormentors were also, of in clumsy spirit, trying to wean her from this. Meanwhile, Caroline's writing followed her fantasizing, away from the painful realities of the classroom.

By contrast, Juliet's piece is much less formally structured; there is a greater sense of 'word-play-in-progress', and a very clear sense of her personal presence in the writing. It seems to read as a simple, expressive flow of her feelings, but she also shows how she has given some sustained thought to her (self-chosen) topic of the 'Two Me's; her writing is rooted in *her* world — playing between the 'within-me and beyond-me'. Thus in a value-laden way, it is personal and expressive, and promises well for further awareness and growth. It is moving, if modestly, towards important issues concerning identity. In contrast to Caroline's piece, it has a wholly different orientation, perhaps best indicated by the distinction made by the poet Blake, between self-hood and identity. Blake's distinction identifies the self-hood as the egocentric, self-protecting, assertive aspect of personality; and identity as being the source of creative energy in the individual, of *dis*interested, outward-going actions. Self-hood, like reason, enhances life when in the *service* of identity; but can be destructive to our real being, when allowed an autonomous, 'split-off' existence.

These two little pieces of writing are unexceptional enough examples of the work of ordinary twelve-year olds in our schools; but they exemplify well the kind of respect and care that a learner's writing requires from a teacher. At best, nothing less than the most attentive critical appraisal possible is needed — by which is meant not, or course, the formal apparatus of 'lit-crit', but, rather, that kind of delicate involvement in the writing which enables us to realize the *underlying* patterns and signals and intentions of the writer. Neither can attention be limited just to the finished piece, as formal assessment demands; the teacher's own acquaintance with a learner and the class — with the whole cultural climate to which they all contribute — will be an essential guide, in responding to any writing.

We are now ready to move on to the actual classroom, and actual work done in English Studies.

CHAPTER TWO

The School, the Group and the Teaching

The School: Some Background Notes

My first teaching post was in a traditionally-run boys' grammar school where I had the good fortune to join an innovative English department. The head of English was one of those rare people who consider it a privilege to teach, whose own standards were of the highest, yet who remained sensitive to the personal needs and whereabouts of any individual learner. Through him and through the achievements of other colleagues, the department flourished; it developed a well-tested, coherent programme for English studies based primarily (but not exclusively) on literary texts, yet there was a continuous fresh endeavour of experiment, within that secure framework. As for teacher-learner relations, these became almost imperceptibly more informal and trusting, over several years, so that English lessons came to be notable for their candour and openness of atmosphere. Such a reciprocation of trust among learners and teachers was an unfamiliar feature of the usual 'staff-boys' relations in such a school as this. But as it was seen to work well enough in terms of 'discipline' and 'examination success', the policies of the department won acceptance, on the whole, from colleagues and parents as well as the boys.

These years were of immense benefit to me, personally and pro-fessionally. But the very successes achieved by this department in widening the scope of English studies, and in promoting relationships on which work involving personal and social experience could be based, eventually sent its members off in different directions. I was eager to become involved in a school that would be both comprehensive and coeducational. In particular, I wished to draw from a wider range of creative disciplines (for example, film, television, painting) and from social studies, in order to develop a richer context for the English curriculum. While a strong commitment to the power and value of literature would remain, a wider notion of art-discourse was needed, to embrace talking, listening, reading and writing in ordinary living, as well as through realized art.

I took over the English department of a newly opened school in Greater

London. It was opened as an 'experimental', purpose-built comprehensive school in the late sixties, and had the odd status of being the 'only comprehensive' in the borough; the idea was that if this school should be 'successful', then comprehensive reorganization might go ahead in other local schools too. On reaching full growth it was a mixed school for eleven- to eighteen-year-olds, with over a thousand pupils. It served both a large council estate and a private housing area. The first year of the school was composed of a full six-form 'comprehensive' intake (that is, a balanced selection of pupils from each range of attainment, according to tests and reports from the primary schools); some older pupils were also drafted in from a small secondary school in the Borough, which closed down as the new school opened. That school had made a good reputation for itself locally, mainly through its ambitious and successfully run Arts and Crafts courses.

The pupils on whose writing the rest of this book is based joined the new school as second-formers when the school was opened, having spent just one year in the former secondary modern school; thus they had been unsettled by shifting to a new school twice over, in as many years. Moreover, their new school was keen to promote its own 'image', so that reference to the old parent back-street school was discouraged among both staff and pupils. Not surprisingly these older pupils were more wary of their new school than were the first-form intake. They were especially sensitive to any hints that they were 'left-overs', whom the new school was waiting to phase out, so that the 'proper' school could reach its identity as a fully comprehensive school (their plight must have become familiar to many pupils throughout the country, during the recent years of changeover to new secondary schemes).

This group of second-year children, some hundred and twenty boys and and girls, had not only gone through 'failing' (their term) the eleven-plus; they had all gone on to lose what had been well established by local reputation as a good, secure family school. Thus they were being exposed once more to what seemed odious comparison with the 'intelligent' children of the year below – or at least, children who had not been selected against. Like their previous secondary school, most of the primary schools from which this group came had been long established and mainly sited in the older, 'working-class' part of the Borough. The group did not settle down quickly in their new would-be melting pot. They did not like having to walk to the other side of town, then up a steep hill to the new glass-and-girder structure at the top; inevitably they were soon being compared, sometimes to their faces by exasperated teachers, against the first year for their 'inferior work and attitude'.

In the previous school this year-group had been rigidly streamed; and in an honest attempt (which I supported) to do something for their morale and education, it was decided to unstream the classes. But the immediate results of this were discouraging; the unstreaming was felt by some parents and teachers, as well as most pupils, to be the harvest of yet another doctrinaire decision from 'above'. Children were tearful at being deprived of friends and groups; there were strong objections from parents of the former two upper streams (but none from the former two lower streams); and there was an outbreak of misrule in *all* the newly reorganized forms, whereas 'anti-social' behaviour had been largely contained before in the lowest stream only. The good intentions of the mixed-ability policy seemed to have failed badly. The school now seemed more than ever an inept and foreign establishment, in the eyes of both children and parents. It looked as if the school was bent on attacking well-established and widely accepted, reasonable distinctions of class and status and ability among parents and children alike; it seemed to be offending both the 'academic' lobby and the 'bring back caning' lobby. The school had a relationship problem with this year-group, which was not likely to be easily resolved.

Along with the rest of the school, the English Department had to face up to its problems here. None of us had previous experience of secondary modern schools, let alone comprehensive schools; the school was still being built around us, with half-finished buildings well behind the scheduled time for completion; and equipment was in short supply. Even so, all the teachers involved had actually made a *choice* to teach in a comprehensive school; we were enthusiastic, and our inexperience with secondary modern schools might even prove to have its positive side too, in that we brought in no shibboleths from the past. A fresh context demanded fresh attitudes and approaches. Our task was to find out the talents, interests and problems of these pupils, and we could only do that in the light of what they expressly revealed and wished to reveal of themselves. In deliberately seeking to see this group as essentially 'ordinary', no undervaluing attitudes, or 'only average' labels were implied; the term was used, rather, simply to imply 'not abnormal', with an undamaged potential for full human development.

In seeking a fresh basis for relationships with this particular year-group, the department felt that the unstreaming which had been carried through with them was likely to be helpful in the long run. For one thing, all the problems associated with streaming were resolved at once — such as over-anxiety and excitement about examination prospects for the top stream; or urgent debates about who should go 'up' or 'down' at the end of the year; or sour, despairing condemnation of the 'roughness' and 'ineducability' of the 'tough' D-stream — followed (more rarely), by over-indulgent comment on their 'animal vitality', and so on. Paradoxically, since nothing much in terms of examination results was expected of this group (all hopes being directed to the 'full entry' first year), the department had free rein in developing a more pragmatic approach to their teaching here — at least until well into the fourth year, when many of the year-group were beginning to show clear academic promise, after nearly three years in their new school.

Yet the beginnings were difficult, and the sense of defeat among those in the year-group often made for a run of unsuccessful, tiring lessons. It became increasingly difficult for us to believe in the possibilities, rather than to see what seemed only too obvious: that the pupils had fixed ideas about themselves and the school, and that this came to be reflected in the feelings of many of the staff about them. They were limited, disappointing and difficult to teach, and not amenable or 'nice' enough to learn properly. As far as English was concerned, we found ourselves forced increasingly to recognize that, to start with, good relationships were going to depend more on acts and dialogues of basic human recognition than even preparing good lessons and presenting them interestingly and pleasantly.

In the grammar school, it had become easy to start with one's own interests, and work out towards the pupils, engaging them in a common enthusiasm for a literary text or a film, and the emergent ideas and values from these. This still seemed a very important aim, but we could no longer take for granted that the formula would work; and when it did not, we had to embark on open discourse with the pupils, to identify their discontents, attitudes and desires more clearly. These attempts to adopt an open approach won some gladdening recognition from the pupils, but also involved frustration and pain on both sides, during the deliberate dislodging of well-tried methods of defence. The human tendency to establish a comfortable routine is powerful, as Tolstoy recognized:

> The teacher always involuntarily strives after selecting that method of instruction which is most convenient for himself. The more convenient the method is for the teacher, the more inconvenient for his pupils. Only that manner of instruction is correct with which the pupils are satisfied .... The business of the teacher is to afford a choice of all known and unknown methods that may make the matter of learning easier for the pupil.
>
> (Tolstoy, *The School at Yasnaya Polyana*)

For good reason, the teacher's traditions and habits of teaching are very much based on what is 'known'. That which is 'unknown' — the as yet unadmitted preoccupations, and intimations of the teacher as well as the learner — tends to be excluded, since it cannot be safely predicted. A new context now demanded entry into that 'unknown' area. Specifically, this involved encouraging greater confidence and activity in exploring the individual, active lives of teachers and of learners; especially, our urgent task was to attend to the learners and their world, and to see how we connected with them (rather than the other way round).

To recognize where a young learner is implies stooping down, and also includes an effort of imagination to recall our own earlier years, and what really happened then, when at the same stage of learning and growth. Jung tells the story (in *Memories, Dreams, Reflections*, 1963) of the Rabbi who was asked why God no longer talked to the people; the Rabbi's reply was that there is no longer anyone who can bend low enough to hear him. The anecdote (one of Jung's favourites) suggests how the teacher might move in two important directions. It urges him to go down in order to explore himself, his own feelings, sensings, imaginings, dreams; it is also an effective reminder of the teacher's actual presence among a class of young learners, bending low to talk seriously to a small twelve-year-old who is finding it difficult to write down intelligibly the feeling-thought that is still only emerging through language. Without such a clear conviction about the need, the importance and the rewards of stooping low, a teacher may well begin to doubt whether teaching young, 'unacademic' pupils is a worthwhile adult activity.

A Policy for the Group

By the time these pupils had reached the fourth year, decidedly happier classroom relations had taken root and grown. The teachers were learning to talk less and listen more, to recognize what individual learners and groups could give to each other, to offer flexible invitations to work rather than give out categorical instructions. Yet while we were learning to listen, attend and respect, rather than always to project ourselves and demand attention, we needed also to discern their real needs and interests, from their superficially declared wishes and wants. With some essential bridge-heads of ordinary trust now better secured, we came to recognize again how those real needs are best served by extending – as collaborators now – local and autobiographical levels of experience, through fiction, plays, poems, myth, film: the rich and traditional sources, in short, of the expressive arts.

While a cornerstone of our policy was to achieve a balance of all language activities, we developed a special concern for the quality of writing with this group. This concern did not come from any desire to reflect the prevailing secondary school emphasis on writing to the exclusion of other language experiences; we wished, rather, to counter-act the feeling which can grow so easily in the secondary school, that to write is not to bring one's own living presence into verbal play, but merely to present one's self for 'correction' by the teacher-markers. Many publications came from the English classrooms, whose main aim was to enhance a closer teacher/parent/learner contact – a revealing of the real worlds and experiences of individuals, both within and beyond their school and family roles. A regular flow of contributions to these publications came from teachers and parents too, to support this intention.

The writing emphasis was, of course, not really separable from other main fields of activity. Throughout the school, we worked to foster links with the live theatre; we developed a quite ambitious programme of film-study; we engaged many outside speakers and arranged visits; we encouraged, and budgeted for, classroom libraries; we pleaded and pressed continually for funds to buy fiction, drama, records, pictures, tape-recorders — all the basic necessities, in short, for a modern English stockroom. Especially and centrally, we gave daily recognition to what might be called 'dialogue-and-dialectic'. Always, there were issues and topics of interest — social, cultural, personal, local, universal — to be explored, in small groups, before the class, at breaks, over lunch and so on. In the staff-room, we were (not entirely kindly) dubbed the 'so much talk, not enough time to chalk' department. We talked, too, with other departments, and developed useful working links with the Art and History people, who had also developed a special interest in the fortunes of this year-group.

The fourth and fifth years of secondary schooling are dominated by C.S.E. and O-level public examinations — and this group was no exception. Virtually the whole year group was entered for C.S.E. in English Studies (a combined Language and Literature course, internally designed and assessed), and the fourth-fifth year examples evidenced in chapters three to eight are in fact all part of C.S.E. course work. Also, about two-thirds of the year sat English Language O-level, and about a fifth took English Literature O-level. No special attention was given to the O-level Language paper until about a fortnight or so before the pupils sat it (the pass rate for those who sat it was high); and preparation for the English Literature O-level was offered in two voluntary sessions each week outside normal school hours — the set weeks were 'doubled-up' with the C.S.E. project work. (Recent developments in a common examination at 16-plus would be likely, happily, to make such elaborate arrangements unnecessary.)

With the Headteacher's cautious but genuine support, the virtually universal entry into C.S.E. meant that public examinations would interfere minimally with our teaching approaches. But the examinations still constituted a serious interference, especially in the fifth year. Any kind of comparative or external assessment ignores the fact that assessment is at best a collaborative appraisal of work-in-progress. Given an emphasis on individual response and growth in the teaching, assessment ought to be an evaluation of what the learner has done in his own particular circumstances, and also an evaluation of what teacher and learner, or learner and other learners, have done together. This would be a continuous process, intimately bound up with the dialogue that developed between the learner's own writing, and the teacher's own comments and reactions. Where an evaluation of lessons or school learning was to be made, the teacher felt as much involved as the pupil, as far as problems and progress were concerned, and was particularly keen to hear the learner's own appraisal and self-appraisal. Such was the pattern in the fourth year, when no marks were given and no gradings made. But in the fifth year the teachers had to comply with the system of assessment required for C.S.E. entry. These gradings had an undeniably bad effect on several pupils, who had begun to gain some confidence and interest in their reading and writing, in some cases almost for the first time in their lives, in the fourth year. One such lad had done a great deal for his C.S.E. projects (which was based on work he had done with six books, chosen by himself, with some teacher-consultation). But he turned down his chance to sit the examination, once he began to suspect that he was unlikely to be given as good a pass grade as some of his friends. He had worked hard at his English studies, and had improved a good deal on his own previous performances. He did not want to end the course with what on his own terms would be a 'failure'; so when the rest of the class was preparing for the examination towards the end of the fifth year, he went down to the workshop and turned out some handsome metalware. For him, it seemed an appropriately creative way of bringing his English work to a good conclusion, given the circumstances.

Greeting Macbeth, Duncan offers service which is tragically rejected: 'I have begun to plant thee, and will labour/To make thee full of growing.' The invitation to Macbeth is to become himself, through Duncan's agency: but he prefers the empty fantasies of 'new honours', that cling to him like ill-fitting robes. Even the more sensitive forms of public examination tend to divert attention away from real learning-growth to abstract, often irrelevant 'norms' of attainment, to make society's rewards available. If a teacher is thinking Duncan-like, positively, about his learners he will only wish to 'measure' the blossoming and flourishing of human beings (or their problems of growing) as a good gardener considers his plans: with reference to soil, climate and other conditions; to the performance of the plant in previous seasons; and to the natural qualities of a strain, or culture. But human relationship and appraisal being more complex even than this, the teacher can never exclude his own intimate involvement and performance from such evaluations.

Marvell's body complains of the soul: 'Thus architects do square and hew/Green trees that in the forest grew.' In the fifth year of secondary schooling neither teacher nor learner can avoid the tension between 'labouring to make them full of growing' on the one hand; and 'squaring and hewing' for public examinations, on the other. With this particular year, the balance was by no means always a happy one. But at least the talking and the writing of the group stayed real, throughout the fifth year. Moreover, the C.S.E./G.C.E. results were in happy keeping with evidence some years ago by David Thompson ('Non-streaming *did* make a difference', in *Forum*, 1974) that non-streaming may have a positively good effect on external examination results. Compared to previous years in the former school, when pupils had been rigidly streamed and setted — there was wide and dramatic improvement in examination grades.

What English lessons were actually about — that is, what the learners understood and drew from them — will be better conveyed through the writings of the group, in the chapters that follow this. The trouble with the teacher's account of things is that it is so easy to announce plans and aims and even 'results', but so difficult to say how it really was, for all those involved. Many writers on English teaching have confessed that, no matter how fine and flexible the syllabus, it can never be more than a crude diagram of only part of the lesson, given that English studies really do incorporate the experience of the learner. It is best, after all, to work from specific examples of what actually happened — as with the writings.

The tendency of syllabus-planners is to depersonalize learning, for they are always tempted to neglect the individual's desire for a personal direction. Neither do changes to programmes of integrated studies and team-teaching necessarily bring about the kind of change in the quality of what is learned. There is even a danger that such programmes might disguise and delay the primary change that is needed. In cases, for instance, where an intensive teaching programme is 'mastered' by a central committee of teachers, all the topics, projects and 'themes' may have been prepared with great thoroughness, but may not have grown at all from consultation with the learners. Even against the declared wishes of the organizers, the learners can become even more remote from their teachers and the course of study as presented on the 'master-plan'.

Yet paradoxically, a policy which begins with people rather than with a syllabus requires even more careful planning and organizing, to ensure success. The four teachers involved with the year-group concerned in these chapters, for instance, developed their own, intimate version of 'team-teaching', through frequent consultations and suggestions to each other on work-in-progress; comparing notes on individuals and class-groups; interchanging learners and teachers within classes, for a particular lesson or series of lessons, or even permanently, in a very few cases (it had been arranged that English lessons for the year-group should be time-tabled together); and bringing classes together regularly, to watch a film, or hear a visiting speaker. Such team-cooperation involved no elaborate organizational changes, but it encouraged each teacher to feel a degree of commitment to the whole year-group, without interfering with the teacher's (traditional) responsibility for a particular class.

There was no syllabus in the department, but there was a 'Statement of Aims', worked out through departmental meetings and regularly revised. The 'Statement of Aims' included a reflection on the need for personal education, and on language as a personal possession; an outline of appropriate resources, with a list of books, pictures, films, and worksheets and extracts available; a plea for variety and balance in the language and drama work; and an outline of a 'block' of lessons, to illustrate how a necessary continuity might be achieved, as well as variety and balance.

To take an example: a half-term programme of work for the fourth year (second term) would cover about thirty-five lessons — twenty-one single (40 minutes) and seven double (80 minutes) periods. In this example, a glance at the outline plans for the year shows that Harold Pinter's *The Caretaker*, C.S.E. set book, will be the main text in this programme, and that two films have been booked for this period for the fourth and fifth years — Clive Donner's film version of *The Caretaker* and Truffaut's *Fahrenheit 451* (these films were also booked for an evening showing to parents). It is usually unwise to plan too tightly over several weeks, but clearly some forward planning will be needed. The play has to be studied and completed, and other kinds of work are to receive special attention in this block — some poetry study; a number of resources related to the Pinter text, and to the films to be shown; private reading, both of 'set' and self-chosen texts; a good deal of talking and writing around chosen and related topics; some inter-departmental link-up, if possible; and always, space for self-chosen topics and directions. My outline plan for the half-term becomes adjusted after consulting other fourth year teachers, and is then extensively adjusted as the weeks go by. But the final summary of what *did* take place still reflects the benefits of forward planing, as well as the need for quick adjustments in the light of unexpected problems and opportunities:

WEEK ONE

Monday: New term greetings and social exchanges. Outline half-term's programme briefly. 'Acrostics' — some verbal games read and written on the pleasures and ironies of family Christmas/return to school/ New Year resolutions.

Wednesday: 'In touch, out of touch' — i. After introduction from teacher, small groups work on Hugh Lewin's poem 'Touch' and on an extract from *Bandiet*, his account of life as a political prisoner in South Africa. (questions on these supplied to group 'secretaries' by the teacher).

Thursday: (double lesson): 'In touch, out of touch' — ii. Soyinka's 'Telephone Conversation' (in *Voices* anthology). Prerecorded tape of the poem by an Irish-Nigerian sixth-former is played, while class read the poem. The class then 'enact' their own readings in pairs, usually boy-girl. The poem is discussed for some minutes (I search for decisions about the tones of voice in the poem). The class then looks at some passages from George Jackson's *Soledad Brother* describing how his sufferings in prison have taught him a special kind of patience. Discussion moves from the passage, to personal accounts of experiences of containing/admitting anger, different kinds of patience (angry, resigned, aware and so on). Bunyan's six month spell in Bedford gaol, Mrs. Durant (from last term's reading of *Daughters of the Vicar*), a recent 'carpeting' of the whole fourth year by one of the deputy heads are mentioned, along with many domestic instances. The class are asked to write a note (half a page) on 'irony' and 'patience', as revealed in the poem, the passages and our discourse. *Writing assignment*, due today week: a short story invited on themes of exclusion and/or intolerance. Some starting points suggested, many alternatives negotiated, while the class settles down to begin this.

Friday (and all Fridays): Private reading of suggested and self-chosen texts, and writing as part of preparation for CSE/O-level work. Many small sets (ten copies each) of select texts are available for class-reading and home-borrowing — including Bradbury, Yevtushenko, Wyndham, Waterhouse, Camus, Graves, Lorenz, London, Brecht, Vance Marshall, Orwell, Lawrence, Hardy, Van der Post, Twain, Wesker, Laurie Lee, Solzhenitsyn, Brontës, Storey, Huxley, Durrell and others.

WEEK TWO

Monday: Introduce Pinter. Short talk by teacher on 'Absurdity and Alienation' in modern plays. Examples given from Ionesco's *Bald Prima Donna* and Pinter's short piece, *Request Stop*. Links established by class with 'Monty Python's Flying Circus' and the range and limits of this kind of humour discussed. A contest develops to relate 'dead-pan' jokes . . .

Wednesday: Copies of *Caretaker* handed out, and class reading of the play begins. Teacher takes part of tramp, having donned his usual overcoat, and an old hat from drama props.

Thursday (double lesson): School hall. Production groups (seven groups of four) work on early scenes in *The Caretaker* — three different parts of the first Act. Class come together to watch dramatization by particular groups. (Writing is collected, late deliverers chivvied to produce by tomorrow . . .)

Friday: Private reading and writing, individual consultations on reading and writing-in-progress. Next writing assignment set, based on opening work on *The Caretaker* (various choices on and around the text, due in on Monday week).

WEEK THREE

Monday: Class arrives late from morning assembly. Return work. One or two stories are read out (with writer's permission). Discussion opens up on these, and on prisons and imprisonment.

Wednesday: Short talk by teacher on film to be shown on Thursday, and passages read out from Bradbury's *Fahrenheit 451*. A short question-naire given to the class on their own book-reading habits (which books would they take to a desert island, which they would consign to heat at 451°F, evaluation of last book that they read for pleasure, and so on).

Thursday (double period): Film *Fahrenheit 451* with whole of fourth year. Film finishes soon after end of afternoon school; about a quarter of the year stay on to discuss the film for twenty minutes or so.

Friday: Private reading and writing, individual consultations. (Reminder about writing due in on Monday.)

WEEK FOUR

Monday: Class-reading of *The Caretaker* – Act One concluded, and Aston's long speech on electro-therapy discussed at some length (writing collected in).

Wednesay: Lesson on 'The Cliché', to introduce tomorrow's lesson on the painter's vision. Teacher presents, and class reads, a passage from D.H. Lawrence's 'Introduction to his Paintings', about Cézanne's fight against the cliché; other, shorter items follow. Class goes into small groups for remaining ten minutes, to 'prepare questions' on the main points in the Lawrence passage. (Short writing task on this for homework)

Thursday: (double period): Co-teaching class in art room, with fifth-year art group. Topic: Van Gogh. Prints and slides presented by art-teacher, passages from Van Gogh's letters presented by English teacher. Also showing of Alan Resnais' short film on Van Gogh. Small group work on selected prints.

Friday: Private reading and writing, individual consultations. Writing on *The Caretaker* returned. New writing topic set, on 'Images of Life' – various options suggested including poetry sequence, short story, discursive/descriptive work on paintings/landscapes (due in Monday week).

WEEK FIVE

Monday: Lesson missed, through late assembly. Lesson plan abandoned . . . .

Wednesday: Class-reading of *The Caretaker* continues with occasional discussion.

Thursday (double period): Short talk by teacher, to introduce a long passage from R.D. Laing's *Sanity, Madness and the Family,* about an interview between a therapist, a girl and her parents. This is dramatized in small groups. The passage provokes intense interest and discussion. A member of the class offers to invite her mother, who works in a psychiatric hospital, to visit the school. Several members of the class ask to change the writing topic set last Friday, to reflect the issues of the Laing passage, and this is agreed. Talk on parent-child relations continues in small groups, without further structuring.

Friday: Private reading and writing, individual consultations.

WEEK SIX

Monday: Copies of the 'Boating Incident' from Wordsworth's Prelude, Book II are handed out, after short introduction. Teacher reads the passage — the class seem impressed, but do not talk readily. Teacher ventures a fifteen minute talk, then asks them to write a note on being 'fostered by fear'. (This is collected in with their homework at the end of the lesson.)

Wednesday: School hall. Production groups work on Second Act of *The Caretaker*.

Thursday: Film, *The Caretaker*, with whole of fourth year. Film finishes soon after end of school. No discussion group this time.

Friday: Private reading and writing. Written work returned, and individual consultations given. (homework: private reading)

WEEK SEVEN

Monday: Set writing topic on *'The Caretaker*: thinking it over'. Various approaches suggested, and individual variations negotiated. Class begin work on this (due in after half-term).

Wednesday: Copies of Thomas Blackburn's poem *Hospital for Defectives* are given to the class. After a reading by the teacher some 'imagist' qualities in the poem are mentioned, and questions are asked about the kind of attention given by the poet to the hospital patients. Some duplicated information is provided from David Ennals' book *Out of Mind*, on mental illness and disability and from Carter's *The Unknown Citizen*, about a recidivist prisoner. These are discussed in small groups (questions provided by teacher to group 'secretaries').

Thursday: Outside speaker, with rest of fourth year, in main hall. The speaker works in a local psychiatric unit, and lives up to her daughter's promise that she will be interesting. Several of the group stay behind after school, to talk to her informally in the school canteen. (lesson originally planned for this session is abandoned).

Friday: 'Refreshment lesson'. Members of the class have been invited to provide an entertainment. Contributions include: guitar playing, presenting discs (with the proviso that each had to be introduced with a two-minute talk), folk-singing (by the teacher), clog-dancing (we were on the ground-floor . . .), parodies, limericks and so on.

No single half term can cover all the activities, let alone the topics, that a balanced English programme should aim to include. Fiction, for instance, was usually prominent in our English work but was confined to private reading during these seven weeks; music and song only had a foothold at the very end; no theatre or other outside visits were organized, and so on. But for all that, the programme can be seen to have offered a fair range and a fair balance of activities; and there were effective contrasts, as well as links, among the topics that were treated. As with other successful programmes of this kind, countless interlinkings took place among individual learners between the various topics. It does not, for instance, need an unusual or eccentric imagination, to see how the Laing passage might connect with the Wordsworth poem, in their common preoccupation with self-direction and parental presences (in the one case enhancing, in the other, destroying); nor, say, to discern a fruitful point of contrast between the stale existences of Pinter's characters, and the creative innovations of Cézanne, Van Gogh or Lawrence.

This example is, it must be confessed, a bare version indeed of what actually happened: it contains nothing of the interminglings of words and ideas, the interruptions, meanderings, cross-talk, irritations, homilies, confessions, comic interludes — all the highly complex experience of several weeks of English work with a fourth-year class. The substance of what happened and what was learned can only be indicated by particular evidence — in this case, by examples of writing from the group. It will be the task of the next chapter to introduce this evidence, and also to introduce a proposal for stages of learning development, that became discernible through the writings of the group. Some of the writings quoted will have come from the work of this half term; and the rest from similar 'work-blocks' during their fourth, fifth and lower sixth years at the school.

CHAPTER THREE

Stages in Writing Growth, and a Case Study

'... you change as you write, you change yourself, you change the way you think.'

(Doris Lessing)

Identifying the Stages

When sorting through the writings of the class on which these chapters are based, and through my comments on these over a three-year period, I was struck by my own habits of commenting almost exclusively on what the pupils had written *about*; there was rarely comment given on aspects of the language that they used, as such, apart from some select emending of syntax, spelling and punctuation. The emphasis of the comments was directed towards those experiences that had been made manifest in the learner's writing; they were concentrated on the context of the experience as reported, not on formal aspects of their language. They offered sympathetic and critical interest by raising marginal questions, inviting further reply to a dialogue that had been first begun in the classroom perhaps, or was self-initiated by the writer — a dialogue that was given the opportunity to continue, through the comments offered by the teacher or (quite frequently) by a trusted member of the class; and where these comments had been perfunctory or inadequate, the writings seemed, chasteningly, to read like only half of the script of a dialogue. The approach to written work became a deliberate policy, which had developed from sharing and comparing approaches with colleagues. It came too from an intimation, which I had not thought over in any very sustained or deliberate spirit, that the best — indeed only — way to promote language growth as a teacher, was through dwelling, as the writer invited, in the world created through the writing. Thus the teacher's task lay first in making as much appropriate provision as possible for entry into that world, which then became the learner's responsibility to encounter and negotiate. Up to that point we had shied away from any of the deliberate investigations of language as such, that were then attracting fashionable attention; our own interest and emphasis as practising teachers had to be centred in the people in the classroom – as individuals, as groups, and as a class. This was, in effect, the basis of our intuitive 'language programme' as English teachers: so that my later attempts to identify patterns and principles in that teaching approach have in turn become particularly concerned with discovering more about those interactions that take place between the individual and the world.

My opening chapter dwelled on the need to envisage learning, thinking and language as acts of the whole person; and some further attention was given to how this principle might be applied to the act of writing. Chapter Two described a particular English programme in a particular context; and this chapter now introduces a proposal for stages in writing growth, to be expanded in Chapters Four to Eight. Each stage is intended to reflect the learner-writer's whole range of learning response – intuiting, sensing, imagining, fantasizing, reasoning.

One of the best savoured pleasures of parenthood is to observe the progress of ordinary children as they reach into a language and make it their own. A normally well-cherished and active five-year-old is likely already to have developed a sound grammatical and lexical grasp of the mother-tongue. Frank Whitehead (*The Disappearing Dais*, 1966) cited evidence from M.K. Smith's work, that the five-year-old's vocabulary is likely to amount to fifteen thousand words, rising by two to four thousand each year up to the age of seventeen. A child of seven or eight has usually reached mature articulation by that age. Of course children may only use a very limited selection of the words they know; much more crucial than the number of words known will be the degree to which there is a corresponding, interwoven growth of meaning, feeling, imagining, skill in coping with different demands and contexts – growth, that is, in personal *and* language development. They will reach out to language in reaching out to life.

Having made that language their own, children negotiate a place in the world – not only as the object of love and nourishing from the parent, but as someone with an individual and creative centre. Edward Sapir has suggested that

All in all, it is not too much to say that one of the really important functions of language is to be constantly declaring to society the psychological place held by its members.

(*Language*, 1949)

In order eventually to convince others that their 'psychological place' as adults is claimed on good grounds, they will need to move towards a more real relation with their environment and with other beings; a clear and convinced sense of their own identity; a capacity to recognize and cope with existential difficulties; a sense of belonging and commitment to the world; and eventually to move towards a sense of integrity, unity, and wholeness of understanding within the shared world.

Reading again through James Britton's 'What's the Use?' (1972), it struck me that the true value of this essay lay not in its reflections on Denis Harding, and certainly not in its disposition towards a duality theory of language, but in the almost 'by the way' suggestions that emerge, about the modes of thinking and discourse that develop when we encounter new experience. My own notes, while reading this essay, identified these: gossip, a first exchange of response to new experience; thinking it over, internalizing, gestating; sustained, objective inspection of the new experience; turning this to use, looking for general possibilities; incorporating into a 'world-view'. Linking these notes with Sapir's reflection on the qualities needed to take one's 'psychological place' as an adult led to a mapping out of five possible stages of enquiry in learning, thus:

1. What do I sense, feel, do, experience in this world?
2. What effect do these experiences have on me, how do I respond, adjust, change?
3. What may I now clearly grasp and identify as beyond-me?
4. How may I connect this with and apply it to other beings and the world that I relate to?
5. What meanings may now be discerned in all of this, what is my world-view, my vision of living?

The pressure to mark out these stages had come from my sifting through two thousand or so pieces of writing that had accumulated from the same mixed ability class as it moved over a period of three years from fourth to lower sixth year. It became gradually clear that five stages of growth-in-writing could be seen to cover adequately just about all the writings sifted (though many pieces could be seen to overlap two stages — or even three, in rarer cases).

A somewhat bald outline of the stages may help to introduce them — but each will need the more detailed explanation and illustration of the chapters that follow. Included in parenthesis after the summary for each there are examples of kinds of writing that are encouraged in English studies, since the sifted writings were all of this kind; but it is possible that the stages could be seen to describe more general patterns of response in learning (they are, for instance, discernible in the work of my present post-graduate and higher degree students in educational studies).

Stage One – Telling[1].

Here the learner records the direct impressions and emotions caused by new experience. Writing tends to be fluent, outward-going, naively communicative, enthusiastic and uninhibited by self-criticism or tentativeness. The writer tends to be strongly context-bound, offering simple, immediate and unsifted recalling of experience. (There is often a strongly autobiographical basis to the writing, and a sense of excitement at the simple narrative events of a story or play – including even a straightforward attempt just to re-tell the story.)

Stage Two – Reflecting.

The writer begins to reflect, to grow aware of feelings, to attend to, and to sift, sense and emotional responses – to respond to responses. The writing tends to be inward-moving, dwelling on the feelings aroused by the new experience, exploring 'inwards'. There is a tendency to exploit new learning for the writer's own subjective purposes, in working out personal bearings and personal needs. (In this sometimes highly self-conscious stage, the writer may need to risk apparently 'eccentric' or 'irrelevant' response to a literary text, or to a direct experience. A story may, for instance, be 're-told' but with changes of emphasis and detail, or even major adjustments of character and plot, as the writer struggles to make subjective sense of the new intrusion of experience.)

Stage Three – Identifying.

Here the writer grows aware of the 'that-ness' of the new experience, and moves outward with confidence into a 'third realm', beyond provisional, self-conscious 'reflecting'; the new world is now encountered. Writing is characterized by acts of imaginative empathy, by awareness of the other's identity and state of being – it shows a fully embodied comprehension. Ordering and reasoning powers are now in full play, now that the experience has grown from conception, through gestation, to birth. There is a disposition to value the new experience for itself, to enjoy the clear, firm outlines of newly gained understanding, to delight in its unfamiliar distinctness. (In response, say, to a literary text, writers may now offer some sustained and detached attention to their own previous responses and involvement – may recognize, for instance, *why* there was a tendency to 'identify' with a character. There is also a natural flourishing of appropriate 'skills' at this stage – for example, how to shape a short story, how to show someone else what is worth noticing about an experience – a poem, a story and so on.)

1. Note: In the original study (summarized by Harrison, 1979) this was termed the 'expressing' stage. 'Telling' is now preferred, in order to incorporate notions of expressing *and* communicating to others. See Chapter Four: *Telling*.

Stage Four – Organizing.
The writer moves out to test the wider relevance of new learning. There is a growing sense of commitment on behalf of others, of the group, the community, the world. With this growing sense of belonging the writer intends to be critical, supportive of, contributing to the aspirations and values of the community. Comparative and evaluative skills develop. (The writer develops interest in synthesizing responses to a literary text or other experience, relating these to wider concerns – social, historical, moral and so on.)

Stage Five – Integrating.
Having established a secure identification of the experience, and having tested its potential worth for actual living, the writer moves towards disinterested, independent speculation on the possibilities of gaining a store of meaning, a vision of living. This stage marks the blossoming of spiritual and religious life, a search for significant pattern, for harmony and integration in relationships. (The writer learns to value art-discourse in the light of deeper, larger moral, philosophical and religious insights; to see realized literary forms as the significant embodying by others of reality, which we too may incorporate, with enriching effects on our quality of being and our vision of living.)

It should be said at once, that while some kind of progression is indicated in the way these stages have been represented above, the writer may well be involved in two or more stages at the same time, and that new experience requires a continual reversion even to the earliest stages of learning response. While these proposed stages imply (and the evidence of the scripts supported this) that no learners are likely to achieve much at all within, say, the fifth stage until they have developed in the earlier stages, their development from then on will involve continuous 'loops of retrogression' to earlier stages, to regenerate the earlier growth achieved in these stages. The stages should not, then, be seen just as (Piaget-like) stages in a learner's growth, but as phases in encountering all new experience and knowledge, which apply to the living, maturing individual throughout adult life. The stages envisage a general and innate pattern, stemming from a tenet that it is normal for the ordinary privileged human individual – one who on the whole enjoys the basic necessities of food, warmth, space and human relationships – to seek and strive for a sense of meaning, a vision of living. Furthermore, it is from among the poor, the cold, the hungry, the oppressed and imprisoned of this world that have come some of the greatest quests of thought that we know; even extremes of repression did not silence George Jackson, or Solzhenitzyn, or Bunyan, or Viktor Frankl. I do not suggest facilely that suffering is good for us, but rather, that the quest of meaning can itself strengthen the human effort to survive.

The Case Of Ian

How do these stages operate within the writings of an individual learner? The case of Ian is chosen to illustrate this; and to anticipate the charge that such stages are likely only to reflect the work of that minority of learners who are positively enthusiastic about writing, the individual concerned came from among those members of the class who were regarded, and who regarded themselves, as deriving very little benefit from their schooling, for whatever causes.

In Ian's case, the cause of his 'under-achievement' was often thought to be his 'attitude', or (in the then vogue term) his 'alienation' from his studies. He seemed to need to give the impression at school that he was 'one of the lads' who were the despair of all teachers. He claimed, publicly and often, to hate school; he always made a show of sitting in the corner at the back of the room, hands in pockets, legs sprawled out, leaning back on his chair and guffawing at Paddy's loud belch, or at Jim's simulated smack of a kiss blown to the girls on the other side. He was famed for his skill in annoying teachers and disrupting classrooms, and acted, in short, according to the long and secure tradition of what one of my own teachers used to denounce as the 'phalanx of louts in the back row'. But Ian's sense of boredom, irritation and frustration with school was deep-rooted, and produced blackly destructive moods in him. Then he would relapse into long and surly silences which excluded both teachers and fellow-pupils from his thoughts, except for an occasional vicious outburst against some individual or condition which had angered him. Up to the fourth year his classroom record was grim. He had done virtually no work in any lessons since transferring from the primary school, and had managed to convince his English teachers in the second and third forms of our school that he was near to being illiterate. Yet he was an athletic, lively lad who played foolball and basketball well; his drawing and painting in the art-room were good; he enjoyed the respect of his friends and peers; and he soon showed in class discussion − when he was in the right mood − that he was no fool in putting over his point of view about things. He managed to settle down to some work in the fifth year, and left school as soon as he could, after sitting for two or three C.S.E.'s, to work in a local hardware shop.

The first piece of writing here, *The Family* was written about half-way through the first term in the fourth year, and was his first genuine *effort* in his English book; until then he had offered a few jumbled and barely readable sentences from time to time, and had succeeded in maintaining his reputation in my eyes as being near-illiterate. Around that time we had begun reading George Orwell's *Coming Up for Air* in class, where George Bowling describes in the opening chapter the daily clamour of his family around the bathroom as he tries to shave. The writing topic for the week had not been based on this, in fact; but while negotiating an alternative topic with Ian, who claimed to have no interest in the set topic (on a Blake poem), he had mentioned that he had quite enjoyed the Orwell chapter. From this we agreed that he should write something about his family life. As in many instances where there has been a long absence from personally involved writing it is interesting to note how both Ian's choice and treatment of topic suggests that of a much younger writer — as though he were suddenly starting up where he had left off many years previously:

The Family

There is six people in the family Mum, Dad, sister, two brothers and myself. We have a mixture of fun and good times and bad argueing times. Often the arguments are started by the most stupidest of things, sometimes if someone is in the Bathroom too long. These petty arguments are often started off by my sister who if you tell here to hurry up and finnish anything she will take twice as long. The main trouble with the family is lazyness everyone of us suffers from this except my mum she will be on the go all day. The worst thing is when my dad gets in a mood, he'll often go like this when he has been proved wrong in an argument, I suppose really he is just a person who has it in his nature to be stubborn, and when you have a person like this, the only way to keep happy is by always admitting he is right whether he is or is not. I used to get on really well with my sister until she started work now I see her only two or three times a week as when she gets home I'm just normaly going out for the evening. Also I hardly ever see my brothers now as they always go out to play. The time in the year when everyone is in a reasonable happy mood is when we go on holiday for a week. As for me I'm in the best mood you'll ever find me when we go to a place like boxhill on a hot and sunny day. I think it is just because of the peace and quiet up there and when you look down and everything is so minute that it give's you a feeling of power.

(Ian, fourth year, aged 14)

Here is a simple, direct telling of facts and feelings about characters and disagreements in his large-ish family, and about a growing sense of being left out, as when 'dad gets in a mood. . . and when you have a person like this the only way to keep happy is by always admitting he is right whether he is or is not.' He feels he is also losing a sense of family intimacy that he once enjoyed, through the simple accidents of growing up and the taking of different directions — his older sister now in full-time work, his younger brothers off to play with their own friends beyond the home. In part-compensation for this sense of loss comes the annual family holiday as one time when 'everyone is in a reasonable happy mood . . " And he finishes by writing about good moments by himself, 'like boxhill on a hot and sunny day .. and when you look down and everything is minute that it gives you a feeling of power ..'. He is on the verge of reflective commentary, in touching on loneliness and being alone here. But over all this is a straightforward, narrating-describing account, that may, perhaps, be regarded as 'setting the scene' for further reflections. At the time it was written, it was encouraging to see that Ian could write with quite reasonable competence, and seemed not to have exceptional difficulties in spelling and punctuation, even if his handwriting looked clearly out of practice.

The second piece, 'How to live' was written after a class discussion on a passage on A.S. Neill, about the aims of schooling. Ian had contributed a good deal to this discussion, much of it in the shape of spirited criticism of our own school. He felt disinclined to write anything further on the topic; and while the rest of the class were quietly writing, (or at least quietly sitting) on their reactions to the discussion, Ian and I had a fierce, whispered and brief debate on the justifications of writing on what we had already talked about. I asked him to make his point against writing *in* writing — and after he had made the obvious ironic protest, he wrote this piece:

How to Live

The only real way to live is to enjoy your live as much as you can. You (M. Harrison) try to make us write about how to live but writing about it really isn't going to make me change my life that much. Although it might make me think about a few points a bit more closely.

When I was younger I used to be frightened at the thought of living just to die but now I'm not really bothered about it, though when the time come's what I'll feel like I do not know. Nearly every lesson you tell us to try and enjoy our lives but how are we meant to enjoy our lives if in every week we have 30 to 35 hours a week at school of which about 28 hours are one big chore and 63 hours sleeping a week. And that does not leave much time a week to live your own live. Even though school only takes up 7 hours a day of most of the lessons have so boring that they put me in a mood for the rest of the day. And the only time I really enjoy myself is when I go out with my girl. Although when I'm in a mood after school, she goes into one and we have a row.

Sundays are the only I really have a good time, because I do what I want, I enjoy myself, within reason.

. . . .

I think a school should try to help people of my age to understand people more easily. From the end of the third year to about the end of the fifth year are some of the most difficult years to get through to people and even more difficult for a teacher to get through to us. I think that the teacher should be able to talk to us in an interesting way instead of just presenting facts and making it into a real boring lesson. A teacher should be really a friend of the pupil.

(Ian, fourth year, aged 14)

Having 'cleared the air' between us in his opening paragraph, he goes on to follow up a major point that had been dwelled on in the discussion — that life is short and that we need to make choices and decisions for ourselves while we can. Ian looks at the way in which time has been taken up in his own life, and he protests about the way he feels that his time and life are being wasted in school. The 'overflow' of strong feeling here seems to confuse his word order, as he claims that even his free time is affected: 'Even though school only takes up 7 hours a day of most of the lessons have so boring that they put me in a mood for the rest of the day . . .' — his quickness to express anger and irritation is evident throughout this piece. Yet it is essentially reflecting writing, where he is taking a look at the ideal of having choice and enjoyment in life, in contrast to the day-to-day realities that he himself has to face. He discerns not only how things outside himself — school rules and conventions, and so on; but also how his inner state — of being 'in a mood' — can ruin areas of enjoyment and good living. And he concludes with a moderate, sensible-sounding phrase about his wish to 'enjoy myself, within reason.' His feeling that he has the right to decide on actions which give him satisfaction is tempered here by avowing that he should act 'within reason' ; he accepts implicitly that his freedom is likely to be restricted by the needs of others.

Having turned away from self-assertiveness in that final phrase, he develops a more clearly reflecting, restrained tone in the second part, which he wrote as a paragraph-long 'afterthought' on 'How to Live'. Without directly mentioning our classroom discussions on Neill, nor the confrontation with me any further, he writes down a brief definition of good teaching, as seen from the view of an adolescent who is 'going through some of the most difficult years to get through to people and even more difficult for a teacher to get through to us . . '. At this point in his writing, Ian has begun to think much more considerately about himself — and about the teacher too, in passing. For the first time since his entry into the fourth year he had come to express feelings that are not angry, strident or scornful. His emphasis is now positive and hopeful: 'I think that the teacher should be able to talk to us in an interesting way . . . be really a friend of the pupil.'

This piece of writing marks a point where, from being a suspicious outsider to the English lesson, Ian became a genuine member of the class. He still had days of dark, brooding silences, and could still be perverse and over-bearing. But he began to take his own progress in writing, reading and discussion seriously, for the first time in several years.

The third piece, on Barry Hines's *A Kestrel for a Knave* and on Ken Loach's film *Kes* was written as part of the C.S.E. course. It is very much on the borderline of the second and third stages of writing. It is a very personal piece, where we are made almost aware of the run of Ian's own private thoughts and feelings, as about the topic of Billy and his hawk. His first sentences indicate how his account will develop:

'Kes': Billy loves a Hawk
rather than another human being. Why?

Billy has more admiration for the hawk than love. He is envious of the way the hawk can fly, just fly off of his own free will, to freedom, whenever he likes.

Billy hasn't got anybody else to love or to respect, his father has left his mother who is not really a mother at all. She is a woman who in the book 'Kes' is described more as a tart who always goes out plastered in make up, and that is just the way Billy see's her. I think this is one of the reasons that Billy turns to the Hawk for, possibly more as a symbol than anything else, a symbol of freedom, the freedom which Billy wants. Billy does not want to go to school but he also does not want to work, he want's to do what a load of people would like to do and that is their 'own thing,' but most People by the time they get to Billy's age, they have conformed to the society's way of thinking, through pressure by others, who say it is right. If people do not conform, they are thought of as revolutionists, and this is what Billy is like, he hates the way of life in there minning town, he realises that there nothing in life, if he grows up the same way as jud did. Home every night from the mine, then out drinking, coming home drunk and then off to bed. That is the pattern of Jud's life. Billy does not admire Jud or his mother, because there is nothing in the two of them to admire and one aspect or meaning to the word love, is when you can admire certain things and qualities in someone or something. Apart from the freedom factor of the hawk, Billy also admires the Hawks stream lining and good look's and one other important factor. and that is its wildness, and Billy has conquered this wildness. In the classroom at school Billy explains in the English lesson how much it meant to him, training this hawk who has only ever had one rule known to him, and that was his rule. The Hawks rule. When I saw the film of the Hawk flying it gave me a kind of funny sensation and I think it probably is the sort of feeling that Billy has. Compared to the Hawk, his family have no real personality. When I saw the Hawk flying it gave a feeling of freedom and peace. A feeling that if I could fly or float about like the Hawk, then that would be the place where everything would be alright and calm and I could rule myself with no-one butting in and belling what to do all the time. Yet also I knew that immediately that hawk spotted its prey, the violence would come.

That could possibly been one of the qualities Billy saw in the Hawk .. Although Billy accepted the fact that violence was part of the hawks life. Although he loved 'Kes', he could go out and shoot another bird for 'Kes', to eat from his hand. Billy has learnt to accept the fact that life is meant to be that way. When 'Kes', is in flight he is like a dream, and Billy thought this until 'Kes' caught his prey and then everything seemed to come back to reality for Billy.

Billy is a boy who is thought of as stupid and lazy boy, but really he is alive more than most other's in his school, and he realises this, and keeps it to himself because I think he realises that if he tried to explain to others they just would not understand and they would think him a crank or something. Yet here is a Hawk who seem's to understand. Billy I think, by just staying with Billy and not flying off. It is a form of understanding of love. And when Billy found him dead he just faced the truth, the Hawk, his symbol of freedom, 'dead' in a dustbin, so Billy did what he thought was the right thing to do and that was not to go out for revenge, but bury 'Kes'. A sign I think of his admiration for him.

I often admire animals more than people because they are not ruled by anyone. Though when I found my rabbit strangled by someone. I felt my heart loose a few beats and I think Billy must have had a fairly tough nature, not to break down or go and for revenge. I know wanted revenge although I did not find it. I think maybe Billy had more sense than I did, He learnt one of the main facts of love it does not say whether he learns the other's.

(Ian, fourth year, aged 15)

'Billy has more admiration for the hawk than love'. This ignores Billy's clearly tender feelings for the hawk as shown in the book; yet it is not a purely personal distortion of what the book is about. Billy is indeed fascinated by 'the way the hawk can fly, just fly off of his own free will ..' though the word 'envious', and the feeling behind it, is Ian's rather than Billy's. This blurring of distinction between the writer's feelings and thoughts, and those of Billy, continues in the account of Billy seeking to do his 'own thing' apart from both family and community pressures. Ian returns continually to the qualities of independence and wildness that he (justly) sees the hawk as representing; and again he gives as strong an impression of his own feelings and preoccupations as he does of Billy's here: 'Apart from the freedom factor of the book, Billy also admires the Hawks streamlining and good looks . . .'. (Ian himself laid emphasis on personal appearance and 'good looks', and took more pains to be groomed and tidy than many lads in the form bothered to be). After this his account becomes openly personal: 'When I saw the film of the hawk flying it gave me a kind of funny sensation . . . a funny feeling of freedom and peace . . . Yet also I knew that immediately that hawk spotted its prey, the violence would come . . .'. Again, while being a very personal account, this is also evidence of fine and clear response, in this case to a moment in the film *Kes*. He seems to realise that both he and the film may be drawing away from the Billy of the book here, and adds tentatively to his last point: 'That could possibly been one of the qualities Billy saw in the hawk . . .' in order to develop his point about ideal dreams against hard realities in life. Ian's final two paragraphs dwell on both the similarities and differences between himself and Billy: 'Billy is a boy who is thought of as stupid and lazy boy, but really he is alive more than most other's in his school, and he realises this . . .'. This, I think, contains both self-identification, and clear insight into the character as presented in the book. Ian goes on to consider the quality of Billy's love (which he has now come to admit) for the hawk, and compares Billy's quiet acceptance of the fact of his death, to his own vengeful feelings when he discovered his pet rabbit 'strangled by someone'. He acknowledges a strength in Billy here: 'I felt my heart loose a few beats and I think Billy must have a fairly tough nature, not to break down or go for revenge . . . I think maybe Billy had more sense than I did . . .' And reflecting thus on Billy's resigned patience, he concludes somewhat enigmatically: 'He learnt one of the main facts of love it does not say whether he learns the other's'. Over all, his account is undeniably personal, in tone and preoccupation; but on balance it may be inferred that he is using himself to understand the book, rather than the other way round. His account here has advanced to an identifying stage of writing and response.

His fourth piece, *Poems by Yevtushenko* represents the organizing stage and was written as part of his C.S.E. Project, in which he was required to choose six books and write about, or 'from' them, as he wished; so that what is reproduced here is about half of one of six sections in his project. He had come across Yevtushenko in his fourth year, when we had read *Lies* in class, and had asked me then for a selection of his poems:

Poems by Yevtushenko
i 'Lies'

This poem I think should be shown to parents and to people who seem to have forgotten what youth is, and who do not see the young as an equal. In a way, I think there should be some kind of youth liberation, just like women's lib. I think that even now though many people are realising that the young grow older quicker, and also they want to know the real world and the real life, not only the life that the older wish the young to know.

The poet Yevtushenko seem's to believe in honesty in life in many of his poems', in this poem, he show's that if you wish to be respected, you have to respect those whose respect you wish to gain. He meant this, I think, when in the last four lines of the poem he wrote 'Forgive no error you recognise it will repeat itself, increase and afterwards our pupils will not forgive in us what we forgave.

The true reality of life should be told to the young as this poem tries to show. Often when a person has not been told the truth's of life, you will hear an old saying cropping up, going something like, 'Well he learnt the hard way,' or words to that effect, which really mean that the child will learn from his mistakes, which can often be harmful mistakes either physcaly or mentaly, and often these memmories of pain which may never have happened had they been told the truth about the consequences, lie deep in there memory, yet they are always' there, and often the thought of revenge could occur.

If a child is not told the truth, and has to wait until later in life before he is able to know the truth for himself, he may think it right for him to deprive his own children of knowing the bare truth's of life. So really the child is often brought up to carry on with the crime thier parents have commited.

Two of the main points in the poem are that really you cannot tell a child that there is a God in his heaven, all that you can do is present the facts, that have given other people prove, and let the child decide for itself. Also the poet points out that everyone should be told that the price of happyness will not be happy for even in love of either girl's, parent's or close friends, hazard's are all around just waiting to be stirred up. And even when the happyness you have struggled for arrives', there is the knowing fact all good thing's have to come to an end.

ii 'People'

When the poet relates people with planets, he is trying to show that although from the outside a planet look's very much the same like any other planet, but inside that kind of revolving ball, there is all sort's of different happening's going on. This is where the relationship comes, for really apart from looks', no-one is particular to the next on the surface, but really underneath the surface, there is a person living in their own world, with many different and original happening's. No-one person lives the same sort of life as the next, for even if they were trained to do the same thing and eat and sleep at the same time, they would still be thinking different thing's in their mind.

In every living person, a history will grow up around him yet when he dies all this history will go with him, for this is really his own personnel possession, and no-one need know whether or not he was good or bad, the only thing's left for those to remember them by is all the material good's which he has owned or made, and maybe photographs and a few writings, which if they are famous writings of famous people, they may be published in books.

When you think you know a person thoroughly, you are really only trying to fool yourself, because you will only know what that person, really wants you to know, and you do the same with them, and I think this can often be the one great thing to a person's privacy. And when that person dies and you realise you did not really know them it is too late.

(Ian had written out all his chosen poems in full, before discussing them.)

(Ian, fourth year, aged 15)

In his account of *Lies* he concentrates on what he sees as the important representative qualities of the poem: 'This poem I think should be shown to parents and to people who seem to have forgotten what youth is . . .'. But he has developed and clarified his earlier self-assertions (as they appeared in the second, reflecting piece) a good deal. He considers how difficult and necessary an art it is to train youth: 'they want to know the real world and the real life, not only the life that the older wish the young to, to know . .'. It is the duty of the teacher, he thinks, to show the young how to avoid damaging mistakes, 'which can often be harmful mistakes either physcaly or mentaly . . . ' Apart from the possible hint of self-revelation of something he has written about many times previously (his revenge-urges), Ian maintains a generous and impersonal argument on behalf of a truthful education for *all* the young, as being the only chance for the young to avoid having to 'carry on the crime thier parents have committed . . .'. Along with the poet he affirms that you can only 'present the facts' to a child but must 'let the child decide for itself;' and that the search for fulfilment will be costly: 'the price of happyness will not be happy . . .'. Also he adds with glum yet simple truth a point which is his, rather than the poet's, that part of facing truth is facing the fact of having to die: 'even when the happyness you have struggled for arrives, there is the knowing (=gnawing?) fact all good things have to come to an end . . .'.

The second commentrary, on *People* is not so clearly concerned with a public issue, being more of a reflection on the difference between individual people. It is less assuredly a 'fourth-stage' piece of writing than *Lies*. But while it is not so clearly concerned with a communal issue or problem, it does attempt, with some success, to offer an objective view of people in their relationships with each other. It is not the very personal, reflecting kind of writing that characterizes the second stage; nor is it specifically concerned with the poem itself, as in the third stage. Here the writer is using the poem as a springboard to make a general and impersonal point about individual as opposed to collective history: 'In every living person a history will grow up around him yet when he dies all this history will go with him, etc . . .'. What he writes does not have a directly social or political reference, yet it may be seen to stem from a sense of political awareness just as surely as an arguing of the opposite case for the common destiny and brotherhood of man may do. It is the objective, impersonal tone and quality of the writing that qualifies it, overall for the fourth stage.

The final piece, was written as set work on Pinter's *The Caretaker:*

True and False Faces

People often play a role which is false to their nature, it often occur's in either a sheepish person, who just conforms to authority, because they are scared to do otherwise. There is also though the average person who play's this false roll, because the authority in society force onto people, situation's in which they do not really wish to be in, but often have to play this false polite roll for the need of money. People play this role whether they are capitalist or communist, or any other political belief.

I have to play a false roll in which it is hard to be myself many times during the day. One Saterday's I have a job in a shoe shop up the high street. Because the shoes in the shop are nearly all above five pounds', people expect the best in everything including service. I suppose they have a right, but sometimes, the amount of abuse I get from some people is really sickening, and it make's me think how meaningless life is to a vast majority of people, who live in a world of money, a world which they were born into.

At my job I have to put on a false face and use an apologetic attitude, when something is wrong with 'sir's shoes. I admit that I like everyone else, except for dropout's only do this work and give this false identity for the couple of pounds a week I get for doing the job. If it were not for the money I'd probably belt every awkward customer to 'piss off' or even something strong. It is not that I do not like work, that I moan about my job, it is just the job that I do, I would probably love my work if I was a photographer, or writer, if I was a writer and was clever enough I would like to be some-one like a modern day Carl Mark, and write my own version of 'Das kapital', only my work's would be my ideal of a completely free world, only this is not possible and there is alway's an authority which grow's out of a revolution, which is alway's needed to start something new. People would only end up eventually the same as they are now, in a rat race, making people think there nice

hard working people. Where as really they are mostly cold hearted
people who are only hard working, not because they enjoy there job,
but because they want money, to by material possession's to keep up
with the Jones's. And some poor soul would stuck at home one night
writing this out again and moaning about the work he put's up with.

One of many other times when I cannot do what I want or be myself,
is when I am at school. If I had my own way, I know that most of the
time I would flirt with the girls' and do very little work, but even when
you try to confirm partly by working, you are still kept down by
teachers' or authority. Of cause there are some teacher's who do
encourage you to be yourself, because really this is the only way to
know who the people you are teaching really are.

Many people often go into discussions with each other what life is all
about, but how on earth will people ever find an answer, while people
are given off a false image of themselves. Often people fall back on
saying God is life, all God is really is or should be is a symbol of peace
and love, not a person, like some excentric preacher's like Mr. B. seem
to make him out to be.

The other day he tried to use his authority on a few of us, normally I
would just go to sleep or daydream, but I listened and what he lectured
about was disobeying and not doing your duty. To disobey mean's
to not do what you are ordered to do. This is one thing which also
make's you have to conform. Who has a right to lecture anyone in
their on carrying out what they are supposed to do. This thing is wrong
in life, something went wrong early in mankind, and when eventually
they grow out of their greed and bossing instincts like some people
already have done. That is when it will be that everyone put's his or her
own thoughts across to someone with equally good thoughts.

There are sometimes though, when a person who uses his so-called
authority to try and keep me down, often bring in my thoughts of the
time although it is often in a temper in retaliation against his bossing
instinct, and this give's the wrong impression. It seem's at school the best
chance you have to air your view's to the top three is when you are in
trouble. What a ridiculous way of communicating with dull people.

There is not any set time in the day when I think you can really act
yourself, I think the brink can just arise at any time, because apart from
authority and law there is alway's a lot of distraction from even your
best friend, at times or sometimes even the surroundings or the
atmosphere can make you act completly unnatural to your normal self.

This represents a considerable personal advance and achievement for
Ian — uneven though it is as a piece of writing — in its blending of personal
experience and reflection, with moments of detached and speculative
commentary on himself and his world. In his shoe-shop anecdote, for

instance, he avoids parading angry and vengeful feelings, but shows a degree of unsentimental compasssion for the affluent people who have abused him: 'it makes me think how meaningless life is to a vast majority of people, who live in a world of money . . .'. He quotes himself as an example of someone who is seduced into a system he would like to despise and reject; that he has to apologise 'when something is wrong with 'sir's' shoes' in order to collect the 'couple of pounds a week I get for doing the job.' He imagines what it would be like to be engaged on satisfying work: 'I would probably love my work if I was a photographer, or writer, if I was a writer and was clever enough I would like to be some-one like a modern-day Carl Mark . . .'. After this he returns to his familiar condemnations of school, but these, too are 'lifted' by an attempt to explain how schools and other man-made systems which demand conformity and obedience have (in his eyes) come to work against man's true needs and instincts: 'something went wrong early in mankind, etc . . .'. Towards the end he relapses into an aggressive attack on the 'top three', and he ends in a state of mind that looks as though it is no advance at all on his earlier piece of writing, '*How to live*'. But, over all, this writing shows a much wider awareness of the constraints and difficulties that are to be faced in his search for fulfilment. While it contains regressive lapses, there is some 'thought-adventuring' here too; and underlying his idealism is a sober acceptance that things will not easily, and may never be, made wholly perfect, even if his vision of life could be acted out: for 'people would only end up the same as they are now, in a rat race, making people think there nice hard-working people . . And some poor soul would (be) stuck at home one night writing this out again and moaning about the work he put's up with' – this ironic glimpse of an idealistic Ian of the future, toiling in his attic for the common good, says much about the progress that has been made in his writing and thinking over the year.

Can the Stages be Justified?

The notion of 'stages of growth' is familiar enough in educational thinking. Piaget and Vygotsky, for instance, both offer five stages in the development of thinking: but these refer only to allegedly 'cognitive' development, and are linked closely with particular age-groups up to adolescence. Smith, Goodman and Meredith (in *Language and Thinking in Schools*, 1976) offer what they called a 'free elaboration' of Susanne Langer's formulations, and describe three phases in 'coming to know', of perceiving, ideating and presenting; or in the words of Whitman – whom they quote – phases where children 'peer', 'absorb' and then 'translate'. But again, their categories assume split-off 'cognitive' aspects of language development, though they claim vaguely to recognize that 'affective' aspects are closely inter-woven here. There have been numerous similar attempts to chart stages in learning response; but most are close to, or even derived from

Bloom's influential yet narrowly behaviourist taxonomy of 'cognitive' and 'affective' steps in psycho-socio maturation, which can only envisage the learner as a *receiver* of message, of value, of knowledge, of morality; and which admits no sense of the learner as an active respondent, a shaper of knowing.

An adventurous attempt to chart 'language development' in children's writing is reported by Andrew Wilkinson and others, in *Assessing Language Development* (1980). Known as the 'Crediton Project', this study admits the manifold intentions and qualities of writing. But their scheme involved even further splitting up into categories of 'cognition, affect, morals and styles', with the result that attention to any particular piece of writing tends to become fragmented from the whole presence of the writer and the writing. Moving nearer to the concerns of this present book is the work of John Dixon and Leslie Stratta on the writing of school pupils. In 'Argument: what does it mean to teachers of English?' (*English in Education*, Spring 1982) they acknowledge that 'literary forms offer important ways of arguing for pupils.' But they, too, urge that while 'personal experiences can still find a place', there are the quite separate processes of 'organising abstract ideas into coherent rational sequences' to be learned. It would be foolish to dispute the importance of reason in the support of thought; yet need there be this renewed division between what is personally understood and what is to be generally proposed? Can we not acknowledge the presence of individual minds (since there is no such thing as abstract 'mind') engaged in thought as individual acts? Chapter Seven (on the 'organizing' stage) will return to this problem.

The search for a more comprehensive version of stages in learning has been more rare, although an entertaining attempt was made by Professor Kieron Egan (in *Educational Development*, 1979). Working mainly from his knowledge of history teaching, Professor Egan recommends four stages — mythic, romantic, philosophic and ironic — which he sees as characterizing intellectual development from childhood onwards. Professor Egan's examples and discussion offer a refreshing critique of some of our more painful educational orthodoxies (he discerns, for instance, how respect for the learner's limits of experience does not demand that all learning be limited to the world already literally encountered). The stages he describes seem well worth sounding out, although I confess that they seem to describe a particular kind of intellectual development — say, of Goethe — rather than a general pattern. Why, especially, should the 'mythic' be consigned to childhood only — why, it might be asked, should children have *all* the fun?

As far as English studies are concerned, Paddy Creber (in *Sense and Sensitivity*, 1965, revised 1982) offered sustained persuasive discussion of some stages which he associated with successive years in the secondary school. He distinguished three such stages: rediscovery of the familiar (first year); the growth of consciousness (second and third years); and imagination and morality (fourth year upwards). Mr Creber's discussion of these tended to centre on the writing-as-finished piece, rather than on the writer-and-his-writing, though this emphasis has changed in the revised edition. But its value lies in its commitment to the developing of an imaginative discipline, which is aimed at offering 'honesty and authenticity' at each of the stages. The weight given there to the quality of the teacher's relationship, and his responsibility in developing the stages, clearly anticipates Witkin's later (1974) insights on the need to aid what Witkin termed as 'reflexive control of the medium' in which the learner has chosen to grapple with and express his experience. In that Creber's constructs are set in the context of an extensive teaching experience, they have distinct value, and particularly deserve the attention of teacher-trainees and student-teachers. Yet as with Professor Egan's stages, we are still left with a sequential kind of development that is seen to do with age, rather than with what happens *whenever* there is fresh learning encounter.

But for an effective understanding of this present proposal for stages in learning-through-writing, acknowledgement ought again to be made to Polanyi's theory of tacit knowing. This is elucidated by Marjorie Grene in her Introduction to *Knowing and Being* (1969):

> A clear illustration, to show how we grow towards a full sense of knowing and reality, is that of someone receiving normal vision with inverted lenses. The first response of the viewer is to 'proximal, interiorized particulars': the viewer is seeking clues to what he sees from a mass of disparate and confusing evidence. From this first response, Polanyi suggests that four aspects of tacit knowing develop. First there is the *functional* aspect, which guides the viewer from disorientation to attend to the 'clues available within my body in order to attend to, see effectively, the things out there. The function of my subsidiary knowledge is to direct me to coherent sight of my surroundings . . .' This is the familiar lesson of gestalt psychology. The bearing of particulars on a total pattern produces the phenomenon of pattern . . .And this leads to the next aspect, of *phenomenal* knowing, where a clear picture of the objects in view has emerged. An aspect is where 'tacit' knowing directs us from particulars to the whole that they signify: that is, its *semantic* aspect. And finally there is an *ontological* aspect, where we are guided 'to the comprehension of something *real* — to a whole of parts, whose significance ranges in ways perhaps unguessed by us beyond its specifiable particulars or even beyond the presently visible outline of the whole . . .
>
> (Grene (Ed), *Knowing and Being*)

(Professor Grene also suggests that the act of reading offers a further clear example of how tacit knowing moves us to full understanding.) Although neither Polanyi nor Grene used the word 'stage', the way in which they discuss these aspects suggests a sequential as well as cyclic process, to show how awareness and reality grow from the process of tacit knowing, from the developing responses of the knower of his experience. That there are clear links in the proposed stages with Polanyi's aspects of tacit knowing now becomes evident: though rather different stresses and terms have been made, since the stages represent much wider kinds and ranges of activity than the particular example of the inverted lenses, even though the analogy holds well for more complex encounters. For instance, I should see the first response as an aspect, or stage in itself − perhaps represented in the inverted lens example as the spontaneous cry of surprise, on first encountering the effects of the inverted lens. Moving from this first naively 'telling' or expressive response would follow the reflecting (functional), identifying (phenomenal), organizing (semantic) and integrating (ontological) stages.

To sum up: the stages might be seen and understood by the practising teacher in two ways; first, as functions of the growing being, both child and adult, to be respected in their own right as authentic responses to living, and to all of which we need regularly to return, in true acts of learning, as we encounter new experience and explore life further; second, as being broad stages of progression, of development in learning and writing. This second view implies some specific support for what may be regarded as a thoroughly respectable 'traditional' view of learning, such as envisaged by A.N. Whitehead (in *The Aims of Education*, 1950) who saw the whole learning process as a movement from exploration, through precision, towards synthesis. Primarily, the stages represent an individual's state of being and acts of becoming − a life-journey from dependence, through independence, to dependability. But the 'cyclic' nature of the stages also allows that mature dependability is not a static state; the mature learner needs as much as anyone to make retrogressive journeys, to be allowed space and time for the earliest stages to be enacted, in the encounter with new learning.

CHAPTER FOUR

Telling

A lesson about writing your language may go deeper than language; for language is your reason, your logos. So long as you prefer abstract words, which express other men's summarized concepts of things, to concrete ones which lie as near as can be reached to things themselves and are the first-hand material of your thoughts, you will remain, at best, second-hand. If your language be Jargon, your intellect, if not your whole character, will almost certainly correspond.

(A. Quiller-Couch, 'An Interlude on Jargon' in
On the Art of Writing, 1916)

This chapter describes the first of five stages in learning and writing response in English studies. These stages mark successive unfoldings of poetic-creative development in knowing and being. The first stage represents an incomplete form of knowing, yet it is seen as an essential pre-condition for all further development towards fullness of learning response. The desire to 'tell' is not merely superseded by 'higher' intentions, but is the primary impulse of all later achievement in learning.

When they were developing their principles of language and art, both Croce and Cassirer laid fundamental emphasis on what they termed as the primary 'expressive' response, from which all language grew. 'Expressive' speech represented a speaker's first attempts to record and to proclaim experience to the world. This view was endorsed in Edward Sapir's writings, and has had widespread influence on assumptions about language that have operated in the teaching of the mother tongue, as with the London Writing Research Unit, for example. In proposing a first, 'telling' stage, this chapter acknowledges the expressive impulse as the primary and essential act of language, but would also wish to include the further act of 'communicating' — especially, perhaps, where writing is concerned. Writing is, after all, nearly always too premeditated an act to be treated as some kind of pure, spontaneous outcry.

The notion of a first, 'telling' stage, then, implies verbal acts of expressing which are also verbal acts of communicating; the two are inseparable, in that they are aspects of the same single enterprise in living language, to bring together speaker with listener. Such a view was affirmed by Georges Gusdorf when he argued (in *Speaking*, 1965) that while expression cannot be isolated ('Pure expression, detached from all communication, remains a fiction, because all speech implies aiming toward others'), neither can communication be separately treated ('I cannot communicate as long as I do not try to bring to the other the profound sense of my being.')

Instances of Now

L.S. Vygotsky (in *Thought and Language*, 1962) recognized the import of Tolstoy's writings on education, and their impact on his own proposals concerning thought and language: 'Leo Tolstoy, with his profound understanding of the nature of words and meaning, realized more clearly than most other educators the impossibility of simply relaying a concept from teacher to pupil.' It seems appropriate that this chapter on 'telling', which depends on the expressive sources of all discourse, should begin with a passage from Tolstoy, which specifically dwells on the spontaneous, expressive-poetic impulses of a young learner, in a lesson that fails because these are misunderstood. The passage comes from *Anna Karenin* (1878) — a novel which Tolstoy broke off from writing in 1875, so concerned was he to return to teach at his free school at Yasnaya Polyana (indeed, a point of interest about this particular passage is that it is one of the rare occasions in the story that Tolstoy lets his impersonal telling of the story slip, by venturing into direct authorial comment on the scene, since he was so eager to ensure that the reader should interpret it in Tolstoy's light). The bleakly conscientious Karenin has been recently partly consoled, after Anna has deserted him, by the award of a distinction for his services to the state, as a senior civil servant. His son greets him with excitement as Karenin returns home to give him a scripture lesson:

> Seriozha jumped up and went to kiss his father's hand, looking at him searchingly, trying to discover signs of his joy at receiving the Alexander Nevsky.
>
> 'Did you have a nice walk?' asked Karenin, sitting down in his easy-chair, pulling towards him the volume of the Old Testament and opening it. Although Karenin had more than once impressed upon Seriozha that every Christian ought to have a thorough knowledge of Bible history, he himself often referred to the Old Testament during the lesson, and Seriozha observed this.
>
> 'Yes, it was very nice indeed, Papa,' said Seriozha, sitting sideways on his chair and rocking it, which he had been told not to do. 'I saw Nadinka' (Nadinka was Lydia Ivanovna's niece, who was being brought up by her aunt). 'She told me you've been given a new decoration. Are you glad, Papa?'

'First of all, don't rock your chair, please,' said Karenin. 'And secondly, it is not the reward that is precious but the work itself. And I could wish you understood that. You see, if you are going to take pains and learn your lessons in order to win a reward, the work will seem hard; but when you work' (Karenin said this remembering how he had been sustained by a sense of duty that morning in the monotonous task of signing one hundred and eighteen documents,) 'loving your work you will find your reward in the work itself.'

The sparkling, affectionate light in Seriozha's eyes faltered and died under his father's gaze. This was the same old tone his father always took with him, and Seriozha had learned by now to fall in with it. His father always talked to him, Seriozha felt, as if he were addressing some imaginary boy out of a book, utterly unlike himself. And when he was with his father Seriozha always tried to be that boy out of a book.

'You understand that, I hope?' said his father.

'Yes, Papa,' answered Seriozha, acting the part of the imaginary boy.

The lesson consisted in learning by heart some verses from the Gospel and repeating the beginning of the Old Testament. The verses from the Gospel Seriozha knew fairly well, but just as he was reciting them he became so absorbed in watching a bone in his father's forehead, which turned so abruptly at the temples, that he got mixed up and put the end of one verse on to the beginning of another where the same word occurred. Karenin concluded that he did not understand what he was saying, and this irritated him.

He frowned, and began explaining what Seriozha had heard dozens of times before and never could remember, because he understood it too well, just as he could not remember that 'suddenly' is an adverb of manner of action. Seriozha looked at his father with scared eyes, and could think of nothing but whether his father would make him repeat what he had just said, as he sometimes did. He was so terrified at the thought that he no longer understood anything.

(Leo Tolstoy, *Anna Karenin*)

Eventually, Karenin impatiently announces that Seriozha will be punished for his inattentiveness, and that his lesssons have generally been coming along very badly . . . and Tolstoy intervenes:

He was nine years old; he was a child; but knew his own soul and treasured it, guarding it as the eyelid guards the eye, and without the key of love he let no-one into his heart. His teachers complained that he would not learn, while his soul was thirsting for knowledge.

(Ibid.)

Tolstoy highlights the contrast between Seriozha's affectionate, spontaneous expression of feeling, his search for human recognition and contact, or indeed sign of any feeling from his father, and Karenin's jaded dullness of spirit. The boy remembers that he must adjust to his father's expectations and injunctions on how he ought to behave, and in doing so he becomes split – one part of him still absorbed in (playful) contemplation of a bone in his father's forehead; the other trying hard to give the answers his father wants. Thus he seems 'dull', cut off from the lesson that his father wants him to repeat, because he cannot give himself as he would wish to his father, yet neither can he wholly falsify his response. But the boy's first openness shows that he is already better developed in feeling than his dull, repressed father. This weakness in Karenin – expressed here as a futilely abstract version of 'caring' through teaching – is revealed elsewhere in his marriage, and his professional life. But even in small, familiar ways that would not have cost him greatly as an adult, he cannot admit his feelings of (childlike) pleasure and pride for having been awarded a 'star'. Nor can he admit the love (which we are given no reason to doubt) that he would like to offer his son (for we see in the passage that Seriozha recognizes some kind of undisclosed intentions in his father here, and seems prepared to find something to trust in him, if only his father would allow that). The existential misery of Karenin's repressions are movingly exposed, as well as the hurt done to his affectionate nine-year-old son; he cannot recognize and share the boy's feelings, and is therefore unable to teach him effectively (later in the passage, we learn how Seriozha has taken his own directions despite the teaching, and has become quite seriously absorbed in connecting up his father's Bible story about Enoch's deathless ascent to heaven with his own concerns and speculations about death, of which no-one has yet told him anything worth wondering about). Tolstoy hints that it is Seriozha who is offering both the worthwhile learning *and* teaching here: 'Are you pleased, father?' – urging him simply to admit his feelings. But the hollow-ness of Karenin's life and work, and his dreary years of service to the advancement of a dead system would then have to be admitted, if he began to admit any feelings at all to himself. Better to retain his self-control, his front of dignity and assumption of authority, than have to face his own atrophied emotional development. Thus his teaching is stale, dead, a matter of directing rote learning and unassimilated memorizing. That Tolstoy depicts him giving a scripture lesson is no criticism of Karenin's choice of material, of course, but a further irony; elsewhere (in *The School at Yasnaya Polyana*) Tolstoy had described how the great Bible stories offered the best possible sources for all the imaginative work done by his own pupils. It is the way Karenin misuses his material that makes it seem so dreary and confusing, since Karenin has no religious life in himself nor even, it seems, any of its simple, expressive beginnings. He learns nothing himself (he has to check the 'facts' himself before inflicting them on Seriozha); and worse, he misuses his splendid source to jack up a conventional morality which traditionally demanded, above all else, only 'duty' and 'obedience' from children. He has no instinct, and no good teacher's skill to find new life in the great ancient stories, through his own 'telling' of them.

It is, we recognize, only through a realized work of art, such as *Anna Karenin*, that the whole nature of thought and intelligence can be conveyed: for thought and intelligence have their sources in individual being, and cannot be generalized about (thus we can recognize Seriozha's intellectual thought and Karenin's lack of it, only through the circumstances and texture of their particular lives). In *Thought, Words and Creativity* (1976), F.R. Leavis termed the knowledge that is the fruit of such living intelligence as a 'specificity of imaginative experience'. Such knowledge is a means of action and living; it establishes, physically and psychically, the primary self-being, and it marks the emergence of 'creative' (rather than only 'reasoning') logic. Seriozha's whole instinct is to think and learn in this spirit, through bringing together all that fascinates him, and creating patterns through wondering and relating – unless or until he is denied by his parent/teacher. In this he is beginning to work, modestly enough, as the poet-novelist-artist works, towards the goal of a comprehensive vision of life (we recall D.H. Lawrence's declaration that the novel 'is the highest example of subtle interrelated-ness that man has ever discovered').

But the beginnings are always in very particular moments or experiences, that still await connection – what Merleau-Ponty has termed 'instances of now' – as in Seriozha's contemplating the bone in his father's forehead. In each case, the moments of experience described may be modest, considering the whole range of life's experience; they may be taken as daily events – one of many hundreds or thousands, which gradually contribute to an increasing complexity and density of pattern. If we take M.M. Lewis's broad distinctions – which can be useful, even if they are akin to the dangers of the transactional-poetic split – between 'manipulative' and 'declarative' speech (in *Language, Thought and Personality*, 1963), any watchful parent will know that his child's first, holophrastic speech is almost purely 'declarative' (a term which usefully covers both the child's urge to express response and to gain attention and communion with the world); and the language to organize, control and make demands of his world may be seen to emerge gradually from this (thus our own son, when small, learned to name and call for the dog, or say and ask for a ball, long before he bothered to use words like 'drink' or 'milk', which he was able to do by merely gesturing and grunting). The germs of a child's expressive language are quickened by a sense of excitement, an engagement – with a parent greeting him in the morning; at a dog barking or rushing around; at the sight of a balloon, Christmas tree, moving car, or ducks. There are moments of recognition which make life concretely and uniquely 'there'; they are savoured as pleasurable (or painful) sensations and feelings of excitement by the individual child, who then takes the first spontaneous steps in building up language as a uniquely personal possession. This first, expressing, speech is, then, an adventuring-out to, and a dwelling-in of potential meaning; it marks the beginning of a to-and-fro process and progress towards a personally-held sense of truth. Neil Bolton, in an essay on the phenomenology of learning (*The Lived World'*, 1982) has argued that 'Expression articulates meaning . . . When we recognize that expression is both preceded by meaning, which guides it, and is followed by meaning, which is its culmination, we can make sense of the way in which expression creates a world of meanings.' Our bodily presence, our being in the world is a pre-condition of our capacity for thought, for the beginnings of expressive speech; and we need, declares Professor Bolton, to be constantly wary of 'attempts to describe lived experience as though it *were* nothing other than the results of reflection. *It is a prereflective world.*' (my italics). The directions of Professor Bolton's argument in this essay serve to quicken and develop his prefatory quotation from Heidegger: 'As soon as we have the thing before our eyes, and in our hearts an ear for the word, thinking prospers.'

In the wake of Tolstoy, the free writing movement of the fifties and sixties realized how such moments of excitement and recognition, caught from memory and from the immediate present, are precious in stimulating a fresh release of writing. They prompt the desire to 'tell how it is'. If the experience written of has been a 'positive' one, savoured and enjoyed, the writing will convey directly the sense of zestful play associated with the experience. If negative — frightening, painful or depressing, perhaps — the writing may come just as rapidly, as a 'pouring-out', a release of feeling. Such writing is always *essentially* self-chosen, in the sense that it depends on the particular and original experience of the writer; but a teacher can help to identify likely areas of interest, stimulate involved talk, or simply offer an appropriate audience as an encouragement to such writing. Harold and Connie Rosen demonstrated this some years ago now, in *The Language of Primary School Children* (1973), where they described how a good teacher is able to follow the 'fine textures of a child's life and . . . able to interpret it.' They showed how personal, expressive use of language could and should be the basis of all school subjects and activities:

> The more detailed the children's observation of snails or the birth of a calf or the more concerned and committed they are to the measurement of foxgloves, the more likely they are to reach an understanding of the object they are describing. The greater the personal involvement, the more likely we are able to reach a more objective view of life.

Such a view (unreservedly endorsed by the Bullock Report two years later) still offers a considerable challenge to our patterns of teaching in the secondary school, where subject divisions have tended to support a bewildering variety of assumptions about the learning process and relationships in learning, as well as different 'language policies'.

Not surprisingly, the insouciance and spontaneity of genuinely 'telling' writing is likely to be more often found, as well as more clearly appreciated among younger rather than older writers — though how far that is due to natural maturing, and how far by Karenin-like disapproval of expressiveness in older learners is an unresolved question. In the two examples offered below, from writing in our younger classes, the sharp simplicity of the experiences does seem to belong especially to the work of young, pre-adolescent writers. The first is a highly subjective, almost 'dream-like' interpretation of an occasion that a first-year boy said he had witnessed; it has strangely fairy-tale qualities, with implications about the identity of love, and the identity of power:

The Horse and the Sparrow

Once there was a sparrow in the road,
And he wasn't afraid,
He flew between a horses feet
And ate the wheat grains on the road.
The horse knew he was there because he lookt down
So he shook the sack that was on his back
And all the grains fell down.
Then the drive came back
And the horse was whipt and then trotted back home.

(Andrew, aged eleven)

Whether the imagery for his poem came from a direct encounter with the outside world, or through a book, or through a dream hardly matters: Andrew's vision has the qualities of a good parable, yet its intention seems much more clearly to re-create the literalness of the events, to tell a moral: he is, the reader gladly recognizes, still very much thinking as a child.

The second poem (which was accompanied by a brightly sunlit illustration of a tree in blossom) is by a second-year girl:

Royalty

The sun how it shone,
Bright yellow-white in colour,
It went behind a cloud,
My long thin shadow ceased.

The sky how it sparkled,
Like a sapphire,
Blue, blue as the sea
Like my blue parasol.

The blue dress that rustled at my feet,
Like the trees in a breeze,
I lifted my parasol, a little faded,
Like a queen.

(Glenis, aged twelve)

In her fantasy of being a queen, Glenis realizes too that she is by no means the ideal beauty of her class ('my long thin shadow – my parasol, a little faded . . .'). But her sense of glamour and belief in her royal self is clear too, and suggests delicately an intention towards self-acceptance and self-delight. It is also a revealing example of the dynamic intermingling between individual world and outside world that is enabled through acts of language. Simeon Potter suggested (in *Our Language*, 1966) that we should really talk of dictionary 'descriptions' rather than 'definitions': meaning shifts according to the word-individual-thing relationship. Writing on how the word 'sun' has changed in some languages to mean 'star' or 'eye', Potter declares that the

rigid relationship between word and thing, between symbol and reference has been changed. The seemingly impossible has occurred and any notions that we may have entertained concerning the indissolubility of the links connecting etymology and meaning have been rudely dispersed.

Such semantic changes, Potter suggests, are gradual, but individually developed. Thus, in the very process of choosing words to convey a meaning, the individual makes an adjustment – however slight – of the meaning that those words may carry; for in each individual there is an adjustment of perception – however small – that is unique. All this risks making unduly heavy weather of Glenis' gentle fantasizing, but the fall of her emphasis in the last line – 'like a queen' – is best understood, I think, in the light of Potter's insight: in her own eyes, she has indeed *become* a queen, she has made the queen herself.

That such writing as this, which is common in the work of younger children cannot be predicted or 'taught' is, strictly, self-evident (and invitations to creative writing need always to be sensitive to this). Such clear successes as these are likely to be sporadic; they depend on the unpredictably wayward directions of the learner's feeling-response to new experiences. Even so, the conditions for regular practice (in the enacting, not mechanistic sense) of personal writing need to be well imagined, to ensure the right opportunities for such spontaneous flights. A further brief illustration of the kind of delicate 'creative-personal' work that can grow from a natural, inner desire to be active, rather than from crudely applied external pressures, is offered in the little piece below:

Nicght

It is dark
It is dark as a dark Blue dress,
It is soft as wool
It is quiet as whisper
It is kind as sleep.

(Debra, aged ten)

Debra was one of a class of seventeen, in a special class for 'educationally sub-normal learners'. She had the good fortune to be with a teacher whose approach to learning was wholly centred on life activities and the expressive arts. He refused to work from any assumptions about the limitations of his pupils, but was eager to fill the day with a great variety of approaches and 'games'. The teacher described his day in a letter, thus:

It is some of this joy (that is, of his own childhood) that I now try to give my class of slow-learners, and I am fortunate to have a headmistress who never seems surprised or shocked. The sun shines, and we must go to the woods; I need a cheque changed, and we all, seventeen of us, walk into the bank. Vast quantities of animals crawl around the class-room; the sink is always blocked; and the children are in anything but their own clothes and every possible craft is practised, especially the art of talking.

Such an extreme of casualness with a class may easily vary according to personal tasks — as long as the essential flow of interrelationship is present. In such an atmosphere, Debra was able to grow from tense silence and inactivity to confidence and engagement, through her ventures into what Merleau-Ponty has termed 'first-hand speech — that of the child uttering its first word, of the lover revealing his feelings, of the 'first man who spoke' (in a footnote to the chapter 'The Body as Expression and Speech' (Merleau-Ponty, 1962)). Through the words she reaches for meaning, and for the first time in her life, has expressed a wish to record it in writing. She gives the impression that she has been quietly absorbed in the writing of her poem, rather than having made a purely 'rigorous' writing effort. Yet writing is a deliberate and complex activity, compared to speech; and Debra has been quickened into willingly accepting the extra 'grain of rigour' needed to fulfil her writing task, through a growing confidence and trust in her surroundings. Her poem recalls the poet William Stafford's view that 'almost anyone can write poetry. One of the most important characteristics a poet must have is a feeling of trust about himself.' It seems clear that Debra has found that self-trust, with a teacher and children who are near enough to her, and capable of making demands on her that she can meet, to reach out to tell her thoughts. Her perception of her external world has been sharpened, made more richly varied and vivid through the analogies she has ventured: an achievement which ought to be proclaimed as being a vital survival-function of art, since our capacity for adaptation (that is, for essential development) depends on the free and rich use of our imagination. She had been encouraged to venture, to take the kind of excursions into her world that she might have missed, for whatever reasons, at an earlier phase of growth; for the adventure outwards may begin within weeks of birth, as is perfectly recognized in Helen Thomas' illustration of the symbiosis between mother and infant, from the account of her life with the poet Edward Thomas:

> I made him pick flowers before his baby fingers could do anything but feebly grasp, and in this way he picked a little bunch of flowers for his father: and finding a trail of bryony, I made him pick a leaf of what had been my bridal wreath. I talked to him, before words meant anything to him but the sound of a familiar voice, of flowers, and birds and of spring, or sitting by his side while he cooed or slept I wrote my letter to David, studying the flowers we have picked. Sometimes I would take him to the pond and dabble his toes in the water, and this he liked so much that he cried when I took him out. But his griefs were easily soothed by my suckling or singing to him, and as he drew the milk from me while he spread his little fingers over my breast I experienced that wonderful pleasure, half-physical, half-spiritual which makes it an ecstasy.
>
> (Helen Thomas. *As it Was*, 1935)

Here is the essential, primary kind of experience through which the human infant becomes individualized. The infant has to await such human realizing in order to become fully participating as a human being. As well as providing the body's milk, the parent intercedes between child and world, relating its strangeness, and providing access through 'telling'. And the quality of the 'telling' of parents and teachers will in turn affect the quality of the learner's own enterprises, in discovering how things really are.

Radical relations

In *The School at Yasnaya Polyana*, Tolstoy reveals how he and his fellow teachers came to realize that they were over-estimating their pupils' power to handle abstractions in language, while underestimating their great and natural urge towards meaning, their capacity to adopt and handle words creatively. Children, declared Tolstoy, can already feel the 'radical relation of words'; they do not need dictionary definitions and rules of expression, as they are already active inventors themselves of new words and expressions. Admittedly, they can soon be made to appear stupid, when confronted by a task which looks easy to the teacher ('describe a table' and so on); but give them the chance to re-tell a story, or some direct experience that has moved them ('the meeting of Joseph with his brother, or a fight with a companion') and their genius for telling is soon kindled. Tolstoy comments that to begin with, their stories are clumsily told, but the children learn to listen eagerly to each other's, and to suggest and accept criticism and improvements. He recognized, through his own classroom mistakes and from his unusual capacity to learn from his pupils, that it is the children's own strong desires to cope directly with their own experiences, which best motivates them in the very complex process of learning and thinking. The zest and also the patience required for learning become available when they feel in immediate touch, when there is no barrier of generality or abstraction to stand in the way of the 'complicated and the living', which for them appears 'easy'. (Such insights are confirmed by the best thinking and practice of our own century, yet such textbooks as those of the famous Ronald Ridout are, incredibly, still regularly purchased by schools, at a time when shrinking capitation allowances have severely reduced the funds available for good books, plays, poems and other essentials of a creative approach to the work.) When a mechanical or abstract attention is given to language — or to any comparable activity — without the charge of context, of lived experience, then an awkwardness and self-consciousness will develop in the individual, such as in the case of Michael Polanyi's piano player, who becomes confused when shifting attention from what is being played to the fingers that are playing, so that he may even have to stop playing altogether, through self-consciousness. An extreme version of this is stage-fright, where the 'anxious riveting' on just one note or word or gesture 'destroys one's sense of the context which alone can smoothly evoke the proper sequence of words, notes or gestures.' ('The Logic of Tacit Inference' in *Knowing and Being*, 1969). There is no doubt that whole classes can be induced away from spontaneous and confident self-expression, into a 'stage-fright' mentality, so that they actually come to feel more 'secure' (as their teacher will woodenly assure you) in doing 'fill-in-the-gap' exercises, than in writing their own stories, poems and reflections. Nor can it be doubted that such exercises mark the death of true language development, as far as that particular classroom is concerned; in such a context, the learners' English will have to develop in *spite* of their English studies.

Vygotsky is indebted to Tolstoy, and anticipates Polanyi in emphasizing the highly individual aspects of the learning and thinking process. The relation of thought to word is to be seen as a restlessly developing activity, 'a continual movement back and forth from thought to word and word to thought. Thought is not merely expressed in words. It comes into existence through them.' Thus even this emphatically natural, spontaneous expressing stage may involve some bodily effort, stress or discomfort, in the release of embodied but still subjectively held form. In Vygotsky's terms, there is the encounter and effort of union between vocal (developing from outside particularities of experience) and semantic (developing from the dim, amorphous whole of the child's world *towards* particularities) aspects of speech. Through this process the original, inviolate self is identified in the world as individual. Vygotsky's now well-known term for this process is 'inner speech', which is a 'condensed, abbreviated' form of vocal speech, and is 'so saturated with sense that many words would be required to explain it in external speech.' Inner speech negotiates between vocal speech and thought; it is 'a dynamic, shifting, unstable thing, fluttering between word and thought.' Vygotsky writes too of the difficulty and unpredictability of discovering and expressing such insight from the 'realm of shadows'. That phrase in particular suggests how the learner must have space to grope around, towards phenomenal understanding; when he is seeking to make the facts of existence his own, to endow them with personal meaning.

Vygotsky recurringly dwells on the enormous demands to be made on inner speech in the learning process; its task is to embody and express in adequate language all that rapid development and active thrusting forward of thought and feeling in the developing learner. He also points out that for the adolescent, 'the use of the word is an integral part of developing processes,' and that the adolescent is likely to meet particular problems in ingesting abstract ideas into his own experience – since he has the same problems as the younger learner in this respect, even though this is largely unrecognized. Vygotsky's view is that the problem which Tolstoy identifies – a failure of meeting between individual particular experience and abstraction – must be countered by grounding all conceptual learning in 'spontaneous, everyday concepts' – that is, in essentially self-chosen, *expressing* response.

Language is renewed – and through language *we* are renewed – by this primary impulse to tell, in the most direct and concrete way possible, how it really was. This is true of the whole range of experience, from infancy to adulthood. Only through the telling can we reveal our experience to ourselves; only through hearing the telling can we directly 'know' what our bodies did not otherwise experience – the voice in the burning bush, Lear's weeping for Cordelia, Hermione's restoration to warm life. If the experience is not realized in the telling, it is as though it had never happened. And politics, religion, history, literature remain as disconnected dreary items on a syllabus, offering nothing to the true growth of the learner.

Telling How It Was

The 'telling' stage, then, is a natural and necessary prelude to the inner, self-revealing activity of the second, reflecting stage, when the implications of expressive experience are explored at leisure, in the subjective living of the learner. It is concerned with conveying the subject's clear sense of actuality, of lived experience. In its nearness to literal events, its healthy tendency is to break down clichéd, second-hand modes of response; for this reason it is a vital stage towards *all* states of knowing and being. It acts as evidence that the experience has managed, in Coleridge's words, 'to excite . . . by awakening the mind's attention from the lethargy of custom.' While it can be encouraged it cannot be forced, any more than good spirits can be forced out of Tolstoy's bored boy, whom Tolstoy told for a second time to 'jump' himself out of boredom, but who simply burst into tears, although he had laughed on the first occasion (*The School At Yasnaya Polyana*). It is less easily generated among fifteen-year-olds than among twelve-year-olds, and is even less readily available to adults in its purest forms of bodily excitation and renewed sense of living. Literature offers a wealth of writing that *seems* to be expressive, but is in fact serving a more complex purpose (outstanding examples here would include Blake's Songs, or Wordsworth's Lyrical Ballads). But genuine examples abound in the letters and occasional journals of writers, as this letter by Van Gogh to his brother Theo, when he conveys his sense of excited wonder at a scene that he just cannot wait to paint. It is a passage that I have introduced at many levels of English teaching, in trying to suggest how that familiar injunction to those who are attempting creative and imaginative writing – 'Don't just tell me – *show* me!' – may be enacted:

From a letter to his brother Theo

Yesterday towards evening I was busy painting a rather sloping ground in the wood, covered with mouldered and dry beech leaves. That ground was dark and light reddish brown, made more so by the shadows of trees which threw more or less dark streaks over it, sometimes half blotted out. The question was, and I found it very difficult, to get the depth of colour, the enormous force and solidness of that ground – and while painting it I perceived only for the first time how much light there still was in that dusk – to keep that light, and to keep at the same time the glow and depth of that rich colour . . .

Behind those saplings, behind that reddish-brown soil, is a sky very
delicate, bluish grey, warm, hardly blue, all aglow — and against it is a
hazy border of green and a little network of stems and yellowish leaves.
A few figures of wood-gatherers are wandering around like dark masses
of mysterious shadows. The white cap of a woman, who is bending to
reach a dry branch, stands out all of a sudden against the deep red-brown
of the ground. A skirt catches the light — a shadow falls — a dark
silhouette of a man appears above the underbrush. A white bonnet, a
cap, a shoulder, the bust of a woman moulds itself against the sky. Those
figures, they are large and full of poetry — in the twilight of that deep
shadowy tone they appear as enormous clay figurines being shaped in a
studio . . . . .

(Vincent Van Gogh, letter, September 1882)

He goes on to describe the urgent task of depicting all this on his
canvas, producing a sketch at last 'which expresses something', and which
encourages him to work even more intensely, squeezing roots and trunk
of the tree directly from the tube onto the canvas, as the brush proves to
be too slow an agent. How he paints, he says, 'I do not know myself',
but he is glad that he did not 'learn' painting:

I sit down with a white board before the spot that strikes me, I look
at what is before me, I say to myself that the white board must become
something; I come back dissatisfied — I put it away, and when I have
rested a little, I go to look at it with a kind of fear. Then I am still
dissatisfied because I still have in my mind that splendid subject, to
be satisfied with what I made of it. But after all I find in my work an
echo of what struck me. I see that nature has said something, has
spoken to me and that I have put it down in shorthand. In my shorthand
there may be words that cannot be deciphered, there may be mistakes
or gaps, but there is something in it of what wood or shore or figures
has told me, and it is not a tame or conventional language, proceeding
less from nature itself than a studied manner or system.

(Ibid)

The point to be made here is not that it is a very skilful, vivid description
of impressionist painting response and method (it is that too): but that it
is a rare first-hand response by an adult, which has all the qualities of the
stage of telling — what we sometimes choose to think of as the child's
vision of life. In the earlier part of the letter his physical excitement comes
over very directly: he wants to convey all that experience of having been
strongly moved to his brother and beloved friend. Even in translation it

comes over as a wholly colloquial piece (several members of a group of English Honours Graduates freshly gathered for their Post-Graduate Teaching Certificate course found, when asked to declare their first response to the letter — that it was 'untidy'!). It shows that overlap detected by Sapir and others, between speech and writing: it taps the resources gathered in speaking, and is decidedly more 'telling' than 'explaining'. Towards the end of the letter, his writing moves naturally towards a reflecting comment on the exciting moment he has described, where he explains and defends his spontaneous method and action. His response to the truth of the moment has led to a further response, to self-validating reflection.

The clear grain of narrative that runs through Van Gogh's letter provides a clear pointer to this stage of writing, for a good deal of writing at this stage takes the form of 'telling a story'. But it would be quite misleading to suggest that all story-telling falls into this stage. The stage of response is revealed by the degree of consciousness revealed in the writing — from the simplest narrating of events to the high organization of a serious novel. Yet the phrase 'telling how it was' points helpfully to a main feature of this stage, since it appropriately suggests the direct, unsifted and naive outpouring of experience that *has* to seek expression and find an audience.

After some hesitation, I felt that the term 'anecdotal' could not be used to describe this stage. In that it echoes Harding's and Britton's thoughts on expressive writing, it is a useful word. And the term has respectable origins too in Dr. Johnson's Dictionary, where it was defined as 'something yet unpublished, a secret history'. But 'telling how it was' conveys better the impulsive and even compulsive element of expressing, since 'anecdote' may also carry many accidental and less reputable connections than those mentioned by Johnson. Empty, malicious and misrepresenting gossip can be retailed as 'anecdotes'; and the word carries a rather too emotionally neutral flavour to describe adequately the more intimate and costly revelations that may come very frequently in 'telling' writing. 'Anecdotes', declared Disraeli, 'are but squalid skeletons, unless they are full of the blood and flesh of reflection' — a comment which may alert us to nurture the more serious possibilities of expressive language, so that reflecting may come into play. There is a natural economy and inevitability in the best 'telling of how it was', as is revealed in the account below by a Sheffield school-boy, written as part-contribution to his 'sixteen-plus' assessment in English. It describes a true, horrifying experience that he had suffered two years previously. It is offered without further comment, other than to suggest that it memorably exemplifies 'telling' as defined so far; it also helps to indicate why the term 'anecdote' will not quite do to describe its rarely affecting quality, and it conveys the sense of how such an incident *has* to be admitted through telling:

An incident involving 'Death'

It was a pretty cold afternoon in October. I felt spots of rain hit me on my face. We (that's my cousin Dave, Steve Mason and I) all decided on taking the horses back in the field then running a little further on Loxley Bottoms to take shelter in some old out-houses. These out-houses had at one time been separated by brick walls. Now it was just like one continuous shelter because people had taken out these stone walls which left a long thick concrete roof unsupported We took shelter in there till the rain died down a bit. When eventually the rain did die down we was tempted to get on top of the roof which was at the most about 10 feet high. Whilst me and Dave climbed on the roof Steve remained inside trying to build a small fire to get us warm. He was knelt down lighting it and taking it all easy whilst Dave and I were having a good laugh.

(Further down the road is a bunker similar and every time we pass Dave climbs on it and acts as though he was on stage.)

Whilst we were on it he remembered about his so-called stage further down the road and immediately began to dance. While he was doing this I was just walking backwards to jump into the field behind it when he gave a tremendous jump in the middle. Straight away the whole thing caved in. It went in the middle, where Dave was, first. Like a sandwich it CAUGHT him in the middle and crushed him. As it fell Steve, who was knelt below it was hit straight on top of the head with the whole lot of it. As he was knelt down his back was bent double and the 18" thick concrete roof was on his face.

Meanwhile, I was lucky. I fell under it all but as it came down on me it caught the back wall and bounced away a bit otherwise I would now be in a wooden box with the other two. As it bounced off, the whole lot landed on my legs and completely crushed one of my knee caps and broke my legs in 3 places. I couldn't move. Whilst people who were around at the time ran to the telephone I tried to free my leg but that was just impossible, the weight was to much for 3 fireman to lift. After an hour the fireman brought out a jack and whilst jacking it up two other fireman dragged me out. I was in great pain. When I was laid there waiting I knew straight away that Steve was instantly killed. As I was trying to undo my boot lace because even by now I could feel two bones sticking out of my leg I could feel Steves head on my leg. To the right of me I had David. The only part of him I could see now was from his shoulders upwards. This was because he was buried in concrete. His back was crushed and blood was pouring out of his ears, his head was split wide open and all I could hear of him was purring sound. I was too shocked even to cry. Ambulance men rushing backwards and forwards and two of them put an oxygen mask to David's mouth but this was no good because the mask just got flooded out with blood. By now blood was pumping out of his mouth like a river.

As I sat there I could feel blood pouring down my leg.

Ten minutes later an ambulance man told me that Steve and Dave were dead. Immediately I went all dizzy and felt sick. They put me in an ambulance, then they brought Steve and Dave in after me. One was laid on the same bed that I was using for a seat and the other was across from me. I realised then that I would never see them again so I turned round to have one last look, Both of them were in a terrible state. From inside the ambulance I could hear sirens from the 3 police cars and above them I could hear people shouting for by now there were quite a few people outside. Then 2 ambulance men stepped in and started to talk to me. They said it might be better if I sat in the front with the driver. So this I did. The ambulance didn't set off straight away but before it did I was again moved. This time I was moved on to the back seat of a police car where I could lay down because my leg was in terrible pain. We then set off for the hospital at a very fast speed. It was now about 7.00 p.m. and dark. As we swerved aound the corners I could see the flashing of the light against the shop windows and the siren was like the ringing of a bell in my ear.

Although after that I never did see Steve Mason or David Wright again I carried on going through pain for 8 months but after that I quickly recovered. Our family soon got back to normal and I was the only one to survive an accident which included 3 people.

(Shaun, aged sixteen)
(I am grateful to David Allen for enabling me to include this passage here.)

Examples From the Group

As will also be the pattern in subsequent chapters, the three examples of writing at this stage that follow are taken from the work of the group which formed the basis of this writing study. All these examples come from writing-in-progress for English studies, during the fourth, fifth and lower sixth school years of the group. Much of the writing comes from writing assignments set by the teacher for class and homework, and some of it is self-chosen; but all the examples are the harvest of the kind of programme for English studies that has been outlined in Chapter Three.

The first piece, by Asta, indicates a rather different background from most of her classmates. Asta's mother worked as a therapist in a local hospital. She had 'passed' her eleven-plus, but the family had chosen the small secondary modern school, which was later absorbed into the comprehensive school, so that she could enjoy the facilities of their Art and Crafts department, which had won good local repute. She was a bright, confident girl who showed by her 'O' and 'A' level passes that she could easily have gained a University place, had she wished. When she chose instead to gain direct entry into a good Art college, there was some staff criticism about her choosing 'too easy' a way of life. In her English work she was enthusiastic, usually among the leaders in any discussion, and producing a wealth of unsolicited 'extra' written work, often vividly and elaborately, illustrated. She was one of the leading lights of her year-group, and was an editor as well as one of the most prolific contributors to their underground journal (described further in Chapter Seven). Asta had a reputation for 'raising the dust' in school; for practical joking in her light-hearted moments (she was arrested with one of the lads in her class at the age of sixteen, for 'colouring' the pavement in the High Street); and for stubborn and spirited resistance when she felt her case had not been properly heard. She was rather too unsubdued to be universally liked among the staff; but she was highly regarded among her own year-group, for her generosity and independence of spirit.

The class were reading Barry Hines' *A Kestrel for a Knave* around the time that Asta's piece was written. They had seen Ken Loach's film *Kes*, and some of the issues of both book and film had been extended through study in class of some passages from A.S. Neill's book, *Summerhill.* There had been much vigorous discussion in several lessons around this time about discipline, curriculum and conventions in schools, which were clearly reflected in Asta's writing here. The passage below represents about a quarter of her whole account:

Exuberance is Beauty

A.S. NEILL

I never realised how closely I was linked. I knew that I had spent one marvellous year at a 'free' school in Epsom when I was five or six. It turns out that this was a Neill school . . .

— I have so many memories of it. It is difficult to know where to begin. To start with uniform was never mentioned, everyone wandered around in jeans and could be themselves entirely, whereas I don't think I can really be me, freezing to death in a miniskirt with a stiff collar rubbing at my neck.

As I said, the grounds were enormous, there were several parts unexplored by me. The main building, as I remember it, had a line of big rooms, and one jutting out at the side. There was a hall with stairs to where the boarders stayed. There was the hut, (I never went in there), tennis courts, the kitchen garden where we used to go and pinch chives, a big hut which the boys used as a garage, with a stage at the end. It always had a smell of its own. There was a place with long benches, whether for woodwork or science I cannot remember: it was always dark in there, that's where we used to see films.

There must have been kitchens — I can remember each individual room, but I can't place them together in my mind. Then there was the paddock, a huge expanse of grass with trees around the edge, and nettles, and a couple of gates, one at either end. There were a couple of big circles where a girl used to make her horse go round and round, and sometimes the old white horse grazed in the corner. Rumour had it that the beast kicked, so we never went near it. The 'big boys', who were always pottering about with motor bikes, used to go tearing around. One day they rigged up a side car in the form of a board on wheels, and were giving rides around the paddock. With Paul Bishop 'driving' and Hesford (I think) holding me on. I think that was the most wonderful, exciting ride I've ever had.

In the winter we'd all go out and make snowmen, the sort where you rolled a giant snowball and made trails. Ann (my best friend) and I made one, and Pete's wife gave us a hat and scarf for it . . . In the summer we sat out there, reading, drawing. One sweltering day we went to lunch, and returned to find all our crayons melted into a lump in the box . . .

Every Friday the whole school met for a meeting. All sorts of points were raised about the school, and the youngest pupil could have his say. Meetings were run by pupils, and not like botched up tutor group affairs either. At the end of the meeting the chairman would say: 'Lost, Broken, Found' and any items under these headings would be submitted. Worthless items of junk such as bashed up combs or plastic bracelets, probably thrown away by the owners, would be handed in by the little ones, and each item was dutifully held up to be claimed. Then the chairman would adjourn the meeting, causing a stampede out through the door.

Next to the room where the meetings were held was a room where the older pupils had a record player. We used to jump out of the window to save walking round. This time was known as 'Richard time', as Richard was the first to exit . . .

I learnt a lot of things in that year. We were taught far more adult things than at the next primary school, where we did embroidery in sewing, and as near to cooking we got was with Playdough; and what we did learn was fun. Of course, I can't speak for the older pupils, but I know everyone was happy there, and we learnt because we wanted to.

I wish Neill's schools would become common practice. The country would be far better for it.

(Asta, aged fourteen (fourth year))

This piece was the first of several autobiographical pieces by her about her earlier experiences at the 'free' school. The memories had clearly been awakened by her English studies; and judging from the volumes of writing that Asta produced on this topic, they released a store of powerful experiences. The desire simply to relate what happened took precedence at the time over any other intention. Her writing contains one or two elements of evaluation; for example, she takes care to ensure that her final sentence has a 'political' edge. But mainly she dwells on direct and immediate details from her memories; many of which are recalled with easy fluency, a clear sense of savouring and enjoying of the memory, and of recording it. Her eye for detail is sharp; sometimes she conveys a moment of naive wonder that she still seems to find a little mysterious ('one sweltering day we went to lunch, and returned to find all our crayons melted into a lump in the box . . .'). More often, she dwells on the events that have been effectively distanced by time and change, even if still very much treasured. She has taken the invitation to 'write without fear' — an invitation that was continuously renewed in their English class-room — and offers a passing swipe at 'botched up tutor group affairs'. But she is, for the present, mainly absorbed in simple recollection and telling. Only briefly, towards the end, does she return to some direct reflection on the qualities of this school, compared to her next one. She raises a wealth of implications for education, implications which were followed up explicitly in later pieces; but this first piece is, over all, very directly and simply involved with the pleasures of recollecting the pleasures of living. (This piece of writing found its way eventually into the school magazine and from there to an issue of *The Human Context,* whose editors asked to publish it as a tribute to A.S. Neill.)

The second piece is by Myrtle, who was transferred from a local girls' secondary modern school to the comprehensive school, at the age of thirteen. She had enjoyed life there, but her earlier primary schooling had been less happy and successful, for she had spent several years suffering from partial but undetected deafness. In her many written accounts of these earlier days, she often referred to her extreme shyness at that time; but when her deafness proved to be easily rectified, her own view was that she quickly blossomed too, in confidence and outward-goingness. As far as formal examination promise was concerned, she was in the middle of the attainment range in her class.

As a trust grew through her English work, her writing between the ages of fourteen and sixteen became prolific: she kept long and detailed diaries; wrote a great deal of poetry, which she carefully compiled into neatly hand-written and illustrated little volumes; and submitted a great deal of writing, beyond what was basically required for English studies. She was a sensitive girl, whose images and ideas seemed like very important possessions to her, as is often so with younger children; and her acute, intuitive flights sometimes gave her an aura of being both naive and wise at the same time — 'wierd', as the Saxons would have termed it. She was weak at mathematics and the sciences, and her spelling and written expression were often eccentric; despite steady improvement here through the fourth and fifth years, she failed her O-level Language paper (but gained a C.S.E. grade one and also a good pass on the O-level Literature paper). The selected piece is typical of her work in the early part of the fourth year. It was a self-chosen piece of work, written into her diary (which she regularly asked to show me) and was not directly related to the concerns of the English lessons at that time. However, it came to have a place in them:

Dreams

When I dream I usually find I loose the middles to them so that when I wake up I have a vivid idea of what the beginnings and ends are, but I have no idea at all about the middles, I carn't even guess what they might be. Sometimes, when I have a complete dream, you can recon anything you like that it will come true, or at least, that there is some truth in it. This happened to me last night and as I recall it now, I realise the depth of truth in it. It scars me. I want more than anything else for this not to be true.

My friend Diana ran up to me and said something. I turned and began to bite my fingernails franticly (a thing I never do and never have done). Then I ran down the main corridor of the school, screaming. Next I was in my tutor group and for some reason my Tutor had kept me behind and would not let me go home, this made me despirit, I knew I must leave school at 3.30 pm. on the dot. At 8.40 pm. I ran out of school with Diana, we ran for a while and then seemed to fly, we were going down Elgin Road. We came to the end of this road, and then I lost all sence of direction and felt this must be the bitter end. All of a sudden Diana and I are outside the grammar school, I knew I had taken the wrong road. Diana and I flew over the houses till we came to the gates of Manor Park. They were shut, the grammar school boys were in the park, behind the gates with our school on my side. As I approached the gates the boys, all of which I recognised, moved aside; Diana followed me. I pulled frantically at the gate; it was locked. I did not know, for a moment, what I was doing outside the gates, then I remembered. 'Don't fight, please, I am sure the whole thing can be sorted out,' I vagly remember saying. 'Its too late for that now' someone said.

I remember looking into the eyes of a boy from the grammer school. At first I did not recognise him, after a while I remembered who he was, and how he had become mixed up in the situation. The next instant the boy had been knocked over, I wanted with all Id' got, to rush forward and help him, but I found that I was unable to move any of my limbs. Then there was an unholy row between our school and the grammar school fourth and fifth year boys, resulting in a fight. For a moment I could not think, then I felt a firm hand on my shoulder.

Turning, I found a Policeman. He asked me what was going on and how I had become mixed up in the fight. I was unable to answer him because I had lost my memory. Someone came up and hit me with a club and . . . the next minute I knew I had woken up. I felt so cold although I knew my bedroom radiator was on. My room was pitch black, for a moment I was unable to move. I felt my face, it was wet, I must have been crying. I was unable to return to sleep, anyway I frightened to incase I had another dream like this. I worried and worried about it until I felt as if I would be sick.

After a good wash I felt better, it was six thirty this morning. I did not rush to get ready for school, there was no need. I tried with all my might to foget it, but did not suceed.

Now I dreading the end of school. I have to go up to Manor Park whether I like it or not, tonight, and some of our school and the grammar school pupils have had a great argument, which probably will result in a fully blown fight.

(Myrtle, aged fourteen (fourth year))

'Dreams' were a favourite topic of hers, and they occupied a great deal of space in her personal diary. Here she writes, Cassandra-like, of her prophetic dream about a local feud. It is an urgent, anxious piece of writing, which gives the impression to the reader that it had to be related not only for her own sake but for the sake of those who appeared in her dream. She asked that it should be read out to the class, at the time, and became even tearfully insistent when I said there might not be time for this. She admits a sense of helpless involvement; she wants something to be done about her fears, but does not know what. When the piece was heard, by the class, it prompted a class discussion and airing of the facts of a feud with a local school, in which several of the lads in the class had become involved at the time. Thus there is an element of intention 'on behalf of the class' in this writing; but in the main, it is a direct, uninhibited outpouring of 'the way it was', where the sheer vividness of the experience has disturbed and prompted her creative impulse to record and write it down.

The third piece, by Philip, indicates well the kind of lad that he was: small and wiry, unassuming and even over-quiet in the classroom, yet showing a lively aggression on the games field. He enjoyed school, worked hard in his English studies. Sometimes the signs of an earlier shyness and tenseness of manner would be on him, but on the whole he had a sunny, confident enough presence. He often declared his liking for school; in fact, for him, writing was yet another enjoyable game. He had no problems of formal accuracy or fluency in his writing, and was always happy to settle down to a task, on invitation. He joined the A-level English set after the fifth year.

The class had read a short story by William Carlos Williams. The story describes a crudely-fought battle between a doctor and his young patient, where the doctor, aided by the girls' parents, forces her to submit to a throat examination, to discover whether she has diphtheria. His aggression is justified, but the narrator (the doctor) also admits his considerable physical satisfaction in overpowering the girl, after being thwarted by her. The story was linked to a small series of lessons on 'The Uses of Force', and the class had considered some of the issues raised, about when force may or may not be justified. The class were given a choice of writing assignments from this topic, and were reminded about the value of being 'true to what was really felt', as in the Williams story:

Hate

I have never really hated anybody or anything enough for it to have come to serious circumstances but I have nearly come to that extent a number of times. I can remember one such time quite vividly. It was around the time of the termination of spring to summer and was a clear, cool evening. I was about seven years of age at the time and of cause the matter wasn't really very serious.

Three of my friends and I were playing some game like pretending to be soldiers. We took turns at being the man in charge who gave the orders. This one of us would carry a stick and if his soldiers did anything wrong he would give a tap on the short-trousered legs of the offender. It wasn't hard but it hurt and I suppose this taught us a bit of discipline.

Anyway, after one boy had been hit it was his turn to be the leader and he started giving out a bit too much punishment and was hitting us harder. It was me who seemed to be getting to the worst of it as he lashed out spitefully at any foot put wrong. I had had enough finally as he drew the stick back viciously, fiercely cutting the back of my legs. It might have been alright if he'd had apologised but all he said was that it would 'teach me a lesson'. I might have been a bit to quick and might have not have been thinking properly at the time but this made me see red. I whipped the stick from him in a split second gave him three hard swipes across the back of his thighs with it. It was then that I realised what I'd done and I turned shamerdly away only to fill pains come across my back and legs as he punched and kicked me to the ground. I felt tears of anger and hate come to my eyes as I lashed out with the strength coming to my body telling me to teach him a lesson. The battle raged on as we forgot about the two other boys looking astonished at each other. One moment I was attacking with the fearless energy of a lion and the next moment was on defence cowardly seeking the security of my house.

By this time we were in the hallway. The vicious punches and kicks weren't felt as I fought for every blow's vengeance. The vase of flowers went flying by stick-brandishing hand cut up anything in its' way. My mother came rushing downstairs and pulled the other boy away only for me to cowardly attack him while he was helpless. When my father came out I chose this as the time to exit upstairs. I knew I couldn't hide and I was called out of the bedroom by my mother. I went reluctantly downstairs and was told to make friend with the boy again. We took a little coaxing until we stood face to face. We shook hands but we both knew that the other would not forget as we stood staring hatred into each others eyes.

Everyone departed home thinking and talking about the viciousness in us. I went to my room and flopped down on my bed. Whenever I wanted to have peace and quiet and think I always did and my parents and sisters would leave me well alone. Tears of pity mingled with my tears of hate as I lay feeling sorry for myself. I find that in times like this things must be done but the situation is hopeless because of my self-pride won't let me go round to the boy's house, apologise, and talk things over. I felt destructive and wanted to destroy everything in my path, but no! Mum would never forgive me if I smashed the grandfather clock at the top of the stairs. Each thought was made nonsense as I thought of it much clearer. That night I hardly had a wink of sleep as I tossed and turned wondering what the next days fate would bring. I woke up after two hours of sleep wanting to naturally stay in bed and contemplate the next move to be taken by either of us. It was then that I realised that my hate had gone. We usually went to school together but I didn't call for him hoping the whole ugly affair would have blown over by then. I went a different way.

One thing I had completely overlooked was that he had had the same kind of emotions as I'd had. It turned out that he'd decided to go to school the same way as me and as we met in the shop we stared at each other for a moment and then we just burst out laughing and we haven't had a proper argument since then . . .

(Philip, aged fourteen (fourth year))

Philip's recalling of an earlier childhood experience, when both his opponent and he broke the unwritten rules of a soldier-game, which suddenly becomes viciously real, conveys vividly the heat and frustration of angry feelings; he admits the emergent vandal that looms from his anger and self-pity, as he fantasises about smashing up the family furniture. But as he broods over his anger, he suddenly discovers that it has vanished, and the embarrassment of the following day's encounter is quickly forgotten in laughter with the former enemy, when he realizes that 'One thing I had completely overlooked was that he had had the same kind of emotions as

I'd had'. Up to this point, his narrative has been vividly expressive, with a strong sense conveyed in the writing of the need to admit, to 'confess'. He went on, in fact, to consider the incident in a clearly more reflecting spirit, mulling over the facts of the incident, and relating it to the issues being explored at the time, and the emergence of such reflecting can be seen in that recognizing of the other's 'same kind of emotions'. He can recognize now with some humour and detachment the rage of his younger self, but he is quite near enough in memory to the actual events not to undervalue the power and urgency of his feelings. In re-enacting through telling, he is provided with good 'food for thought' towards a healthily-reflecting conclusion; the impetus is naturally towards the next stage.

In *The Prose of the World*(1974) Merleau-Ponty dwells on painting as an embodying language, then writes:

> The task of language is similar. Given an experience, which may be banal but for the writer captures a particular savour of life . . . the writer's task is to choose, assemble, wield and torment these instruments (i.e. words) in such a way that they induce the same sentiment of life that dwells in the writer at any moment, deployed henceforth in an imaginary world and in the transparent body of language.

Just as in the language of painting, there is the same 'migration of a meaning scattered in experience that leaves the flesh' in order to lodge itself in the realms of language, and to acquire 'the dignity of expressed meaning'. Thus these pieces of writing tellingly reveal who their creators *are*, and what their experience of the world *is* (not who or what they 'ought' to be); in this, they mark the beginnings of true learning.

CHAPTER FIVE

Reflecting

'Teacher says', Linda told the old lady softly, 'that maybe if we wonder and wonder, then things will begin to happen.'

'Is that what he said? Ah but that is so right,' the old lady said. 'But now you run into the house. There's a little tin on my kitchen shelf and in it there are wineballs. You get us each a wineball out of the tin. Then I'll sit in my porch and you sit in yours, and we'll think about storks. But we'll think better each in his own porch, because thinking often gets lost in talking. And maybe your teacher is right — that if we begin to think and wonder, somebody will begin to make things happen.' Lina had dreams in her eyes and would not hear words anyway.

(Meindert de Jong, *The Wheel on the School*, 1954)

We have admitted new experiences, through 'telling' them in writing. There now emerges an intention to wonder about their impact on ourselves, to reflect on these, to seek out meanings in their forms that relate unmistakably to our already existing patterns of living and knowing. This second, reflecting stage might be regarded as introspecting — 'each in his own porch' — in some contrast to the form-releasing, outward-bound directions of the first and third stages; and the language used will have intimate connections with our inner dialogues, the language of meditative responding to response.

Where Is Fancy Bred?
The reflecting stage is born out of intense inner activity in the learner, out of subjective, intuitive states and responses in learning, where there is a suffusing and confusing of experience, and the learner has not yet come to distinguish the subjective feelings aroused by an experience from the clear identifying of it, to which learning is directed. Yet to be so 'con-fused' is to be more complexly involved in new encounter than the first impulse to 'tell' about it would indicate. The point of change from the first stage is when the individual embarks on a kind of meditative play around the field of new interest, and around the experience of having told something of the

feelings and emotions aroused. It marks an advance from the close, literal response of the first stage, and is a natural prelude to the third 'identifying' stage; without this, the next stage can never be achieved as an act of authentic, individual perceiving. In this reflecting stage, the individual becomes, in a strict sense, self-conscious — of those already expressed responses to events, people, places, problems. It is a phase of relatively free interplay between form and feeling, an intermingling of expression with impression, as a prelude to the firmly 'out-there' defining of later stages. These intuitive, non-deliberate modes of responses are not just confined to the child's mind, but are just as indispensable in adult experience. They are akin to what Wordsworth termed 'wise passiveness', when the onlooker receives and retains the impressions of the world, savouring the feelings engendered by experience.

In the free subjective play of this stage the learner can, for instance, 'become' a character in a book, or even imagine that the reader is 'writing' the book, as part of the journey to 'possessing' the story for him/herself. A more simple example of such confusing and suffusing of forms with subjective feeling may be found in the apparently 'irrational' reactions of a child (or, indeed an adult) to an 'unfriendly hill' or a 'laughing field' or a 'prim chair' and so on. Such examples abound in art-discourse, and in a chapter on 'Language' (*Philosophy in a New Key*, 1957) Susanne Langer dwells especially on the young child's capacity to make strikingly original connections of this kind. She recalls the 'mood' of a particular armchair from her own childhood memories, and suggests:

> A mind to which the stern character of an armchair is more im-mediately apparent than its use or its position in the room, is over-sensitive to expressive forms. It grasps analogies that a riper experience would reject as absurd. It fuses sensations that practical thinking must keep apart. Yet it is just this crazy play of associations, this uncritical fusion of impressions, that exercises the power of symbolic transfor-mation. To project feelings into outer objects is the first way of sym-bolizing, and thus of *conceiving those* feelings ... The conception of 'self', which is usually thought to mark the beginning of actual memory, may possibly depend on this process of symbolically epitomizing our feelings.

This passage reflects and expands her more general feeling (Susanne Langer, *Feeling and Form*, 1953) that for those who are sensitive to art, 'feeling does inhere somehow in every imaginal form'. However her description of subjective reflecting as an activity which 'fuses sensations that practical thinking must keep apart' raises some awkward questions about how we can come to apply reflecting activity to effective knowing (thus raising the phantom of her sense of a split between 'representational' and 'discursive' symbolism). Mrs. Langer's account, in fact, carries strong suggestions of the workings of fantasy as distinct from what Coleridge termed the genuinely 'esemplastic' operations of the imagination (and we remember, too, his warnings against the parasitic tendencies of fantasizing, in feeding off the prolific activity of the imagination). Fantasizing may indeed be regarded as a familiar element in writing at this stage; but as with 'narrating' in the first stage, it is the quality of the fantasizing that should determine the stage. At one (almost pre-expressive) extreme might be what Harding (1937) termed the fantasizing of 'hallucinatory participation', which might almost unconsciously relate inner 'adventures'; or there could be a perfectly impersonal, highly developed vision of life, through fantasy-fiction, as in the best fairy-tales. But it is the early stages of inner play with shapes and impressions — such as described by Mrs Langer in her passage on the armchair, which might at best lead 'inwards' towards more deliberate introspection, or 'outwards' towards a clearer realizing of outer form — that characterizes fantasizing at the reflecting stage. Certainly such fantasizing is a natural phase of response, which should be nurtured in the learner. Through such dwelling in new experience, whereby both form and subject are suffused in each other, the learner is enlarged into new awareness.

These processes of fusing and confusing between seer and seen occupy some of Merleau-Ponty's most significant thinking on the nature of learning. In his chapter called 'The Body as Expression, and Speech' (Merleau-Ponty, *The Phenomenology of Perception*, 1962) he writes of a 'taking up of others' thought through speech, a reflection in others, an ability to think *according* to *others*, which enriches our own thoughts'. (Evidences of such a capacity to 'think according to others' will be seen in the stories by Andrew and Lynda, towards the end of this chapter.) These directions of thought are daringly developed by Merleau-Ponty in his later, specific preoccupations with the painter's art, which offer inferences both for learning in general, and for all creative enterprises. In his essay 'Eye and Mind' (1974) he dwells on the inter-changing of roles between the seer and the visible, as one reflects the other, and quotes Andrew Marchand's experiences of walking in a forest: 'Some days I felt that the trees were looking at me, were speaking to me . . . I was there listening — I think that the painter must be penetrated by the universe and not want to penetrate it . . . I expect to be inwardly submerged, buried. Perhaps I paint to break out.' Merleau-Ponty goes on to suggest that we should take the term 'inspiration' quite literally here: 'there really is inspiration and expiration of Being, action and passion so slightly discernible that it becomes impossible to distinguish between what one sees and what is seen, what paints and what is painted.' Again, the term 're-flecting' may be taken, he suggests, as something literal, an actual event: commenting on the marvellous ways in which an interior is 'digested' by a mirror in Dutch interior paintings, he suggests that 'the mirror appears because I am seeing-visible (voyant-visible), because there is a reflexivity of the sensible; the mirror translates and reproduces that reflexivity.' In human relationship 'man is mirror for man. The mirror itself is the instrument of a universal magic that changes things into a spectacle, spectacles into things, myself into another, and another into myself.' Merleau-Ponty's description of the inspiring-expiring, active-passive aspects of the painter's reflectings as a 'technique of the body', implies an even closer correspondence to Michael Polanyi's notions of 'in-dwelling', than to Susanne Langer's thoughts on subjective reflecting; for while Susanne Langer's account is persuasive in its particulars, it is evident that she tends to regard such reflections as characterizing a particular ('representational') branch of thinking, rather than being a stage in *all* genuinely creative thinking and learning. In this, she works against the grain of her own concern for the validity of poetic truth. Paul Ricoeur ('The case against reference' in *The Rule of Metaphor*, 1977) has pointed out how the splitting of thought and feeling has produced so general a prejudice that many authors whose aim is to refute logical positivism often fortify it while opposing it. And he concludes: 'to say, with Susanne Langer, that to read a poem is to grasp "a piece of virtual life", is to remain within the verifiable-unverifiable dichotomy.' The act of reflecting is a stage in the manifold, unified activity of thinking. Thinking involves sensing, feeling, perceiving, intuiting, imagining, questioning, representing, inferring and so on; but to split this activity into discrete parts is to reduce it to something much less than the sum of its whole.

As an illustration of the learner's creative capacity to 'think according to others', to reflect not just the directions of an argument but even textures of tone and phrasing, a short extract from an established writer is given below, followed by a piece from a twelve-year-old girl who had read a long passage from his work in class. The passage is from George Sturt's well-known account (in *The Wheelwright's Shop*) of the 'very fascinating art' of the master-wheelwright, in nineteenth-century Farnham. The passage itself offers a revelatory account of the 'inwardness' that a craftsman needs with his materials:

> The timber was far from being a prey, a helpless victim to the machine. Rather it would lend its own subtle virtues to the man who knew how to humour it; with him, as with an understanding friend, it would cooperate — twisting it, turning it 'end for end', trying it for an inch or two this way and then an inch or two that, a skilful wheelwright was able to get the best possible product from his timber every time. Can you not imagine a little the joyous sensations running up his wrists and calming his nerves as he feels the hard wood softly yielding to his wishes, taking the fine, clean-edged knife-shape under the faithful tool?
> (George Sturt, *The Wheelwright's Shop*, 1923)

After reading and discussing the whole passage, the class were given some 'open' questions for writing on the passage, such as 'What is happening here, between the wood and the man?'; they were invited to answer these 'as they wished', preferably as a continuous account, in poetry or prose. Sarah's contribution was too long to quote in full — longer, in fact, than the original passage from Sturt — but the following brief extract shows how she 'reflects' the passage from Sturt, above:

. This page to me seems really to come to life. I can actually imagine the faint fresh 'woody' fragrance of clean white wood. And I sense the joy in which the craftsman felt when carefully bending and moulding the ever-changing textures of the wood, while it gradually yielded to his skilled and sensitive fingers. He actually felt the wood. He didn't hack harshly through the rough grain like a sharp-edged machine would, but he carefully and subtly followed the grain line deep into the heart of it. 'Man's ingenuity' — used in this context the phrase was referring to the resourcefulness that man always has ready to fall back on. The wood would not curve with one method and so the ingenious man finds yet another way of confronting this problem. And so finally, the wood yields and the clean white curve is continued — The writer associated the stock of wood with the countryside, expansive and wide. This association took root because of the wood the stock was made, elm. An uncultivated tree that grew wild and free in the woodlands. And he has tamed part of that tree and carved and moulded it, and now in its fragrant simplicity, it stood before him . . .

(Sarah, aged twelve)

(Her account dwelled on various kinds of other crafts, including horse-training and different kinds of teaching; she also included accounts of different textures, like the 'feel' of her mother's shawl, and finished by considering Sturt's thoughts on mechanization, which she didn't agree with — and her own tone became rather assertively generalizing at this point, as indeed does Sturt's.) Sarah's written response here is a prose-poem in that there can be no distinction made, without great damage to her intentions, between the delicate rhythms of her feeling-revelations, and any 'extractable meaning'. The passage includes some 'telling' response (as in the sense of excitement-in-discovery at the beginning), and also evidence of a later, identifying response (as in her well-made point about the meaning of 'ingenuity' in its context); but it illustrates in particular the kind of 'con-fusion' between learner and what-is-to-be-learned that Langer and Merleau-Ponty have identified. There is no doubt that Sturt 'lives' in the second passage; neither can there be doubt that the passage contains Sarah's own highly individual presence. As for the teacher's response to this piece, Sarah's work was warmly praised; and she was invited to think further about whether it might not be better, as far as the craft of teaching was concerned, to think about the learner as 'the customer' rather than as the wood waiting to be shaped.

Mediation in Reflecting: the Teacher's Role

Intuitive activity is spontaneous and self-directed, but this does not lighten the teacher's task as agent and enabler in the learner's personal effort to meaning. In fact the learner may need especially tactful mediation at this stage. The growth of patient attentiveness, and of sustained exploring do not follow automatically, even after true excitement has been generated through the 'telling' of fresh experience. All teachers will have experienced that unhappy phase when the mood of the class changes as the sense of excitement fades, to be replaced by an odd sadness, an emptiness and inertia. The pupils seem to become obtuse, with fixed mentalities, apparently waiting to be returned to the reassuringly safe, if boring, routines of teacher's chalk-and-talk, or whatever. Such a fading of vitality is caught in the account below:

> The class has not been so good lately, it is being slowly sucked down into a state of lethargic triviality. Nothing is taken seriously, it takes too much effort, and some of us can't be bothered to waken our senses, but instead, let the situations drift past, living in a world of nothingness. A certain group — me included sometimes — cluster round one desk in the room, totally oblivious of the world going on around them. They sit with waxen, stupified faces, which seem to convey their dullness of mind and boredom of life . . . But these are not a stupid group of people, they are alive and aware, yet when I look at their sad empty faces, and when I am with them, I find it hard to remember. This group and most of the other people's minds in the form need to grow and develop with age and experience of life, but they are regressing and slowly changing into apathetic yes-men. Sometimes that form is alive, flowing with vitality and power of feeling — everybody is enthusiastic in discussion then, and in a way more keen. Everyone is a strong individual, thinking and with a great personal awareness of people and life around them. But then someone might under-estimate us, and give us work which does not stretch us, the form notices gradually that they need not make the effort, it is far easier to sit back and let someone think for you. It is hard to overcome this laziness and indifference again . . .
>
> (Sarah, aged thirteen)

'But then someone might under-estimate us . . . '. Sarah's (the same who wrote the piece on Sturt in an earlier term) lucid account of why the class have become 'bored', offers an awkward challenge to the would-be effective teacher. Instead of taking experience to themselves, the class have now cut themselves off; connection seems lost between the experience and the way to meaning. The class have lost the confidence that their experiences and feelings have import; and the teacher too, it seems, has lost confidence in the next step. How can we sustain and deepen the commitment to new forms of knowing, and not fall again into the role of the know-all teacher who purveys knowledge as a commodity, with the pupils as 'consumers'? Such a 'consumer' mentality is adroitly exposed in the Taoist story (from Arthur Waley's *Three Ways of Thought in Ancient China,* 1939) which comments on how intellectual inertia needs sometimes to be quickened by devious and ingenious method:

> A monk asked Ts'ui-we, 'For what reasons did the first Patriarch come from the West?'
> Ts'ui-we answered, 'Pass me the chin rest.'
> As soon as the monk passed it, Ts'ui-we hit him with it.

Ts'ui-we anticipates his students, and works surprises; Tolstoy, we may imagine, would have appreciated his unexpected invitation to quicken inner activity in learning. Such an element of serious play — serious in its intentions, yet play in that it is intended to relax — is an essential enabler of reflecting activity. It is difficult to live with uncertanties, which may seem intolerably diffuse and untidy both to the learner and to the over-prescriptive teacher, who is tempted to impose a rigid learning scheme on the learner without further ado. Sometimes the teacher may enable an advance through creative teasing, as with the wisely unpredictable monk; at other times a deliberately gentle offering of space is needed, so that emotion may be amply 'recollected in tranquillity', and the poetic process may continue. There can be no by-passing of this stage, unless language is reduced to cliché and learning becomes a mere sorting of dead items of knowledge. Thus the teacher's ingenuity is continuously put to the test at this stage, when the learner may seem to require the teacher least, yet is paradoxically in special need of support, in the gradual task of interpreting and making meaning. In the movement towards reflecting the learner becomes vulnerable through talk and writing, in ways that may not even be noted at a conscious level. Learners may reveal almost unawares how events have made an impact on their emotional life, how part of themselves has become touched and involved, in ways which may not have been formulated at all clearly, as yet. Specific and continuous reassurance may be needed, that the natural, relatively untaxing 'pouring-out' of the 'telling' stage *is* likely to lead somewhere.

A good account of the role that the teacher can play at this stage was offered to an earlier generation by the psychologist and educationist William James. In *Talks to the Teachers* (1899) he recommends that the teacher should always be seeking 'associations' between various aspects of work and experience. The teacher should begin with 'the line of (the pupil's) native interests, and offer him objects that have some immediate connection with these'. James goes on:

> Associate the new with the old in some natural and telling way, so that the interest, being shed along from point to point, finally suffuses the whole system of thought.

This is the abstract statement; and abstractly, nothing can be easier to understand. It is in the fulfilment of the rule that the difficulty lies; for the differences between an interesting and a tedious teacher consist in little more than the inventiveness by which the one is able to mediate these associations and connections, and in the dullness in discovering such transitions which the other shows. One teacher's mind will fairly coruscate with points of connection between the new lesson and the circumstances of the children's other experiences. Anecdotes and reminiscences will abound in her talk; and the shuttle of interest will shoot backwards and forwards, weaving the new and old together in a lively and entertaining way. Another teacher has no such inventive fertility, and his lesson will always be a dead and heavy thing.

(James, Talks to the Teachers, 1899)

A teacher who plans to put into practice what James says here about the need for creative flow in the classroom, does not have to assume a show of theatrical abilities (though they doubtless help sometimes) but, rather, the kind of creative attentiveness which allows a freeing from rigid patterns of behaviour and thought. The more the teacher can demonstrate this kind of creative play, the more he or she is likely to generate a similar confidence and engagement in the learner.

The learner's search for discovery of relation may be tentative at first — depending a good deal, perhaps, on the degree to which there has been previous encouragement or discouragement of such personal reflecting — and may sometimes be barely discernible from simple 'telling' response. 'Creative' listening or reading implies a play of intuitive faculties; learners can be encouraged to discern their own links between new events and their own subjectivity.

As far as speech is concerned, the kind of tentative, exploring dialogue as recommended by Douglas Barnes and others is likely to be important. Yet even an informal small group arrangement with a flexible study programme may not meet the particular needs of individual pupils at particular times. Barnes himself suggested (1971) that it is 'the meanings which children take away from the lesson which really matter'; and although 'talking it through' is often likely to help the learner's writing, the meaning may sometimes need writing out, *rather* than talking out, in order to be discovered. But talking or writing, the learner is securing specifically *personal* connections at this stage, when language has a heuristic function. If the learner's writing is rooted in what is felt to be of personal import, then the writing itself will act as a kind of excavating process, turning up the part-known meanings that wait to be revealed from beneath the surface of experience.

Through language, the learner's unique reflections are discerned; though they may well still be very provisional, in that the learner is much more concerned to see how an experience 'fits', to understand it in terms of one's self, prior to presenting them clearly beyond the self, fully fledged, to be recognized by the world (I recall my own frustrations as a student, when having to submit work to a tutor as a 'finished' piece for due critical demolition, when it had in fact only reached a stage of having been written 'for myself'). The more involved the learner is at this stage, the more he may sometimes be 'unacknowledging' — both of the teacher and of the experience (for example, the text being studied). The lack of acknowledgement may manifest itself in apparently 'irrelevant' response — for example, where a poem or piece of fiction connects so powerfully with a learner's personal experience, that dwelling on the actual experience becomes a more urgent task than dwelling on the study-topic; or it may be evidenced by a whole-hearted 'ransacking' of a text (which is not to be confused with uninvolved plagiarizing) when the writer wishes so much to make the text his own, that he interweaves personal patterns into the very fabric of the text. Thomas Wolf has pointed out how, as far as reading goes, the etymology of the Teutonic 'raedan', from which our own derives, implies not merely the decoding of texts, but a whole complex web of acts of bringing together, sorting, discerning and understanding; as the modern American says, 'I read you' (Wolf, *Reading Reconsidered*, 1978). Thus, if this stage is to have its due place, we have to recognize how idiosyncratic the process of 'making it one's own' may be. It cuts across conventional 'comprehension' questions, for instance, of the kind which dwell only on what the text is 'objectively' about, and it requires a radical shift in even advanced work from a sudden application of traditional 'analysis and criticism' tactics.[1] But even if this is to be seen only as a stage — though a stage with its own validity, and one in which the teacher ought to be

1. That this has been increasingly, if belatedly, recognized in recent years is shown in the Schools Council Project Report, *English 16–19* (1979) by John Dixon, which describes experimental approaches to 'varieties' of writing in A-level work. The experimental alternative A-level syllabuses which enable such variety in their course work component seem so far to have justified the hopes and aims of the teacher and Examining Boards involved. (There are however, the different and, in my view, altogether more dubious issues of the English-as-Communications 'model' at A-level that are raised in this book, which will be reviewed later in Chapter Seven).

very closely involved — it might be thought by some to dodge teaching responsibility. Doubters may perhaps be reassured by the uncontroversial suggestion in the Bullock Report that 'what a teacher has in mind may well be the desirable destination of a thinking process; but a learner needs to trace the steps from the familiar to the new . . . to make a journey in thought for himself.' (That, for a start, might liberate both teachers and pupils from the linguistic drills that the Report itself recommends.) The Report indicated too, that the teacher cannot abdicate from being a necessary agent at this stage.

Caul of Shadows

In *Stations* (1975), Seamus Heaney writes of a 'caul of shadows' which protectively surrounds emergent forms of experience. Heaney's phrase echoes insights from the great Romantic writers on the fostering of personal experience, both 'active' and 'passive'. It is a legacy which other living poets have drawn on, to describe thought-processes:

> Your whole being rests lightly on your float, but not drowsily: very alert, so that the least twitch of the float arrives like an electric shock. And you are not only watching the float. You are aware, in a horizon-less and slightly mesmerized way, like listening to the double bass in orchestral music, of the fish below there in the dark. At every moment your imagination is alarming itself with the size of the thing slowly leaving the weeds and approaching your bait; or with the world of beauties down there, suspended in total ignorance of you. And the whole purpose of this concentrated excitement, in this area of ap-prehension and unforseeable events, is to bring up some lovely solid thing like living metal from a world where nothing exists but these inevitable facts which raise life out of nothing and return it to nothing.
> (Ted Hughes, note on 'Learning to Think', in *Poetry in the Making*, 1967)

Through this analogy with fishing, Hughes emphasizes the absorbing play of the inner search for connection with an image; it is a calm and gradual, yet also daintily quick process that lifts the 'cloud of unknowing', enabling the new forms to emerge. Openness and patience are required in waiting for the idea to form itself. The learner must be alert to ensure that the words which contain ideas do not merely slip away; but they need to be protected, 'cauled' in the shadows of being, until they are ready to be brought to light for full identifying. The reflecting stage offers just such a protection in allowing for implicit patterns of response that still await full realization.

Coleridge (in *The Ancient Mariner*) meditates on how the fresh play of imaginative contemplation may generate life-renewing forms. Through suffering, the mariner has been halted in his greedy exploitation of his world. In his anguish at being condemned to live in a dead world, he cannot himself escape into death. But after prolonged suffering, he comes unexpectedly to connect, as a child awakening, with the living world again, in being moved to find the forms of his imagining lovely in his sight:

> Beyond the shadow of the ship
> I watched the water-snakes.
> They moved in tracks of shining white,
> And when they reared, the elfish light
> Fell off in hoary flakes.
> Within the shadow of the ship
> I watched their rich attire —
> Blue, glossy green and velvet black,
> They coiled and swam, and every track
> Was a flash of golden fire.
>
> (Coleridge, The Ancient Mariner)

This fresh, symbol-making activity in the subconscious — wondering, dreaming, reflecting, connecting — marks, as he blesses them 'unawares', the renewal of the mariner's life-journey into full awareness of being, as the albatross — emblematic of his earlier blind and greedy lust to bind living forms to himself — falls away from his neck, and leaves him free to live again.

Some Examples

To conclude this chapter, three examples are again offered from the work of the group on whom the writing-study was based. Each of these is specifically concerned with response to a literary text, at a stage where the writer is still so personally involved that the learner's own, personal connectings are at present far more urgent and important than what is 'out there', as a text. From the teaching point of view, it should be said that for each of these writing examples a wealth of suggestions and possibilities for writing were offered, but in no case was there a requirement to write in any particular way. In each case the subject and mode of writing was self-chosen, to enable the kind of personal 'reflecting' that is envisaged in this chapter as a development from the first, 'telling' stage. All three examples here are taken from written work on literary texts.

The first piece is by Andrew, a robust lad, a good footballer and swimmer, who worked hard at his school subjects and was one of only a few in his group who showed any flair for mathematics. Only an error in the system could explain how he ever came to be on the wrong side of the eleven-plus examination before joining us. Andrew was one of the most energetic of the team who wrote, edited and produced the year-group's 'underground' magazine (described further in Chapter Seven). His independent disposition developed into a deeply earnest questioning spirit, as he grew in years. The piece that follows was written about half-way through the fourth year when he had immersed himself in Jack London stories; and it is London's influence which is evident in this short story — in the scene-setting, the description of Joe McBride, and the circumstances and terse enacting of the plot. The assignment was based on an invitation to write on some aspect of their private reading, as part-contribution to a project for their C.S.E. course. The work did not issue directly, then, from English-in-progress at the time, except that private reading itself was a regular weekly activity in English lessons.

Unemployed

Joe McBride pushed back his chair. It slid easily across the floor and stopped in the corner, chipping the wall. Flakes of plaster spattered onto the worn chair. Its wine red covers were dusty, the colour had passed, with the years it had seen, into weakness. A spring had forced itself upwards, conclusive evidence of its age, pressing hard on the cover, revealing its shape.

Its twin chair was snuggled into another corner. Together they formed a perfect triangle with the door, stationed halfway along the northern-most wall. A modern table that looked as though it came straight from a cafe stood in the middle of the triangle.

The carpet was moss green, also looking dusty, decrepid with age. It was almost threadbare near the corner chairs but it sparkled in the other two corners, a shiny green. That was the untrodden land.

A bureau squashed down small areas of the rich green carpet but it stole onto the threadbare areas. It was littered with ornaments. Cheap ornaments with telling marks 'Blackpool' or 'Skegness'.

Above the bureau was a damp spot on the wall. It was easily visible for it had coloured a rich brown with saturation. The wallpaper was a feeble coffee colour. At a touch the walls were very cold partly due to the dampness but also because of the very cold weather.

The fire, opposite the bureau, choked in the fire-place. Smoke whirled up the chimney or swamped into the room. No heat. Not even a glow could be seen through the coals.

McBride was a robust fellow, his broad shoulders forced his hands deep into his trouser pockets. His grey flannels tapered from his beer gut inwards to his ankles, just touching the tops of his black shoes. His massive abdomen was covered with a lumberjack's shirt, green in emphasis. He had a heavy jaw which thrust forward pulling the skin tight to the bone. His head was round, a curved balding scalp. A shiny patch of flesh shone through is scanty hair which was smarmed back across his temples. His eyes were deeply set; dark chestnut eyes. He was forty five.

He crossed the room and snatched up a white cup which was cracked and without a handle. A thin white foam had formed on the surface of the tea. McBride shook the cup, anticlockwise. The white disappeared, sucked into oblivion down the produced whirlpool. He gulped down the tea and breathed a long gasping breath. He put down the cup.

Putting his head round the kitchen door into the tiny room he spotted a piece of cake on the sideboard. He took the cake and plodded back across the room. Falling onto his chair he picked up his paper off the chair arm. 'Over nine hundred thousand unemployed' read the headlines.

As regular as an alarm clock Joe McBride awoke at ten to eleven. He had fallen asleep in the chair. He grunted and shook his head. Becoming conscious he stooped down and tied the laces of his shoes. Getting up, he went into the hall. He grabbed his coat and pulled his floppy cloth cap across his head. Smacking his lips and rubbing his hands, the door slammed behind him.

Outside it was cold and Joe's breath turned to mist and floated away. He pulled his coat in closer and thrust his hands deep into his pockets. Turning out of his road, Joe walked past the docks.

The sea was a dirty grey, there was no horizon; the greyness continuing into the sky above the town. The docks were full of laughter piercing the icy air. People turned in curiosity but they scowled as if it were a crime to joke in the cold weather. They walked off, away from the docks, from the cheeriness, away from the life of the town. The docks buzzed, they were electric but their warmth was exclusive to the men already there, working behind those gates.

A waft of hot air hit Joe's face as he swung open the door of the 'Anchor'. It was quiet. Two old age pensioners sat at a corner table, teethless and dribbling into pints of beer. They watched the entrance of the younger man before huddling back into conversation. Joe drank alone at the bar.

The labour exchange was very low and an old building. The doors were a cold light blue. The chipped and dirty brickwork was a collage of varying shades of brown and red-brown. The colours were just visible through the layers of dust and grime which had settled there.

Outside there was a long queue of men, two deep from the wall. They stood sullen and grim-faced, in cloth caps and donkey jackets, rubbing their hands for warmth or eeking out cigarette butts. The clouds of tobacco smoke rose until they lingered a while above the bowed heads of the men before they were caught by the breeze and blown towards the back of the queue.

The men shuffled along the pavement and filed into the exchange. Soon afterwards they returned into the cold, counting through their money, sums flashing across their minds. The queue shortened quickly and Joe walked into the hall. The line split into five small groups here and it looked like a river delta. Joe came to the front of the queue to collect his unemployment benefits.

The officials sat behind wire mesh pivoting on moving chairs. They wore sports jackets or two piece suits; there was a little more than a wire fence between the men.

Joe withdrew his cards and folded the stiff cardboard flat onto the counter. He pushed them under the gap in the wire and waiting, biting his bottom lip between his teeth. The official folded the money and the cards into Joe's flattened palm. Joe took it folding over the notes, pushing them into his pocket and dropping the couple of odd coins after them. He turned away and slowly left the exchange.

On leaving the building Joe kept his head low and looked at his shoes. This was the humble position expected of him; shouldn't he feel grateful to society for keeping such a useless article in circulation? His inclinations were to keep his head lowered but he felt a strong revulsion for the labour exchange official and for his old employers. He wanted to hold his head high. 'Swines' he whistled through his teeth.

Now there was a knot in his stomach, a battle between his pride and accepted humility. He was the unintelligent, their smart jackets had told him that. The knot was tugging hard. He sought an outlet for his rage. Turning into an alley way Joe swung his fist through a dusty pane of glass of a half demolished house. It shattered noisily so Joe moved off quickly, finding solitude in the pub. He broke into his dole pay for a couple of pints.

(Andrew, aged fifteen)

Andrew had been given no formal lessons on 'how to write a story': yet it can be seen that his story-writing competence is already there. Through his admiration for London's work, he has developed a strong involvement in the craft of writing, and he maintains a quite effective tension throughout the story. But there is evidence that this is more than just an exercise in impersonal writing in the style of a favourite author; his choice of a tough, Jack London-type here enables him to discern and describe elements and movements in himself, to reveal some half-admitted feelings about his own emerging thoughts about the way things are in the world. One small lapse in the story amusingly suggests the involved adolescent-writer rather than the assured and impersonal creative writer in whose persona he has sought to write, when he depicts the penniless and hungry Joe abstractly reaching for food — 'Putting his head round the kitchen door into the tiny room he spotted a piece of cake on the sideboard. He took the cake and plodded back across the room . . .' More significant a sign of his personal involvement is in the last paragraph, where his story moves to a brief and sudden climax, an act of angry violence. Joe feels a 'knot in his stomach, a battle between his pride and an accepted humility', in his rage against the label of being the 'unintelligent'. We have an earlier glimpse, too, of reflecting connections being made, when Joe is outside the Labour Exchange, watching the men as they 'returned into the cold, counting their money, sums flashing across their minds'. This counts in the story as an effective contribution to the element of social (and self-) criticism in the story; the men take their degradation too patiently (thus the final act of violence is felt to be cleansing and justifiable) and waste their ingenuity and life in mechanically counting and checking their money, 'in the cold'. How far Andrew is writing with full and deliberate awareness here is difficult to decide. Certainly, it is a very successful detail as far as the story goes (and in later work, Andrew showed a recurring need to discuss his own dispositions towards, and revulsions from, the pleasures of purely mathematical problem-solving). To sum up: it is the singular closeness of writer to hero in this story, that characterizes this as a reflecting, subjectively preoccupied piece; although it has to be admitted that some real sense also emerges, of the feelings of a quite separate person, of the plight of an unemployed man in his forties. In this, there are elements of third stage, identifying writing; but these are less prominent than the elements of self-preoccupation and self-projection here.

The second example was written by Lynda, in the first term of the fifth year. Lynda was of the kind who would have been a good choice for 'head girl' in a school that still had head girls; she was reliable, sensible, capable, well-liked and well-trusted by all, except for occasional outbursts of irritation from her class-mates at her apparent 'perfection'. She had shown unusual artistic talents in her earlier years of schooling, and her paintings were boldly imaginative, with a very good sense of colour. Some domestic difficulties might have explained a loss of confidence in her schoolwork around the time of the eleven-plus, but by the time she had reached the fourth year of secondary schooling, her confidence seemed fairly well restored, and she was in the 'middle' range of attainment in her class. She was quite unafraid of speaking her mind, but she usually preferred writing to talking in class, and would spend many discussion lessons quietly working on one of her (usually extensive) stories, for which she had a special interest and flair. She usually transformed any direct invitation to write personally, or questions on a book or poem, into a story of her own making; and she worked only very gradually from this into the kind of more formal literary commentaries demanded by the conventional kind of examination question (she *never* attempted directly personal writing, and naturally, was never 'pushed' in this respect, although her stories were often strongly laden with personal feeling and experience). During her fourth year she attempted one or two stories of near to full novel length, including one particularly successful tale based on Viking legends and a monster-fairy tale, based loosely on Viking stories, which she had written to read out to her younger sister.

At the time of writing, the group were studying a selection of short stories by D.H. Lawrence, as part of their C.S.E. studies. The stories had proved to be successful in this 'mixed ability' class, in that they offered abundant personal access for all the class, even the inexperienced readers, while well-motivated readers such as Lynda became engaged at new levels of subtlety, through the best stories in the selection.

The story below, which was based mainly on a class reading of 'Odour of Chrysanthemums', but partly also on her own reading of *Sons and Lovers*, offers an interesting blending of sensitive response to the details and implications of the original stories, and of 'telling the tale for herself'. It is in many ways a highly conscious, deliberate piece of writing, and in its careful re-creation and development of the original sources, it can be seen to be moving towards considered literary commentary. The scene that she has clearly borrowed from *Sons and Lovers*, is one where Walter, having endured a cold ignoring of his presence from his wife and family, walks out to a warm and cosy reception at the local pub; and by interweaving this with her 'Odour of Chrysanthemums' source, Lynda manages to include as one of her central characters, the husband who only appears in 'Odour of Chrysanthemums' as a corpse:

Man and Woman – man and wife?

The pub was perched on the corner of a line of long, dirty, terraced houses. It was alive with light and sound, and an excess of light spilled out onto the dark road.

He had just finished his shift at the mine and he ambled down the hill with three or four of his work mates. They reached the overflow of light from the pub and he hesitated. The laughter and enjoyment was pulling him, but then he thought of his wife at home, waiting and maybe worrying. He made a step down the hill, but then slowly was brought back to the pub by the encouragements and arguments of his mates. He would not be long, just a quick pint and then he would be off.

Inside was warm and full of life, so unlike the dead darkness of the cold night outside. Glasses tinkled and sudden laughter erupted from the corner where the piano stood. Everything was alive and full of movement. Warm, glowing faces showed for a moment, smiling as he approached the bar. The fat barman bellowed with laughter as his order was made and within seconds a brimming frothing pint was handed over.

He was a bit conscious of being in here when he should have been at home. He felt he was neglecting his responsibility to his wife and home, but the mock sneering at his quietness, drew him back. Soon, he had forgotten her because he didn't want to remember that dim cold prison of a house where she would be waiting. He knew that she would nag and grumble unceasing about her lot, but the persuasions of his friends were too strong for him.

The evening wore on. The 'quick pint' became three. The air was laden with smoke and sound. He boasted at the corner table of feats done in the mine. The others egged him on to more and more exaggerated stories of his heroism. Then the barman broke the spell with a tired 'Time'.

The smoke whisps whirled as men got up, kicking chairs and clanking bottles and glasses. Muttered 'goodbyes', and the breath of the unfriendlyness of outside, invaded the room for a moment as the bar door swung to and fro.

Outside the darkness seemed blacker in contrast with the light and he identified this with the scene that he would meet in the small, dirty, tired block of terrace houses that was his home. Each step brought him nearer to his doom. If only he was strong like she was, but he was weak. He stood the abuse that flooded at him without a word, meekly bowing his head and accepting the angry torrent that he was to face. His other friends didn't stand for it. They ruled their wives but he was ruled and he resented it.

He was now going along the row of dark houses. He walked over the squares of light and dark cast by the windows. Each little cubicle was cosy and closed, each with its own family settled around a roaring fire while he was walking towards a cold angry welcome. His footsteps sounded back at him accusingly and he found himself thinking of an excuse to soften the verbal blow. Why should he offer an excuse and give her the right to accept or refuse it? He was a man to give orders not to receive them. When he ordered men in the mine, they jumped to it without question. Why couldn't he have that sway in the home? He was pushed and hustled by a woman whose will was stronger than his, and he, like the coward he was, accepted without any resistance. How he resented it. When they had first been married he was the boss and rightly so; boss in his own home and she had been the meek one, craving his affection. Now she had taken over and ruled the house and him and it encroched on his sense of authority and maleness to be in such a situation.

He knocked on the door (he didn't even have a key) and waited, stamping warmth back into his feet and regarding the smutty plants in the plastic window box on the sill. At last the door opened and he entered.

She looked at the clock on the black mantlepiece. The fire threw orange shadows across the wall and softened the edges of the sideboard with a warm glow. She shrugged and returned to her knitting, but after a moment or two she looked at the clock again. The hands had only moved a fraction. Where was he? In the pub I suppose boozing with his mates!

The house was warm but not cosy. There was too much tension for that. The mantlepiece was littered with papers and bills. The bills were especially depressing, always there, menacing and waiting. The most urgent ones were jammed behind a plastic horse and foal, bought on a forgotten holiday long ago.

The clickering fingers entwined the brass candle-sticks on the chipped sideboard, a wedding present from someone or other along with the glass vase that was green with stale water and the remnants of leaves and stalks.

Wedding! How long ago that seemed. He had been the one who asserted himself and she had been contented. To be dominated was what she had always wanted. Domination to her represented security, the security she had lacked in her childhood.

When she brought her washing to the dirty courtyard where the woman dried their washing she heard of the family life of the other women and was secretly jealous. They had the security of a husband who made all the decisions and the wife to follow loyally. Why was she bound to such a husband? She was the head only because she couldn't bear to watch the slow deterioration of what she had built up in this area. Respect and friendship would all be ruined because he would come home drunk. Everything would go down hill. She was like the whip to a lazy animal.

She sometimes felt lost and depressed. Her spirits would sink while uneasiness rose in her. All through her life, security and lack of re-sponsibility had been her goal and she felt crushed and miserable. She was in conflict. On one side, she longed to be dominated and reponsi-bility passed over to its rightful place, her husband. But on the other, this desire was pressed back and hidden by her sense of pride. The thought of all that she stood for in the town, buckling and slowly cracking to crumble before her eyes was too much for this other side so she was torn. She knew herself that pride would always win whether she wanted it or whether it asserted itself unconsciously. She was chained to him so she must accept this and try to change him through herself.

To keep their heads above debt and gossip she had to nag and grumble at him. Nag and grumble. How she hated it and hated herself for doing it. It was so alien to her character.

Time dragged on and on. She dropped a stitch in her effort to hear his faltering footsteps. Then the agony of speaking harshly and watch him cringe under the lash of her tongue would come.

Time dragged on. The clock ticking, blended into the silence, softening the unending minutes, seconds and maybe even hours. Then her heart jumped. The muffled thud of feet stamping on the step. She put down the wool and resigned herself to her fate as she slowly plodded off to the door.

(Lynda, aged fifteen)

What Lynda offers here is by no means simply a borrowing and revision, but more an effective re-creation and development of hints from Lawrence. The original scene in *Sons and Lovers* is only briefly depicted:

He closed the door behind him, and was glad. It was a rainy evening. The Palmerston would be the cosier. He hastened forward in antici- pation. All the slate roofs of the Bottoms shone black with wet. The roads, always dark with coal-dust, were full of blackish mud. He hastened along. The Palmerston windows were steamed over. The passage was paddled with wet feet. But the air was warm, if foul, and full of the sound of voices and smell of beer and smoke.

'What shall Yer 'ave, Walter?' cried a voice, as soon as Morel appeared in the doorway.

'Oh, Jim, my lad, whereiver has ye sprung from?'

The men made a seat for him, and took him in warmly. He was glad. In a minute or two they had thawed all responsibility out of him, all shame, all trouble, and he was as clear as a bell for a jolly night . . .

(Lawrence, *Sons and Lovers*, 1913)

Lynda has developed this outline into several well-detailed paragraphs, which highlight the confused loneliness of a man who has lost touch with his wife. In the course of her own story, she follows the stream of thoughts and feelings of both husband and wife, with skill and subtlety; and with both characters she successfully conveys the strife within them- selves, as well as between each other: 'If only he was strong like she was, but he was weak . . . ' And of the wife: 'Nag and grumble. How she hated it and hated herself for doing it . . .' The details given by Lynda (whose own parents had separated) are disturbingly true to life, in their close observation of a failed marriage. This, with her acute literary insights into some main themes of 'Odour of Chrysanthemums', and her unusually inward sense of both the man's and the woman's feelings, makes her writing seem unexpectedly grown-up, and focally aware. But it is above all, I think, a reflecting piece, holding the original stories within her subjective intimations, and 'testing' them to seek connections, from which her own, quite individual story springs. The strong degree of involvement in the writing, and the closeness to an admired author, make this story comparable in its qualities and motives for writing to Andrew's Jack- London-type story.

The third example is by Alan, a small, reserved, rather solitary lad, who looked very young for his years. Being so unobtrusive, he tended to be disregarded in the ordinary to-and-fro of classroom contact; and my first real recognition of him did not come until he had been in my class for over a term. It is a moment I recall with some shame. I asked him why there was so little writing in his book, and why he had been absent of late; and he replied, with some bitterness, that he had been playing occasional truant since the year began, by coming to school for registration and then slipping away unnoticed, and this was the first time he had been challenged. He promised to turn up, and I promised to respect his presence more; and the embarrassing interview was soon forgotten, with the one good outcome of increased recognition on both sides. Later in the year he teamed up with a newly-arrived immigrant lad, and they maintained an unbroken, silent friendship together for the rest of their school life. Little was expected of, or achieved by, Alan in terms of formal academic achievement. He was indisputably of well-below-average attainment in English and in all other subject areas. Yet he could talk lucidly and thoughtfully, on the not-so-frequent occasions when he was relaxed, and discussing a book or idea on a one-to-one basis. He was no fool, and was very aware, without being unduly anxious about it, that others in the class despised him as something of a 'weed' (his word). Underlying his diffident and hesitant manner, in fact, was a quiet strength and independence of character which I found well deserving of respect; his personal presence, too, contributed unobtrusively to the rich character of his class. He left school with one or two low-grade C.S.E.'s, and secured an apprenticeship in a local firm.

The piece quoted below represented an unexpected advance for Alan, and provided ready evidence that he was far more proficient in writing than he had previously been prepared to admit (his longest piece to this point had been an ill-written half page that had given rise to doubts about even his basic literacy). Blake's 'Sunflower' poem had been read and discussed in class, and the class had then worked at the poem in small groups, working out suitable questions on the poem. In consultation with his one companion, Alan had worked out four questions, and went on to say that he would like to answer them, as his next writing task. It will be seen that while he makes some attempt to offer direct answers to his own questions, he also frequently uses those only as a stepping-stone, to connect the poem with his own (as yet not at all clearly sifted) preoccupations:

Sunflower

Questions   1.   Why does the sunflower want to climb so high?
2.   Why did the youth quote pine away with desire?
3.   Who is the pale virgin?
4.   Is it a sad or happy poem?

Answers

1. To me the word "climb" means to move to a greater height this is what the sunflower wants to do it wants to get nearer the sun. The sunflower isnt worried about time he does what he can and then accepts it not like people they are worried about time I dont think a person has been happy or satisfied if all he does is worry about time. You have to accept time some people try to recent time but what is time? Time is when someone gets more mature. Some people are worried about time, as in the end they die. They shouldn't worry as time will still go on as long as we and other living things live. but when everything dies time to will just die

. . . .

2. This means the youths feeling for work and sex relations. This is where the youth was told sex is dirty and filthy so the youth got pleasure by some other means. This to me is the worst thing a parent or adult can teach. Your find more women getting raped and more little Kids getting beaten up and killed. Youth will want to try it out like a boy finding whats in a box so I think more damage is done. This to me is nature you cant tell a dog not to have sex with other dogs. Just because weve got a lump of flesh which recieves vibrations from the ear this makes us completely diffrent which just isnt right. Every person has got a ceartain pecentage of disancy — like a annimal. How many dead dogs do you find or other annimals? you dont as they have got free relations I dont think people would go about and jump on some girl and make love to her as our human decency is to strong to allow us to. So I think if they all stopped preaching society would get along much better.

. . . .

3. This means in my mind of a girl who has'nt followed her nature or rather desire. Shes been told its wrong to have sex. This alsoe puts in my mind that all the others girls have gone with their desire but shes held back her desire just as her mother and father have told her. The word pale I think is the virgin weakining with desire Shes just stayed put like a lamp-post likes shes been told by her parents she is also at that stage where I think shell wipe of the snow and go and enjoy herself like her parents have and freinds.

. . . .

4. No, to me the first part is happy but when you come to the 2nd
verse this to me is where I think it turns to sadness. The first verse
is all based on freedom but when humans come into the poem it just
locks all the freedom out completly. But the humans get ther break
of freedom like the sunflower does at the end of poem. The poem
says the youths came out of their graves to aspire and then it goes on
to say the sunflower wishes to go there. The sunflower seems like
humans it wants to break away from routine the flower dose'nt want
to go up like its supposed to the flower wants to go down in the
earth. If freedom was granted to every-thing on earth I think this
earth would be a greater and content place. These things the sunflower and youth are just meaningless to me they just want to
change there life with each other one wants to rise the anther wants
to go to a grave nothing in this world will be content. This is the way
I look at the poem I looked at this as myself would look at it not
like society would like me to look at it.

(Alan, aged fifteen)

There are many kinds of personally-reflecting excursions and (as far as
'identifying' is concerned) misprisions here, which enable him to pursue
his own enquiries — almost at the expense of the poem, it seems. For
example, he chooses in his first question to reinterpret 'golden clime'
(a phrase whose meaning was made clear in class discussion) as 'climb', so
that he can more readily talk about the good sense of growing up in his
own time, without anxiously hurrying the process of growing — ('I don't
think a person has been happy or satisfied if all he does is worry about
time . . . '). His phrasing becomes a little muddled here, and his line of
thought is at best marginal to the meaning of the poem; but his main line
of thought is clear enough in *itself*, and seems to be of central importance
to the writer. In paragraphs two and three he is closer to the context of
the poem, and recognizes the import of 'where the youth pined away with
desire' — but again, he translates the poem into his own terms and
preoccupations, and asserts how youth needs to explore the adult world of
'work and sex relations' ('world' is entirely his own insertion here) without
being brow-beaten by a 'parent or adult'. In a vivid though somewhat
enigmatic sentence he declares how he sees no good reason why human
beings should be imprisoned by other people's moralities, simply because
they have an enlarged brain which can receive language: 'if they all
stopped preaching society would get along much better . . . '. In paragraph
three he is struck by Blake's phrase about the 'pale virgin shrouded in
snow', from which he develops his own objections to preaching about sex,
and the anxiety-raising pressures of parents and other adults. Around this
point his account becomes a good deal less coherent. Random impressions
and obscure phrasings multiply, some of which may well be more at-

tributable to the poem, than to Alan's personal confusion (as, for instance, when he admits that he cannot understand whether the youths and the sunflowers are reaching up to the sun, or down to their graves!). His concluding sentence offers a good clue to the spirit in which he has attempted his writing. Confused and sometimes incoherent his account may be; but his claim that he has sought to be true to his own feeling and reflecting is justified in what he has written. His answers suggest the peculiar impact made on him by the poem; having been encouraged to make what *he* wishes to make of it, he has taken the poem to himself, and discovered something of himself, as well as of the poem, in his reflections. In doing so he has shown a far greater depth and range in his thinking than I had presumed was likely. He, too, could reveal the strange operation of the mind:

> That ocean where each kind
> Doth straight its own resemblance find;
> Yet it creates, transcending these,
> Far other Worlds, and other Seas.
>
> (Andrew Marvell, *The Garden*)

CHAPTER SIX

Identifying

No-one believes more strongly than I do that what our senses know as 'this world' is only one portion of our mind's total environment and object. Yet, because it is the primal portion, it is the sine qua non of all the rest. If you grasp the facts about it firmly, you may proceed to higher regions undisturbed.

(William James, *Talks to Teachers*, 1899)

Realizing Actualities

There is, after all, something very satisfying in being able to visualize and hold for oneself a clear, well-embodied insight, or 'fact'; to enjoy through defining, just as the firm round solidity of a polished stone and the wonderful tension around a globule of mercury satisfy eye and touch. This is the stage when the learner is prepared to identify 'beyond-me'; to define — and to celebrate — those specific qualities which make up the other-ness of all that lies beyond personal being. It is a movement outwards, a bodying-forth of formed concepts; a movement which secures the 'third realm' between person and world. To be 'objective' in this sense is not, then, to renounce the notion of 'in-dwelling'; for having identified an aspect of the world the learner offers a personal investment in the new knowledge. He or she may then take significant steps towards the wider, communal involvement that characterizes the fourth, organizing, stage. The identifying stage, then, is not an end in itself; rather, it empowers the learner to take personal responsibility for the new knowledge. It generates new growth, new cultural interactions between the individual and the world.

This identifying stage is the imagining stage, in the fairly strict sense that a clear image or version of the 'beyond-me' is formed, which has gradually emerged from preliminary 'telling' and reflecting play. As has been suggested by the two previous chapters, it is important that learners and teachers should recognize the patterns and actions that lead to identifying, in order to keep in touch with actual processes in coming to know. On first encounter with unknown things we are simply alerted — to the taut liquidity of the mercury, to a voice on the telephone that is known but not immediately identified, to the cruciform shape of a tree in winter. If we admit (through 'telling') the new experience further into the reflectings of our consciousness, we are then still further involved by a more disinterested attention, which was first generated by the initial alertness or curiosity, and is now carried by a more sustained questioning. Thus the learner is moved beyond former limits of self-hood, into what we commonly recognize as 'impersonal commitment' to a problem, or issue. The learner, in short, comes to care for what is learned, to care for its truth.

The actual experience of the third, identifying stage is well conveyed in a passage from an early chapter in D.H. Lawrence's *Women in Love* ('Classroom') when the school inspector Birkin interrupts Ursula's lesson in elementary botany, on catkins. As he enters, he switches on the lights, so that 'the classroom was distinct and hard, a strange place after the soft dim magic that filled it before he came.' Swiftly, Birkin intervenes to identify the purpose of the colours in the catkins, with definitive emphasis:

> 'Give them some crayons, won't you?' he asked, 'so that they can make the gynaecious flowers red, and the androgenous yellow — It's the fact you want to emphasise, not the subjective impression to record. What's the fact? — red little spikey stigmas of the female flower, dangling yellow male catkins, pollen flying from one to another'.
>
> (D.H. Lawrence, *Women in Love*, 1921)

As this, and the opening passage from William James suggest, it is suggested that this identifying stage should include a grasp of specific 'facts' and concepts in the sense, say, that a Physics or Biology teacher might use the term. But this is to be matched with an equally important claim that such 'facts', if they have not merely accrued as clichés, are understood individually and bodily; and that we cannot exclude the original feeling-activity that enabled our 'objective' understanding of new concepts. There is a danger, when attempting to free the handling and ordering of 'facts' from over-subjectivity, of distorting their true nature (that is, as experienced and actualized by a living thinker); this happens, for example, in depersonalized modes of 'rational-scientific' discourse. We are alerted to this danger, indeed, in the 'Classroom' chapter of *Women in Love*, when Birkin is disturbed by yet a further intruder, the self-styled 'artistic' Hermione, who torments him with the bullying, yet 'conscience-harrowing question' about why there should be a need to objectify, to 'rouse to consciousness' at all. As Lawrence himself has acknowledged elsewhere (in *Morality and the Novel*), 'We shall never know what the sunflower is'. Even so, we *know* that this appreciation, the 'shock of recognition' into other-awareness, may be experienced in our actual living. Without it, we should be imprisoned in whatever emotions happened to be colouring the present moment of our lives, never able to dwell beyond those moods of the moment, to put our feelings to the test, in the surrounding world. Our versions of sensed experience would then be in danger of becoming too subject-bound to be adequately communicated to others, for their comprehension and affirmation. The outward journey of the identifying stage is vital, then, in learning, and in all areas of learning, not least since it envisages an enlivening of objective or 'scientific' insights, rather than accepting merely 'dead universe' notions of existence. Such a principle — that to recognize the actuality of a form must include a recognizing of its livingness — underpins the fruitful insights of Marjorie Grene's enquiries into the philosophy of biology:

> Perceptions of form — the shape of an oak-leaf, the walk of a cat, the metamorphosis of a butterfly — the grasp of such configurations and changes of configuration, are among the basic insights by which the subject-matter of biology is singled out. A certain freedom within form . . . is the criterion by which we see a shape as 'alive'.
> (Marjorie Grene, *The Understanding of Nature*, 1974)

The painter's/poet's vision extends this recognizing of living configurations, of a 'certain freedom within form' to all natural objects, so that the principles of physics itself are affected by 'in-dwelling'. As a boy, I had the good fortune to be *shown* physics at school; to experience in a darkened room the astonishing 'facts' of the refracting of a pencil of light as it enters and leaves a glass prism was to be brought, through ingenious teaching method, to recognize the true links between physics and poetry. Such a memorable presenting of 'facts' subverts any unhappy view that scientific information and method must be poured into learners as they were into Gradgrind's little pitchers. (There is likely to be less room for full imaginative play in the science laboratory, in that any established science is bound by less flexible paradigms than can operate in English studies; but it is now a familiar principle in the teaching of science that there should be an emphasis on the *experiencing* of science, on enabling a sense of living contact with moments of discovery — for example, through historical and narrative accounts, as well as guided 'trial-and-error' problem-solving and imaginatively presented experiments.)

Identifying involves a fresh attending, a bodily meeting with the new 'facts', a clear grasp of their firm 'bounding-lines'. That term is Blake's, from a passage which dwells on the ethical power of authentic identifying:

> The great and golden rule of art, as well as of life, is this: that the more distinct, sharp and wiry the bounding lines, the more perfect the work of art; and the less keen and sharp, the greater is the evidence of weak imitations, plagiarism and bungling . . . The want of this determinate and bounding form evidences the want of ideas in the artistic

mind, and the pretence of plagiary in all its branches . . . How do we distinguish one face or countenance from another, but by the bounding line and its infinite inflections and movements? What is it that builds a house and plants a garden, but the definite and determinate? What is it that distinguishes honesty from knavery, but the hard and wiry line of rectitude and certainty in actions and intentions? Leave out this line and you leave out life itself.

(William Blake, *Descriptive Catalogue XV*)

Here Blake visualizes all human achievement — all concepts in architecture, the arts, the sciences, morality — as contained within the living tension of that 'distinct, sharp and wirey-bounding line' which alone can reify individual intention. And the beholder or learner will, in turn, need to enact the same imaginative distinctions, in order to understand the original creator's achievement.

Thus, identifying involves far more than rote-learning; indeed, it involves a *subverting* of rote-learning, for it requires a creative inter-acting of the sympathetic imagination with perception. Through this, we may come to feel and understand — we come to *identify* — the innovations of form in Giotto's frescoes, the integrity of Marvell's 'political' poetry, the nature of the harmonic liberation achieved by Monteverdi, or Solomon's judgements on which mother should keep the child. In short, we identify 'with', in order to identify 'objectively' the particular qualities of a concept, or form, or decision.

As with the other stages, it is envisaged that there are both younger and adult versions of this stage. Empathic flights of imagining, such as very young children are capable of in their play and fantasies and art are authentic, if not mature, versions of this stage. At an adult level, a craftsman's inward grasp of the qualities of his materials; a good farmer's knowledge of his land and stock; or a capacity to recognize one's marriage partner's state of mind without the intrusion of one's own 'viewpoint' (or to disengage oneself from, and recognize clearly one's own state, for that matter) come to mind as natural examples in ordinary living. But in order to understand the full force of an idea (or identifying) that has been individually grasped, it is helpful to turn to an example of original discovery, by a man who felt oppressed by over-handled, worn-out 'facts' that he was expected to accept in his profession as a painter, even though he felt no personal recognition of them; and who struggled through to a freshly embodied 'objective' view, derived from his own contemplating of the world. The example is Cézanne's dramatic contribution to new forms of painting at the beginning of this century.

Cézanne and the Cliché

> Throughout my youth I wanted to paint that table-cloth like freshly
> fallen snow ... I know now that one must try to paint only: 'the plates
> and napkins rose symmetrically', and 'the light-coloured rolls'. If I
> paint 'crowned', I'm finished, you see. And if I really balance and
> shade my napkins and rolls as they really are, you may be sure that
> the crowning, the snow and all the rest of it will be there.
>
> (Paul Cézanne, quoted in Merleau-Ponty, *The Phenomenology of
> Perception*, 1961)

Commenting on this passage, Merleau-Ponty adds, with teasing simplicity,
that the problem raised first by our body and then by the world, is that 'it
is all there'. He returned often to Cézanne, as a source from which to
develop his thought on the nature of the body's inter-acting with the
world; but earlier than this, and with comparable insights, came D.H.
Lawrence's interest in the great French painter. In an essay on Cézanne
which has won some recognition as a piece of original thinking on the
nature of Knowing and Reality ('Introduction to his Paintings' in
Phoenix, 1936) Lawrence discusses how real knowledge comes from being
bodily aware within our living, rather than from mere 'camera-vision' –
those accretions of conventional consciousness which are the source and
harbourer of the cliché, and which for the painter were exposed with
potentially humiliating effect through the rapid development of the
camera, in the nineteenth century. In this essay Lawrence presents his
own view of 'in-dwelling', in declaring how each individual bears his or
her own responsibility of bodily existence, in order to know the world. He
describes what he sees as Cézanne's 'heroic struggle' to break away from
surface, impressionist effects, in order genuinely to *re*-present nature as
he saw it. He was seeking an essential reality that would challenge a five-
centuries-old quest for verisimilitude, which had worn itself out: 'A cliché
is just a worn-out memory that has no emotional or intuitional root, and
has become a habit.' Cézanne disregarded what he saw as mere further
refinements in tricks of the trade, to prop up a dead tradition through
disguise or embellishment. He went back instead to the basic shapes of the
cylinder, sphere and cone, simplifying further into planes, in order to construct a fresh version of the latent structure of objects. Lawrence sums up
his achievement by contrasting it with what he sees as the lesser achievement of Van Gogh (though he ignores Van Gogh's interpretative painting
in order to do this). Van Gogh's response was, declared Lawrence, suffused
with personal feeling; whereas Cézanne's body of imagery was drawn up
from the very core of his being and projected into the world, for all to
see its distinct existence:

Van Gogh's earth was still subjective earth, himself projected into the earth. But Cézanne's apples are a real attempt to let the apple exist in its own separate identity, without transfusing it with personal emotion. Cézanne's great effort was, as it were, to shove the apple away from him, and let it live of itself. It seems a small thing to do; yet it is the first real sign that man has made for thousands of years that he is willing to admit that matter *actually* exists.

(Lawrence, *Phoenix*, 1936)

Cézanne, then, was not so much looking for ways of expressing his emotions, as seeking to communicate the truth that he perceived about the three dimensions of the world. It was a painstaking building from his own intuition 'that matter *actually* exists', which led him to lay down the groundwork for cubism, and for the great adventures of Picasso and other artists of the twentieth century 'renaissance'. 'I am convinced', Lawrence declared

that what Cézanne himself wanted *was* representation. He wanted true-to-life representation. Only he wanted it more true-to-life. And once you have got photography, it is a very difficult thing to get representation more true to life: which it has to be.

(Ibid.)

For Cézanne, such a sense of reality, such a way of knowing, is achieved by the full experience of the body — not just relying on the eye, and on memories recorded by the eye:

for the intuitive apperception of the apple is so tangibly aware of the apple that it is aware of it all round, not only just of the front. The eye sees only fronts, and the mind, on the whole, is satisfied with fronts. But intuition needs all-a-roundness, and instinct needs insideness. The true imagination is for ever curving around to the other side, to the back of presented appearance . . .

(Ibid.)

This fully bodily entering into the object, and then letting it *be* in its own right *is* knowing, for Cézanne, and for Lawrence. In Lawrence's terms, it involves the body in effort to bring new vision and new consciousness into the mind; for the mind, when left to itself in separate existence, will become a tyrannical guardian of clichés, worn-out memories — 'All sorts of memory, visual, tactile, emotional memory, memories, groups of memories, systems of memories.' Whereas Cézanne 'wanted to be a man of flesh, a real man: to get out of the sky-blue prison into real air.' The object, insight or idea is then endowed with its own distinct living-ness, uncluttered by the dead accretions of past memory and experience. As Lawrence declared elsewhere (in a letter to Middleton Murray): 'You can't give a symbol a meaning. Symbols are organic units of consciousness with a life of their own and you can never explain them away.' Thus Cézanne's apples live as real forms, conveying their own meanings to those who will see them with a painter's questioning gaze.

The fact that Cézanne's discoveries emerged as an advance from the work of the Impressionists, suggests that in general movements of thought and culture, too there is a clear movement from reflecting to identifying stages of insight. Paul Klee (Jena Lecture, 1924) suggested that the movement developed from the 'under-brush' of the Impressionists to the 'bedrock' of the new painting.

Historically, Cézanne offers an outstanding example of a high, adult level of insight into particularities, and through them into larger, more general patterns of form. A native example is to be found in the work of Gerard Manley Hopkins, whose notebooks and journal show not only rich, Van Gogh-like 'expressive' descriptions of natural objects and landscapes, but also an emerging identifying attention to what he termed the 'inscape' (the inner form and reality) of natural life. His love of quick visual observation was sustained throughout his life, which he would sometimes record with the naively 'telling', at times seemingly tasteless first-hand response of the artist in his role as a voracious would-be analyst of life – and of death:

> I saw under a stone hedge was a dying ram: there ran slowly from his nostrils a thick flesh-coloured ooze, scarlet in places, coiling and roping its way down so thick that it looked like fat.
> (Gerard Manley Hopkins, 1873, in *The Journals and Papers*, 1959)

Tasteless or not, this we recognize as providing the essential clues towards a full artistic-human response – just as Leonardo and Michelangelo 'discovered' human form, in part, through their hours spent in the city mortuary. But Hopkins often advances, even in his note-books, on this kind of rapt, expressing-exploiting description, for he believed that 'when you look hard at a thing it seems to look hard at you; only by constantly refreshing the mind by looking hard and long in this way can you remember or believe how deep the inscape in things is.' He records how this experience of inscape is also accompanied by a physical sense of 'instress', and in an empathic flight, 'the individual beholder becomes mystically one with the whole.' Thus he is able to identify clearly and unmistakably the inner quality, the essential pattern as well as the visible outline of the object beyond himself:

This is the time to study inscape in the spraying of trees, for the swelling buds carry then to a pitch which the eye could not else gather . . . in these sprays at all events is a new world of inscape . . .

(Gerard Manley Hopkins, *Journal*, 1871 — 'end of March, beginning of April')

After which there follows a closely detailed description of the buds of the male ash tree, which may perhaps be judged as being both a 'scholarly-botanical contribution to knowledge,' *and* as a highly individual, 'poetic' attention to the object, in which Hopkins is absorbed. In short, these note-books, as we might expect, provide evidence of the necessary preliminary stages of response and enquiry, that sometimes — but by no means always — lead to the realized achievement of Hopkins' remarkable poetry. It gladdens the reader, to discover so many daily events and impressions that aroused the poet's curiosity and pleasure-in-encounter. Indeed, the journals enable an added respect to grow for the singular achievements of one who is often acknowledged as the one real poet (as far as writing verse goes) of Victorian times; for often they demonstrate the poised delight of learning-involvement, where the will-to-discover seems in harmony with the natural process and rhythms of the body — work as an 'absorbing game', as Lawrence termed it. They offer a reminder that, satisfying as it may be to reach a stage of firm identifying, to 'capture' the prize of the idea or insight or fact, it is the *process* of learning which really takes up our living; the process ought therefore to be experienced as something intrinsically satisfying. Writing on 'The Essence of Hunting', Ortega y Gasset suggests that:

It is not essential to the hunt that it be successful. On the contrary, if the hunter's efforts were always and inevitably successful it would not be the effort that we call hunting, it would be something else. The beauty of hunting lies in the fact that it is always problematic.

(Ortega y Gasset, *Meditations on Hunting*, 1972)

Everyman's Venture
To return to the everyday world of secondary school writing, the out-standing quality of identifying writing lies in the strength and clarity of what has been contemplated beyond the self. It is a venturing-out, in the spirit of Cézanne, or Hopkins, if not to their degree and depths. The vast majority of people do not make their rare kind of journey; and even when they do, what most people usually 'discover' has already been discovered by someone else, in terms so similar that the differences do not matter, as far as encyclopaedic 'knowledge' is concerned. But on the other hand, the concerns of most people may be a good deal nearer to those of Cézanne and Hopkins than most educational systems and most people themselves

commonly realize. For most of us, it may be enough that we should be able to enjoy the enterprise of identifying for ourselves, through being enlightened by the insights of others. And our acts of recognition may be seen as an important advance on earlier, more randomly self-involved reflections. To recognize how the swan shaped itself for take-off and beat its wings against resistant water to move into flight (as the empathic Saxon poet of riddles saw it); or to recognize what happens to light as it goes through a prism (as the young schoolboy was brought to see it), is to experience a kind of epiphany, to use Joyce's term: a bodily awakening of the mind to new kinds of awareness, so that although the recognition is not original as far as History is concerned, it is so for the individual learner. Thus such an experience cannot be seen as a purely mental process, detached from bodily feeling and engagement. The fullness of the experience was well recorded by one of my adult students, who wrote:

> The importance of the getting a degree side of this course decreases weekly as I become more and more immersed in the joy of at last thinking and talking away some of the fuzzy nonsenses of my life. But it's not just this, it's a feeling of the reality of it *all*, mainly because I'm beginning to find that suddenly, just a little, I can relate things to things. As yet exactly what is happening is vague to me and is hardly possible to put into words, but it's slowly and inexorably emerging. My great fear is that it will suddenly sink again. I just thought today at the tutorial (as I've often done before) how totally unrelated are the things I learned at school, to each other and to life. Even things that were so obvious still seem to remain in boxes shut and locked in my mind – e.g. you mentioned tonight Galileo's discovery that all matter falls at the same rate. I learned something like that in Physics, yet I'm sure if you'd asked me I would have said heavier things fall faster. When I get home I want to do somersaults and things.
>
> (M.B.)

This account by an adult freshly re-engaged in the pursuit of learning points well to the changeover from a reflecting stage ('talking away some of the fuzzy nonsenses of my life') to an identifying stage (her excited grasp of Galileo's discovery and her felt sense of its value – 'When I get home again, I want to do somersaults and things.') Not that all fresh insight produces quite the same dramatic, 'Eureka!' reaction. It may perhaps be much more appropriately expressed in cooler terms, when the involvement has been felt as soothing and restoring to the body's nerves; but sensate experience will just as inevitably have been involved, and will have drawn energy from what Polanyi termed (in *Knowing and Being*, 1969), the 'heuristic power of a problem'. Our learning-encounter is a mode of 'being-in-the-world'; we undergo our living through our learning, we live through participating with what we learn.

Face-to-face

For Merleau-Ponty, to observe *is* to participate — to offer a dialogue with the world. In *Signs* (1964) he declared how for the painter '*that* object and *that* colour' in the world, and in the painting command us 'just as imperiously as a syntax or a logic' to view them as they *are*. And in *Eye and Mind* (1974) he emphasized how the painter's view is not a 'view upon the outside, a merely "physical-optical" relation with the world'; it is, rather, the 'painter to whom the things of the world give birth by a sort of concentration or coming-to-itself of the visible.' Then, in an illuminating passage he visualizes his notion of 'field-being', or that 'third realm' which is lived between facticity and ideality:

> When, through the water's thickness I see the tiling at the bottom of a pool, I do not see it *despite* the water and the reflections there; I see it through them and because of them. If there were no distortions, no ripples of sunlight, if it were without this flesh that I saw the geometry of the tiles, then I would cease to see it *as* it was and where it is — which is to say, beyond any identical specific place. I cannot say that the water itself — the aqueous power, the sirupy and shimmering element — is *in* space, all this is not somewhere else either, but it is not in the pool. It inhabits it, it materializes itself there, yet it is not contained there . . .
>
> (Merleau-Ponty, *Eye and Mind*, 1974)

Here Merleau-Ponty provides the picture of a world that is lived, dwelled-in, that has its own powers, rather than waiting to be manipulated; a world where our identifying is born from that lived connection, and through reflection, into the field between the seer and the seen. The painter understands, above all, how to trust his vision, his direct intuition, before it is weighed down by accumulations of memory and fixed patterns of response. Through individual contact with the visible, the painter creates new 'fields' on the canvas, so long as his vision remains untamed. The directness of the link between painter and world is highlighted in a passage from David Holbrook's *English for Meaning*, where he recalls Jean Renoir's biography of his father, *My Father* (1962), whose painting activity, declared Renoir, was like a swallow hunting for insects: 'Renoir's brush was linked to his visual perceptions as directly as the swallow's beak is linked to its eyes.' Extreme actualizations, such as this one, are rare even in the best painting, and there may be good reason why they are even more rare in the medium of words, where the temptations of ready-made versions of experience lurk in every phrase. But unless learners are encouraged — even coerced at times — to discern shapes through direct, personal intuition in the pool of experience, their thought will remain undeveloped in terms of truly incarnate response. Such response requires a kind of daring that risks being misunderstood, or even seeming eccentric, as is illustrated in another of Arthur Waley's deceptively slight anecdotes from Taoist sources:

> Chuang Tzu and Hui Tzu were strolling one day on the bridge over the river Hao. Chuang Tzu said, 'Look how the minnows dart hither and thither where they will. Such is the pleasure that fish enjoy.' Hui Tzu said, 'You are not a fish. How do you know what gives pleasure to fish?' Chuang Tzu said, 'You are not I. How do you know that I don't know what gives pleasure to fish? Let's go back to where we started. You asked me what gives pleasure to fish. But you already knew how I knew it when you asked me. You knew that I knew it by standing here on the bridge at Hao.'
>
> (Arthur Waley, *Three Ways of Thought in Ancient China*, 1939)

The story makes no sense unless we too have identified with the moment that Chuang Tzu savours (we cannot 'change' our feelings, we can only select from them, or pretend to change them, in coping with them for whatever reasons). Having recognized the truth of Chuang Tzu's moment of recognition for ourselves, Hui Tzu's objection seems heavy indeed; and Chuang Tzu's deft verbal play adds to our pleasure in the story. Hui Tzu is cornered into admitting that he, too, was witness to the poet's encounter on the bridge; and if he admits the experience, how can he *not* know the answer to his question?

Some Examples

As far as writing at the identifying stage is concerned, it is characterized by a steady movement towards more clearly formed, better ordered pieces than those in the reflecting stage; and by a tendency towards more impersonal (but not unfelt) treatment. Such writings usually indicate a readiness by the writer to be able to accept and welcome tactful *comparative* evaluation (whereas at the early stages, evaluation can only be usefully offered in terms of the learner's own previous performances). Where response to a literary text is concerned, learners show a readiness to write on behalf of the text rather than themselves, to keep close to the spirit of the text, and to seek out its forms and patterns; or where there is dwelling on self and on personal experience, it is in the spirit of impersonal evaluation, where the learner has found some fresh ground of strength and confidence, from which to contemplate past or present experience.

It is no accident that all writing examples chosen for this section are centred on a literary text. For all the variety of resources and approaches that were adopted in English studies, the department retained a commitment to literary studies as an indispensable centre for the flourishing of creative language work. We gauged the progress of our English teaching by appraising the amount and quality of reading that our classes were engaged in, as evidenced in their talk to us and to each other – during lessons, during breaks, over lunch – as well as in their writing. 'Good teaching' Raymond O'Malley has said, 'is "simply" the art of causing much good reading to occur. It is enough in all conscience!' (*Use of English*, 32, 2, 1981). Writing as an examiner, Mr O'Malley adds that good examining 'permits and even encourages good teaching thus defined', without damaging the purposes of the examination. The writing examples that follow were in fact all written for C.S.E. assessment. They are un-exceptional enough in themselves, but I should suggest that each reveals good elements of both personal contemplation, and of a willingness, having dwelled in the text, to put its qualities first – beyond the self, as it were.

Given the reservations offered already about the wrong kinds of exam-ining and assessing in secondary schools, it may still be conceded that occasional work under assessment conditions can help to concentrate the mind, in formulating just what has been identified, and to what depth. But the learner is not, of course, to be pushed to a point where an essential personal orientation is strangled, in favour of 'what the exam requires'. For this reason, if any writing was to be done under 'test' conditions (which never happened more than once each term), the class were given the questions to be set a week beforehand, and they were also invited to negotiate their own questions, so that they might write on a topic of genuine interest to them. They were also allowed to consult the texts and to have up to half a page only of notes, during the test.

The first example, by Asta (who wrote on Free Schooling in Chapter Four), was written for such a test to complete a session of work on a selection of short stories by D.H. Lawrence. Asta chose to write about *Daughters of the Vicar* and *Odour of Chrysanthemums* during the one hour test, in answer to the (negotiated) question, 'How do people avoid, and how do people discover life in these stories?' The passage represents just the half of her essay that dwelled on *Daughters of the Vicar*.

Discovering life

In 'Daughters of the Vicar', I think Miss Louisa discovers a great deal of her own feelings. Towards the end of the story she begins to find out just what *she* wants, rather than doing what is more expected of her by her family. Although they are very poor, the children are brought up with a great deal of pride. They tend to look down on everyone else, although they are somewhat worse off than many others. They are almost totally isolated, and so have little contact with outsiders to see what they are really like. The strange family is very tightly knit, but in such a way that each member is isolated.

Louisa is somehow unable to make contact with other people. When she goes to see Mrs. Durant and finds her hurt from pulling up a cabbage, she is suddenly admitted into a completely new environment and she doesn't really know how to react, how to cope with the situation.

Durant was in a similar predicament. He was beginning to get some ideas from reading, and was quite fit, but even from his years in the navy he was quite attached to his home and to his mother. He felt 'spiritually impotent'. He could not make contact with women, and this drew them together somewhat. Being the younger son also made this great bond between them, as seems to happen in many families between mother and younger son, especially when the older ones have left home or died.

From the time that Mrs. Durant becomes ill, when her son comes home from working in the pit, Louisa has to become 'mother' for Durant, cooking and cleaning, but the thing which strikes her most is when she has to bathe his back. Such an intimate act is carried out by what are, in reality, almost total strangers.

So then again another strange relationship forms between Louise and Durant. A need and desire for one another builds up, but both of them, through their family backgrounds, are unable to do anything. Then when Mrs. Durant dies and there is no longer any good reason for her to stay in the household, her innermost feelings break forth despite Durants seeming dumb passiveness, and because the inner self is finally stronger than the cover she is protected by, all ends well, and Durant himself even becomes a fuller person. Louisa finds out about the peculiar relationship between mother and son – how even on the mothers death bed they play a sort of game, and how Durant is not strong enough to break away from the game. He goes to work even when he wants to stay. I think the sudden realisation even makes Louisa more aware of her *own* family background.

(Asta, fifth year, aged fifteen)

The writing shows Asta's capacity to become engaged *beyond* herself, through the Lawrence story. Her writing here is sober in tone, with a quite close attention to the details and direction of the story (the 'reflecting' groundwork is still well visible). In the first paragraph she identifies both the inner and outer isolation of the children in the family, although she has already hinted at Louisa's development beyond this. She is also quickly alert to Alfred Durant's plight – 'He felt "spiritually impotent". He could not make contact with women . . .'. She sees how the circumstances of the story enable Louisa to 'become "mother" for Durant, cooking and cleaning, but the thing which strikes her most is when she has to bathe his back. Such an intimate act is carried out by what are, in reality, almost total strangers . . .'. Her involvement in this critical meeting between Louisa and Alfred is close, and she interprets skilfully the impact on Louisa: "her innermost feelings break forth despite Durant's seeming dumb passiveness

. . . Louisa finds out about the peculiar relationship between mother and son — how even on the mothers death bed they play a sort of game.' Asta has maintained an absorbed, concentrated commentary here, without any personal intrusions, in her intention to convey the qualities of Lawrence's story. Her account of this story (and of *Odour of Chrysanthemums* too) showed how she had been touched into a more sober kind of contemplation by these stories, than was usual for her. Her writing was typically ebullient and assertive, usually too carefree or volatile to linger patiently over patterns of experience that needed sustained attention. It was good that she should have 'schooled' herself to dwell with care on this story, and it marked a distinct point of development in her work.

The second example is from Jackie's work. Like so many of the pupils in her year, and in the group whose work has been selected here, Jackie began to gain much more confidence in herself and in her schoolwork, after an initially uncertain year of settling down into her new school. Along with most of them, she had 'failed' her 11-plus exam and started her secondary schooling in the small local secondary school which our school came to absorb. Reflecting once on her schooling, she declared that she had enjoyed her education up to joining us, although she had learned to regard herself rather humbly, as being average-to-dull in her schoolwork. Yet she was a deft, personable girl who came to be respected as one of the leading individuals of her year, helping, for instance, to edit the year-group's 'underground' magazine.

No one in this unusually fluent year produced more pages of writing than Jackie; and while these began by being rather dull and over-'correct', her sheer fluency became astonishing as she began to experiment in her writing, and to write from within herself. She gained several O-levels and grade 1 C.S.E.'s at the end of her fifth year, including good passes in English; she hoped to take up a University place to read English, but went eventually to a College of Education. One of her final activities as a schoolgirl was to work in an education 'Shop' run by the Advisory Centre for Education (ACE) at a Butlin's Holiday Camp. She was employed to give advice and information on comprehensives 'from the inside', where her services were thought by the organizers to be 'outstanding'.

Edward Thomas was written as part of Jackie's C.S.E./O-level Literature project, and was her first real venture beyond 'notes on the lesson' into her *own* response to the poems. We had read these poems during some after-school sessions on the O-level Literature set books, but her topic here was self-chosen. Jackie was becoming keen to be skilful in writing about Literature; and it was good to see in this piece how well she was beginning to identify and evoke the mood, tone and feeling of what she was reading (the passage here represents about half of what she wrote for this assignment):

Edward Thomas

The five poems I have chosen to write about are Manor Farm, Women he Liked, The Sun used to Shine, As the Teams head-brass, Celandine.

These five I feel are all happy if not wistful poems. The easy rhythm and the stillness is all connected with each of the different surroundings. I will write about each of them in turn and you will see the similarities between each of them.

The Manor Farm is one of the happiest poems that Thomas has written, because it sends over the typical serenity of the old country-fied English on a Sunday. The poem indicates a great age and hospitality when the poet uses such words as, 'ewe trees, manor house, church'. All these are of a comparable age and in turn give a serene and peaceful effect. The lines, 'with tiles duskily glowing, entertained the mid-day sun: and up and down the roof white pigeons nested. There was no sound but one' represents a richness, interspersed with a warmth and hospitality, typical of an old English Manor house. There is a picture of something asleep and contained in the manor as if some richness had been preserved. The weather in the poem has been a typical Winter, cold and frosty and now, 'The rock-like mud unfroze' and little rills or rivulets are trickling down the road. The catkins are a sign that the spring has arrived and now the sun was trying to tempt the manor farm and its surrounding's to wake up, 'But the earth would have her sleep out, spite of the sun', and so you get the picture of a very mild peaceful and sleepy winter.

The poet regards England as a happy old man really, and the words, 'Smiled quietly' suggest an easiness, contentness and a quiet contained happiness about the poem. The last line, 'This England, old already was called merry' gives a contented drowsiness and sense of richness to the poem. I think this is a lovely whole-some image of a typical countryfied image of Merry Old England and some pockets of England still contain this richness, just as you see it in people . . .

. . . The poem, As the Team's Head-Brass, again is about the easiness, remoteness, and beauty of the country. Thomas has been for a walk and now he is sitting on a broken elm bough. Usually elms in Thomas's poems suggest a sinister feeling but this time it is as if the elm is defeated by being broken and so is not so sinister anymore. You get a line, 'The lovers disappeared into the wood' near the begining of the poem and this suggests a happy naturalness. The poem is set in an Autumn scene, as Thomas is watching a ploughman 'narrowing a square of yellow charlock.' A calm and easy atmosphere is sent over, the farmer obviously enjoying his outdoor life — his work and pleasure is all one to him. Occasionally the ploughman leans over to Thomas to ask or say some-thing. The weather is talked about first, as obviously this is more

important to the ploughman than the war. Although there are long
intervals between words spoken, there are no uneasy silences, just an
easy atmosphere. Thomas notices the calmness, and remoteness of the
farm. There's not much relish for the war here, because everythings so
distant and remote. What farmer would want a war anyway? His
country-life would be lost.

Celandine, the last poem, I'm going to write about, deals with
Thomas's memories and the poem has a wistful quality about it, but
not an unhappy one. Words such as "recalled air" suggests the memories
belong to someone older. The celandine to Thomas here is a flower for
reflection almost. Although when he just thought of the girl here, it
saddened him, but suddenly seeing the flower again, his memory
becomes so clear and sharp that his shadow overtakes him and its as
if he's reliving the events all over again, and for a time this makes him
happy again.

But really this poem seems too good to be true – too nice almost.
Here Thomas only appreciated the dress and not the person inside.
There is no real warmth or love conveyed in the poem, its as if Thomas
is 'imprisoned by his niceness' and can't appreciate warm living human
flesh, and the person for what they are. He only sees a person by what
they dress in and not for what they really are.

These are the poems I have chosen, To me all these poems have
something special contained and preserved in them i.e. richness and
memories. They all appreciate nature and are happy poems which have
a sense of fullness about them. The slow rhythm of life pumps through
all of them like a life pulse and the sense of easiness conveys itself
strongly. These are the points that connect themselves in all of these
poems that I have written about.

(Jackie, fifth year, aged sixteen)

There is nothing remarkable about Jackie's studies of Thomas here,
except that it conveys such unstrained appreciation for a poet whose
qualities are often of the best, yet lacking in any obvious or dramatic
appeal that might be supposed to attract younger readers. Through each
of the poems she has chosen for commentary, she follows the narrative
line closely, while her appraisal remains largely implicit. She conveys
Thomas's moments of experience as closely and faithfully as she can.
Thus in commenting on a line from *As the Team's Head-Brass* she writes,
'although there are long intervals between words spoken, there are no
uneasy silences, just an easy atmosphere'. The phrasing of her own commentary is close to the movement and feeling of poetry here. Her sense of
closeness with the language of Edward Thomas eventually gives her the
confidence to offer an evaluation of one of his poems, 'The Celandine'.
Her evaluation – a perfectly original one, so far as I know – is finely

recorded, and conveyed with a sense of personal regret almost, that Thomas is not at his best in this poem, as she sees it: 'But really this poem seems too good to be true – too nice almost . . . it's as if Thomas is "imprisoned by his niceness" and can't appreciate warm living human flesh, and the person for what they are . . .' – But she moderates the sting in her criticism by making a further judgement, a general one this time, in her final paragraph of the piece: 'To me all these poems have something special . . . The slow rhythm of life pumps through all of them like a life pulse and the sense of easiness conveys itself strongly . . .' – Jackie's engaged, quickly receptive response here has the mark of someone who recognizes both the text and also the person who provided the words and experiences of the poem. We see her involved in the process of identifying the poetry and the poet who has engaged her attention, then moving gradually to her final remarks on the special qualities, the 'inscape' of the poems, to borrow Hopkins' famous tribute to the distinctive other-ness of living forms.

The third example is from Penny's work. Penny had the misfortune to spend a good deal of her third and fourth years in the school wearing a temporary spinal and neck support to improve her posture. She was a tall, attractive girl, though not surprisingly she was self-conscious and awkward in her movements during this period; she tended at times to be rather more moody than the girls with whom she liked to sit in the classroom, and would sometimes lapse into bleak, mournful silences. Her class performance depended greatly on her moods. She could be fluent, if jumbled in both her conversation and her writing; and then she could lapse into hesitant, rambling speech for days on end, and refuse altogether to write. At best her writing was very sporadic, and she wrote less than any other girl in the class, over two years – (and less than any lad, except for two almost total 'non-writers'). Her spelling and punctuation were often very eccentric, and she showed no improvement at all here. She felt, and indeed was becoming, lonely at school. She sought out the company of the livelier, extroverted girls, yet found it difficult to keep up with their lively chatter; and she could be perverse and off-putting, where teachers were concerned. On one occasion, for example, she was talking with calm ease about a book that she was reading, then announced in stiff, chilly terms that she did not intend to write on the book because she did not feel like it; and that I was 'not likely to get any writing from her until I forced her to do it.' Such rebuffs were frequent, and I resigned myself to the thought that you cannot win them all. Yet Penny managed to finish her C.S.E. course, and gained a modest grade. She also consistently attended nearly all the voluntary O-level Literature classes that were held outside school hours – mainly, I had supposed, to attach herself to her more hard-working and enthusiastic friends rather than for love of the work. But my assumptions were unjust to her; she asked if she might take the O-level Literature exam at the November sitting, and she duly sat and passed. She must have worked very hard for this, despite the very small amount of written work that she submitted to the school.

Two closely related examples of Penny's work are given below, since they reveal an interesting progress from identifying a text, to identifying an aspect of her own experiences. Both pieces came from work-in-progress on Harold Pinter's *The Caretaker*, a book which inspired more written response from her than any other text or topic on the whole two-year course. The first piece is an extract from her first general evaluation of the book:

The Caretaker

Davies is a frightened man, and he is confused and worried and I feel very sorry for him. You can't really tell what sort of man he is, for I think he covers up his real self with his put on agression, and bullying-ness. His only nice self comes out at the end of book when he's almost pleading with Aston, to let him stay. Then he finds it to late and he stands there stuttering. He suggests thing to Aston. He says 'I'll give you a hand to put up your shed, thats what I'll do,' and Aston turns round on him and says 'no'. I think that if davies was allowed to help someone, do something he might change in some way, as long as he suggests it first of all. I don't blame Aston for chucking him out. He is in some ways a devious old man, always treing to see what he can get from other people, espesially their pity for him. David never says no or thankyou to anyone, he says to Aston when he is handed a pair of shoes, 'Not a bad pair of shoes', but immedeatly, he says as though to spite him, 'Don't fit though.' He never says, thankyou for showing them to me, or I'm sorry but they don't fit. But I suppose nobodys ever been kind to him, and when he meets kindness he does'nt reconise it, and therefore hurts the other person, and people who know him and have met him, just wan't to keep well away. Not like Mike who wants to make fun, and scare this old man.

Davies has got no feelings for anyone, but expects others to care about him. When he's down at the monestry and he say's to the monk, 'Now look here, I'm an old man you can't talk to me like that, I don't care who you are.' But yet he thinks because he's an old man, he can go and talk to anybody, how he likes, with out upsetting any one else.

The people he meets along the road, and askes money off, don't take any notice, they prefere not to notice him, as though he was not a human being at all, but some ugly old monster that they should keep away from, or even cross the road when he's coming.

Davies can be very comical, with the things he says, but he does not know. The first night he slept with Aston, he wakes up and starts jabbering. Aston askes if he was dreaming and davies turnes round and say's 'I don't drea, neaver have done in my whole life.' Aston says he was jabbering and Davies replies, 'I tell you what, maybe it where them blacks. Them you got, next door. Maybe it were them blacks making noises, coming up through the walls.' This is really funny but yet Aston does not laugh he sits and mutteres to himself, not taking much notice of what Davies say's, and Davies not taking much notice of what Aston say's.

Davies probably knows nothing of life or real beauty. He sits allday or he says he walks, he does not notice flowers, or trees, and beautyful things of life, all he see's or cares about is himself, not a thourght to any one else. When other people care about him, like Aston, who brings him to his own house and invites him to stay, not one things does Davies do for him. He's all talk saying what he's going to do and what he's not going to do. I think if he did not have these wills, even only saying them, there would be no other apparent reason for him living. No one would know, or miss him, Its a shame, that he cannot change him self. But he is him-self and no one else can say they are the same. He is a person in his own right even if he has no other rights at all in the world. Or though he likes to think he has, he says, 'I've got more rights, I've got more rights than anyone. I have you know,' and yet, in a way, he has. People have dashed his hopes and desires, and I thank he's got rights to have, them back againe.

(Penny, fourth year, aged fifteen)

Penny shows here that she is quite willing to discuss the book with some objectivity. Having chosen to write about the would-be Caretaker himself, she is not hostile to Davies, and seems especially concerned to stress that he has been disadvantaged: 'Davies is a frightened man, and he is confused and worried and I feel sorry for him . . . if davies was allowed to help someone, do something he might change in some way, as long as he suggests it first of all . . .'. But she accepts Aston's eventual rejection of this 'devious old man, always treing to see what he can get from other people, especially their pity for him.' She recognizes that 'Davies has no feelings for anyone, but expects others to care about him . . .'. Yet while her response to Davies is clear — detached without being rejecting — she is not yet clear about how to understand Aston, and simply notes without comment that he 'sits and mutters to himself, not taking much notice of what Davies say's . . .'. She returns quickly to her main discussion of the less problematic Davies, and concludes with an unusual defence of him: 'Its a shame, that he cannot change himself. But he is himself and no one else can say they are the same.'

At this point her writing seems to be reverting to a subjective-reflecting stage — and somewhat defensively so, too. At any rate, she cannot take her critique of Davies any further at this stage, and she ends her account on a note of unresolved sympathy for Davies, which, as she seems half-aware, does not fit in with the view of him that she has already identified, as a self-pitying, fearful and devious old man.

The second piece on *The Caretaker* reveals the kind of advance in her self-understanding that she needed, in order to come to clearer terms with the 'messages' of the text. It was, for Penny, an unusually forthright piece of writing which shows how, helped by her thoughts on the text, she has at last won through to some important self-identifying insights. So keen was she to place this writing 'out there' that she invited her friends to read and discuss it, and she responded to a suggestion that it might go in the school's writing magazine, by producing a carefully corrected 'manuscript' copy for the editor:

> *The Great Need . . .*
> is to be ourselves, and to be loved, to have
> friendship. It is very hard sometimes.'

Reading about all those confused characters in Harold Pinter's 'The Caretaker' makes me realise that friendship and love are the most precious things in life. If you have both, you are happy, content, Then things go wrong: perhaps sometimes you prefer not to be your real self and to pretend you are someone better or cleverer than yourself. I am always saying that to myself; what will Miss so-and-so think of me, oh how I wish I was better than my friend, she's so pretty, or she's so much cleverer than me. How I wish I was someone else. But as I go on wishing, I never really try to be someone else, because I somehow know that I'm me and nobody's going to be the same as me. Sometimes it takes a few days to make myself understand that, and in the mean time I am trying to be that someone else, in the way I write and speak and dress, even going as far as to copy her every movement. It's stupid, and it seems even more so as I write it here.

I often have arguments with my friends, the ones I love best, and I find it's easier making up with a really good friend, than making up with a casual friend, for you know their feelings, and they also want to make up as much as you do. But sometimes hatred can develop over a stupid argument, and you find yourself hating even the person's name. Revenge grows up inside you, and you either go and swear it's someone else you like, and unintentionally hurt them as well, or you go and destroy something, like the present this friend recently gave you for your birthday. I must admit, I am often very jealous of my friends, because they can make other friends more easily than me — boy friends too. Sometimes I can't really care. But when I find that every night my friends go out with them, I feel really sad and depressed. Back comes that feeling of wanting to copy them. Oh, I go out with my friends too, but not as often as they do. I always have something to do — it's just that interests clash. But I must not mind, I am me and no-one's the same, whether I'm mean or good.

Without love, you are, like Davies the tramp in the 'Caretaker', almost nothing. All he has to think about are the imaginary attacks he sees coming — he's lonely, and he's frightened — 'I keep to myself, mate, but if anyone starts with me, they know what they got coming —' God help me from ending up like that.

(Penny, fifth year, aged sixteen)

It seems that Penny has encapsulated the personal anxieties of several months in this writing, and has been able to give them shape through her own emerging self-belief and self-criticism. The writing offers a summing-up, an appraisal, and a clear and emphatically phrased decision on action for the future. Through identifying and providing herself with some essential insights and self-insights for her own living, she can afford to shed her own subjective fears and love-excluding defences. This may not all happen as swiftly or as clearly as the insight-through-writing was achieved; but she recognizes her directions now, and the reading and writing done in her English lessons have made their small contribution to this.

CHAPTER SEVEN

Organizing

(i) This, then, is style. As technically manifested in Literature it is the power to touch with ease, grace, precision any note in the gamut of human thought and emotion. But essentially it resembles good manners. It comes of endeavouring to understand others, of thinking for them rather than for yourself . . . It gives rather than receives.

(ii) Although style is so curiously personal and individual, and although men are so variously built that no two in the world carry away the same impressions from a show, there is always a norm somewhere; in literature and art, as in morality.

A. Quiller-Couch, 'On Style' in *On the Art of Writing*, 1916)

This chapter on the fourth, organizing, stage will seek to show how the movement from spontaneously expressing, through self-conscious reflecting, to aware identifying of other-ness may advance now to an organizing stage. It is envisaged as a stage which grows from the natural (if not inevitable) quickening of a certain creative unease in the learner, on behalf of a humanness that is held in common with others. Strengthened with fresh awareness of new forms of knowing, the learner now moves outwards, in generous concern for people in groups and communities, and for the well-being of their − of our − world. Such a movement may be seen as a direct consequence of achievement in identifying. Enriched now, through receiving, we aim in turn to become transmitters of meaning; having dwelled in learning, we have drawn strength to participate in and contribute to the world. Our new commitment may take infinite forms, of course, but its characteristic intention will be to organize what is known, on behalf of all; we labour for a common purpose − 'for the race, as it were'.

Creating Possibilities − a fifty years' war?

The increasing (and, let it be admitted, overdue) interest that schools came to show in the social and political contexts of learning during the seventies reflected movements in several parts of the curriculum (notably in ecological and environmental studies) to foster a more critical consciousness in the study of humanity's relationship to the world. These new emphases have been reflected in English teaching, and where they have sought to enlarge the scope, say, of literary studies, they are likely to have beneficial impact; for how can we experience plays, poems and stories without also considering the cultural-social life of the community in which we dwell, or in which the literature has its context? Once identified, the 'truth' of literary insight remains to be applied to ordinary living; and the learner's natural wish is to move outwards to do so, unless actually curbed from taking such a direction by a teacher, or other outside force (such as the wrong kind of examination, for instance). If the third stage marks discovering, in the sense of coming to identify, to particularize and analyse, then the fourth stage marks a synthesizing stage, when links are built up between individuals and people, books and people, books and other books; and a social context and background come increasingly into focus. Such a development is a mark of the learner's ever-deepening involvement with the larger movements of humanity, which makes new demands of awareness and discipline. Not only is the learner moving towards increasing commitment through self-adjustment (as well as self-assertion) within the peer-group; the peer-group too, if healthy, is learning to venture beyond itself, to discover its relation to other groups and to the larger community. There is a refreshed sense, at this stage, that to use language creatively is to announce a claim on the world that is to become the learner's through a shared inheritance. Such enacting of language proclaims the taking up of responsibilities in that world.

These natural directions in the learner need, then, to be fostered in English work. But recently renewed concerns for the social and political aspects of learning may also have been responsible in part for a deplorable split of approaches which has been developing in Advanced Level English and elsewhere, between 'literary' and 'communication' versions of English studies. Of course, neither the (justifiable) concern for social and political contexts, nor the (unnecessary) error of assuming some kind of inevitable split between 'either' literature, 'or' social concerns, were inventions of the seventies; it may be recalled how the battle waged fiercely enough in the thirties to produce delayed shock-waves even today. The influential linguistician J.R. Firth, who adopted highly determinist structure-and-function principles as a basis for much of his thinking on language, doubted (in *Speech*, 1930) if 'there could be such a thing as individual speech behaviour'. And in *The Tongues of Men* (1937) he saw speech as the 'telephone network of our society', as a 'network of bonds and obligations'. He claimed that schools should aim at conditioning the range of specially prescribed roles available; this he viewed as 'sense', unlike the 'nonsense' of literature. For society's sake, he declared, 'more plumbing, less poetry is the motto for modern education'; and his prescription was 'to make our young people actively and critically aware of the sort of language which is used for them and against them every day of their lives.' This was to be done even 'at the expense of all the pretty talks about books other people have read.' Firth's positive proposals here, nourished as they were by a well-based scorn for over-gentility in literary studies, deserved some assent. The learner needs living language, not museum relics, and he needs to meet it through his own living concerns. But the possibility of best achieving what Firth desired *through* the study of literature had already been urged by F.R. Leavis, who wrote as scathingly as Firth against 'belles-lettrism' in literature, and declared that literary studies must move outward from the literary sources, into the world:

> The prior stress must fall on the training of sensibility . . . But a serious concern for education in reading cannot stop at reading. Practical criticism of literature must be associated with training in awareness of the environment — advertising, the cinema, the press, architecture, and so on, for clearly, to the pervasive counter-influence of this environment the literary training of sensibility is an inadequate reply.
> (F.R. Leavis, *How to teach Reading: A Primer for Ezra Pound*, 1932)

Whatever reservations in detail might be offered against the exclusiveness of Leavis' stance against 'mass culture' (some would surely have to be offered now, for instance, where film and television are concerned), his achievement was to have realized both the vast socially educative powers of literary studies, and also the need for radical changes of approaches in teaching, to ensure their living 'relevance'. The 'uses' of literature lie, in fact, in the very kind of watchful intelligence that literature (and the other arts, we should add) contains, and that it generates through us, as engaged readers. It was — and is — a daring claim; even the thrustful George Sampson did not manage to place literary studies quite so emphatically in the land of the living. Sampson realized well enough the need for aware social criticism, when he urged that 'behind print, even of the largest circulation, there is merely a man of no special importance . . . We want to create people who can use print, not people who are intimidated by print.' (Sampson, *English for the English*, 1921) But in a quite separate chapter on 'The Induction to literature' Sampson adopted tones of over-reverence, 'as we reach the English that is not a routine but a religion'; and although he wrote essentially well on the reading and teaching of literature (he termed it 'a kind of creative reception'), he reverted to the high-church claim that 'it is almost sacramental', and to Arnoldian phrases about the 'class of young barbarians whose souls are to be touched with the magic of poetry.'

Such over-reverence might understandably have provoked such a self-consciously 'progressive' reaction against literary studies as Firth's, who scorned their seeming unconcern for actual or real issues. But the counter-thesis offered in *How to Teach Reading* — that critical awareness is trained best through literary experience — was swiftly followed up by F.R. Leavis and Denys Thompson, in their influential *Culture and Environment* (1933). This book (with its sub-title, 'The Training of Critical Awareness') aimed to provoke thought among teachers and students about prominent problems of the day concerning literary and other studies — advertising, mass-production, the uses of leisure and education, the quality of education and tradition. Written so compactly that it now seems to be almost a collection of memorable aphorisms in the form of questions: (' "Lord Northcliffe went down to the people to lift the people up". How would *you* describe the process described here . . . What do you think ought to be meant by the Standard of Living?') its influence was felt well into the post-war period. Such contributions in its wake as the *Use of English* pamphlets were concerned to work from a sound literary grounding towards such questions, in a spirit that seems now to have faded — at least as far as publications on English teaching are concerned. In the new Language programmes that have been advanced in the last decade or so, there have been signs of reversion to the old simplistic choice between 'either' literature 'or' language study, or to what the Bullock Report itself con-demned as the misuse of literary texts through 'filleting' them for social studies.

Such language programmes have proclaimed the need to study language 'forms' in order to cope with culturally and linguistically 'plural' class-rooms, in advocating that language studies should be at the centre of English work. Firth's crudely forthright plumbing versus poetry distinction is not usually directly echoed, and the literary and other arts are not usually specifically excluded from such programmes. But it becomes impossible to conceive how there might any longer be proper room for them, so vast is the ground of knowledge 'of' and 'about' language to be covered in such a programme, say, as the Schools Council backed *Language in Use* (1971). And even when literary studies remain, the danger is that a kind of adulterated pseudo-'structuralist' approach emerges, whereby literature becomes no more than 'secondary source' material for the revealing and criticizing of social/cultural patterns. Writing against this trend, Peter Abbs has declared that 'if literature is employed solely to spark off a discussion of "issues", moving ever away from the metaphor to the abstraction, then imaginative texts are being roughly abused. They are not being conveyed, but betrayed.' (*The Reconstitution of English as Art*, 1981)

Teachers must still face the choice, then, of teaching the mother-tongue through imaginative enactment — through art-discourse; or through anatomizing it (as was the effect of many of the *Language in Use* papers). But having chosen imaginative enactment, they still need to ensure that art-discourse should provide a basis for social and moral discourse, too. Without this, the language of social and moral politics will be still-born, powerless to struggle against the tyranny of received ideas from established factions and power-bases. For our survival's sake, art cannot retire in refined distaste from the contests of the time, since it is only through art that the oppression of clichés, or the weight of dead authority, can eventually be resisted. This was Solzhenitsyn's theme, when delineating the unifying powers of 'true literature':

> One is still presented with newspaper headlines: 'None of their business, interfering in our internal affairs!' — while in fact there no longer are any internal affairs in our cramped little world. Mankind can only be saved if all men are concerned about everything. True literature — which is one of the most sensitive, delicate instruments at man's disposal — has already been one of the first to detect, assimilate and promote this feeling of growing unity of all mankind.
> (Alexander Solzhenitsyn, *'One Word of Truth'* — *The Nobel Speech on Literature*, 1970)

Such a view acknowledges the best principles of English and literary studies (and also reminds us, by implication, of their honoured place alongside historical, environmental, scientific and other disciplines). It alerts us also, to recall how we damage our living, when language is anatomized, or when art-discourse is withdrawn from the events of the day. As teachers, we are challenged to review the English syllabus at all levels, in order to ensure that English studies actually reflect the issues of our times, in the choice of texts, and in the creative-critical spirit to be nurtured.

The Impact on Schools
The view that schools should foster greater social consciousness has steadily gained ground in recent years. There has, for instance, been a notable growth in various kinds of community service, both within and outside normal school hours. Many experimental directions have also been taken in the encouraging of critical involvement in social issues within the curriculum, in contrast, say, to the dull information-peddling of 'civics' courses in the fifties and sixties. Social studies are now a familiar option for O and A level in further education colleges, if not in so many sixth forms. The much publicized Schools Council Humanities Project was eagerly adopted by many schools in the early seventies, in the hope that it might provide, among other things, a possible cure for new headaches caused by the raising of the school-leaving age. (Several packs of this Project reached our own stockrooms at the time, although it must be confessed that they were quickly relegated to providing occasional support-

material only; as far as developing modes of wider awareness was concerned, they could never have matched a programme for English studies which depended for its coherence on the quality of literary-imaginative response.) In the seventies, the Inspectorate joined in the general plea that political education should be included in the school curriculum, and inevitably such views came to be reflected among English teachers. In 1975 the NATE journal devoted a whole edition to the social context of English teaching; this was followed up in 1982 by an issue on 'Social Class and English Teaching', where the editors claimed that 'As class differences and their relationship to advantage and disadvantage in our society survive and as language is clearly associated with class differences, then it is the responsibility of those in education to keep such matters alive in their conversations and their work.' (*English in Education*, 16, 2, Summer, 1982). A number of English departments launched pro-grammes that directly involved their pupils with the local community. Our English groups ventured too with tape-recorders and notebooks into the local markets and onto local estates, to record and document interviews; one result of these expeditions was an increase of visitors *to* the school — a docker, a street-seller, a probation officer, and so on.

Ventures like these brought fresh directions to the existing scope of English studies, but their very worthwhileness sharpened even further the problem of how to include all worthwhile options in a limited timetable. The problem is now highlighted, for instance, in the moves for reform at A-level. Several Examining Boards are now experimenting with departures from the traditional 'Eng-Lit'. exam, which in its old form has neither solved the problem of how to ensure genuine personal creative-critical engagement in the writing of candidates, nor enabled candidates to dwell on the social-cultural implications of creative-critical studies. The need for greater flexibility of approach in the teaching of literature was advocated in the Schools Council English Report edited by John Dixon *Education 16–19: The Role of English and Communication* (1979). In recommending a much wider variety of written response to literary texts in Advanced level studies, and in describing some already established and successful experimental approaches by various Boards in several parts of the country, the book argued valuably for necessary change. It offered much evidence, not least from the work-in-progress of A-level students themselves, of the many kinds of thought-adventuring that the learner may be encouraged to take, when once given the root nourishment of significant art-encounter. My own involvement over several years as a moderator for one of these experimental A-levels has convinced me that such experiments are right, and that they should go further.

Yet by contrast, the descriptions of and proposals for a 'communi-cations' version of English studies in this Report are dismaying. Here the book works largely on an ill-based assumption, that there is a need to marry 'academic' with 'vocational' education (where and why did the learner-as-individual suddenly vanish?). This emerges, it seems, from an unquestioning dependence on assumptions drawn from the Schools Council Writing Research Unit, concerning 'poetic' writing (that is, literature) on one side, and 'transactional' writing (that is, communication, or 'the language to get things done') on the other. I have dwelled already on the dangers of such a bifurcation in the learner's modes of thought, since all human transactions need, eventually, to be seen to serve the quest for a greater (poetic) truth.

In failing to acknowledge that the nature of language cannot be reduced to notions of 'tools' or 'skills', the book itself fails. It breaks the back of its own argument by consenting to face both ways. Such a contortion would rob literature of its essential living context; it would rob life-studies of literature, which offers, to recall Solzhenitsyn's words, 'one of the most sensitive, delicate instruments at man's disposal' for the interpreting of life. Any versions of 'communications'-English', or 'cultural-studies' English which are not rooted in the study of literature and the other expressive arts, are likely to weaken the lifeline of art-discourse that sustains the learner, in striving for authentic and individual strength-of-being; for only a strong life-line here will ensure that social and cultural orientations are genuinely personal, not merely imprinted from outside. If our approach to literary studies at Advanced level is worth revising, then it is because of the essential worthwhileness of artistic experience in the learner, and because we recognize that such experience ought to be as widely available as we can possible arrange, and work for. There is certainly a case for extending artistic experience (into film study, for example) and for extending the range of response invited from the learner. Yet *English 16–19* seems at times even to be admitting a case *against* quality, in being willing to take seriously the empty generalities of 'vocational' or 'commercial' English, or worse — as though the art of sensitive language usage could ever be reducible to so many skills ('how' to debate, 'how' to write a letter, 'how' to offer a personal relationship), rather than to work within lived contexts of imaginative encounter. Any English course which evades this can only succeed in locking us away from our own humanness; it will work against the learner, in whose individual living such concepts as 'society', 'morality', 'justice' or 'education' can alone be embodied.

Against 'Art for Art's sake'

The case having been put against 'language', 'communication' or 'social-cultural' versions of English which ignore art-expression, it now remains briefly to restore a balance to the argument.

The 'organizing' stage envisages a new venturing from art-encounter, where the learner develops forms of political, social, ethical and environmental awareness and commitment. This view of learning offers a value-judgement about art, and art response, which runs counter to 'Art for Art's sake'; indeed it would regard the notion of 'Art for Art's sake' as a perversion of the true purpose of the arts, which act as both an expression and an agent of creative change in culture. In an essay on the politics of art called *The Artist and his Time* (1967), Albert Camus foreshadows Solzhenitsyn, in arguing that the 'ideal of universal communication is the ideal of any great artist'. He goes on to emphasise the necessary *communal* experience that Art must embrace:

> In order to speak about all and to all, one has to speak of what all know and of the reality common to us all. The sea, rains, necessity, desire, the struggle against death – these are the things that unite us all. We resemble one another in what we see together, in what we suffer together. Dreams change from individual to individual, but the reality of the world is common to us all.
>
> (Albert Camus, from *Resistance, Rebellion and Death*, 1967)

He declares that art which turns away from serious treatment of such communal concerns, by prostituting itself as a 'meaningless recreation' for commercial gain, or by turning esoterically inwards, into dream-refuge, leads in both cases to 'an art cut off from living reality.' Art, declares Camus, is born of a desire to express truth and to unite people in common understanding. Such aims imply a commitment to Freedom, since oppression breeds solitude and lies. His commitment, his moral sense, does not demand of him that he become a 'preacher of virtue'; but it does require him to be communally aware:

> Cut off from his society, he will create nothing but formal or abstract works, thrilling as experiments, but devoid of the fecundity we associate with true art, which is called upon to unite. In short, there will be as much difference between the contemporary subtleties or abstractions and the works of a Tolstoy or a Molière as between an anticipatory draft on invisible wheat and the rich soil of the furrow itself.
>
> (ibid)

If then, the richest art is that which is most engaged in exploring the common bonds of mankind, we are bound to be just as involved in the nurturing of that communal sense, as teachers of English studies.

Literature's commitment to Freedom, as advanced here by Camus, reveals a principle that is held in common between writers of such different political colours as Conrad or Solzhenitsyn or Camus on one hand, and Gorki or Brecht or the Kenyan Ngugi wa Thiong'o on another. Brecht's art, for instance, offers a criticism of 'nature' through criticism of social organization. 'Many of us', he has said, 'find the exploitation that takes place between people just as natural as that by which we master nature: man being treated like the soil or like cattle,' (Bertolt Brecht, *The Messingkauf Dialogues,* 1965). We approach great wars like earthquakes, he claims, as if they were great 'natural' forces, beyond human influence; whereas war, like the organization of labour or of trade, is a *social* phenomenon, subject to individual and collective human decisions:

> It's not we who lord over things, it seems, but things which lord it over us. But that's only because some people make use of things in order to lord it over others. We shall only be freed from the forces of nature when we are free of human force. Our knowledge of nature must be supplemented with a knowledge of human society if we are to use our knowledge of nature in human way.
> (Bertolt Brecht, *The Messingkauf Dialogues*, 1965)

To return again to the more modest concerns of the Secondary School classroom: in proposing a fourth, organizing stage in which there is a growing sense of commitment by the learner on behalf of others, it is important to distinguish what is meant by 'commitment' here, from that kind of 'sense of responsibility' that, for example, joining a corps of monitors or prefects is still supposed sometimes to foster, where the 'sense of responsibility' consists of complying with and executing school rules as prescribed from above. Nor is it meant to cover even the kind of 'community work' which many schools now encourage, and which is sometimes declared to be a kind of antidote to the otherwise seemingly self-centred pursuit of qualifications and a good job that the academic side of the school seems often to develop. The distinction offered implies no lack of respect for such work; indeed, when there are clearly discernible links to be found between classroom learning and such work, no distinction would need to be pressed. But the qualities of 'commitment' and 'responsibility' that a school aims for do bring into focus some questions about where all the learning in a school should be leading to.

School learners are not normally required to play a critical or truly creative role in their school society, although they are expected to understand it, and learn to cope with it. The roles required of them, both at home and at school, are on the whole compliant-supportive ones – helping around the house, looking after younger children, acting as monitors, helping the elderly and so on. There are good reasons for all this, in that school learners clearly have many demands to face at earlier stages, without having to face adult commitments. But there is a danger that healthy drives to develop a sense of *critical* involvement in group and community, and to work for common ends may be frustrated for want of appropriate encouragement. And while it is true that 'earlier' stages of growth are experienced by adults, the converse is also true; A.S. Neill confirmed how, given the right support and framework, even young children of seven upwards can take an intelligently contributory interest in the game of communal life. Casual observations of any self-organized children's game reveal this to us; yet we tend to do little to encourage such participation in most aspects of the school curriculum.

A non-compliant awareness in the learner, of the group and its interest is not always convenient in schools, and can provoke awkward tensions when too vigorously advanced, or too strenuously resisted. In planning the English curriculum, our aim should be to ensure that the learner is truly prepared for this stage — is trained in critical awareness, through the earlier stages. If this is achieved, there will be no need for any external ablation through censorship; the learner's own self-discipline will be guard enough against thoughtlessness or intemperance of expression.

Some Examples

The first example was written by Andrew (who produced the Jack London based story in Chapter Five). In the fifth year, Andrew came to feel more acutely than most in his group, that his most sincere interests in learning were leading in a quite different direction from the demands of the examination syllabus. At around this time, he was veering between somewhat stiffly dressed (but safely 'high-grade') writing, and much more informal reflecting as in this self-revealing response to a poem by Yevtushenko:

I have no doubt that I am not fully aware of myself. I feel like an ocean. A very deep and dark ocean unexplored and partly unexplorable. There is a great mystery in the sea and man has very little knowledge of it, much in the same way that he has very little knowledge of his own depths. Yevtushenko talks of the depths in man in his poem 'People'. He believes that everyone is more than we so often believe . . . we are each autonomous beings. Our deep fathoms contain other mysteries not found elsewhere . . . every time I experience something that leads to a greater understanding of other people or myself, another bit of puzzle is completed.

The emerging sense of a division between the kind of writing needed to acquit himself in an examination, and the exploration that he needs to discover himself and others, is made explicit in *A Sane Revolution*. Here he admits the tensions of trying to maintain personal bearings through his writing, and of formulating a statement not only on behalf of himself but of his whole peer group. It was written for CSE assessment in the term before the main public examinations in the fifth year, as an attack on the fifth-year examination grind:

A Sane Revolution

'Let's abolish labour, let's have done with labouring!
Work can be fun, and men can enjoy it: then it's not labour.'
                                D.H. Lawrence

Work, according to Lawrence, can be fun but I have rarely found any degree of amusement in my work in school. I am not disagreeing with Lawrence, but saying my exam work at present is completly devoid of interest. Through all my schools years I have never approached any work with a great deal of enthusiasm although I may have been interested in the subject. The fact is that I have to write about a particular subject to suit the requirements of exams or to be acceptable to the teacher. I am not free to write as I please about a subject even though I may have been told to explore it.

Last week I handed in a history essay which was about African nationalism. The essay subject was of great interest to me and I prepared to write about the struggles of Nkrumah, Kenyatta, Lumumba and their peoples. As is usual with a History essay I had to cram it with facts and dates. A further country I had to deal with was Rhodesia and in the course of talking about the proposed sell-out I sympathised with the black majority. Of course this was not on. I was simply told (yet again) what a history essay should or should not be and according to the standards of public exams, politics was not to be included. I am not trying to blame the teacher for reprimanding me because it was basically the fault of the exams but wherever the blame falls it was a realisation for me on how restricting the current exam system is. Thus a subject that I am genuinely interested in I am not allowed to write freely about. True in this school I could turn to my English book and write a proper essay about the subject in question, but even then I would feel that I should write it in a particular way. A certain amount of data is not uninteresting but I could not feel free to put facts into an English essay. Time would also restrict me. We are set regular homeworks which have to be handed in on a certain date and about a certain subject. This then cuts down the time which I allocate to English. I am so taken up with education and enjoyment, primarily the former, that I cannot spend enough time on reading books or writing, which are the main forms of an interesting education. I feel I cannot write as inspiration takes me because of the large amount of homework in all subjects that we are required to produce pushes aside this enjoyment of taking the cork out of the bottle. I also try to get out at least two of three times a week and mix my friends because I feel I must not get cut off from people and personal relationshops. I cannot wait for inspiration to overtake me because of the deadlines. This exam, for example, I am writing because it is Thursday evening and it has to be in tomorrow, before which time I want to have produced a piece of work of which I am proud. 'Edna, the Inebriate Woman' is taking much of my attention at the moment, and it thoroughly deserves it.

However I feel I must not grumble too much about our English department because it does provide an outlet for many of my thoughts: Thoughts are repressed in other department of the school as in the example I have already given when I was as good as told not to think! There are severe implications behind this. The denial of imagination, the practice in academic subjects is an enforcement of conformity on the individual. Our character is a product of our thoughts and feeling not of our actions because they are a subsequence of our thoughts. Therefore the repressing of our thoughts, is the repressing of our actions and, as a consequence, of the moulding of our character.

This rejection of our individuality must be even more severe in the schools where there is no outlet. I know several pupils in secondary schools where there is no English literature and the English lessons are devoted to grammar. There is art one might say, but is this a general mode of expression? In schools there is little expression in an art lesson. I have not taken art here but experiences from my old school tell me that art is taught. Genuine individual expression cannot be taught because it then takes a contrived form.

In fact I am sometimes unsure that my expression is not contrived. I am not sure that my thoughts are completely my own because of the education I have already recieved which may have stereotyped my reactions. Very rarely is it that I can say I have written a completely original essay. I bet you have heard about conformity in schools before! It is not uncommon that I write an essay, hand it in and get reasonable remarks about it but I am aware that it is not very good. These essays are very contrived and probably a collection of several views on the subject that I have heard before or that have arisen in class discussion. In such a way I write an essay without the use of deep thought or imagination. I have pre-conceived ideas which are perfectly stable and tie in with one another. My ideas are usually those that I am expected to have by other people. This assures me that my individuality is partly supposed.

I was not very aware of myself or my environment during my years of infant, primary and the first stages of my secondary education and thus I cannot remember what forms my education took. I am sure that my thoughts suffered similar negligence for me to be so unaware of my childhood. Certainly the boy in the poem called 'Written by a boy who committed suicide afterwards' was greatly affected by the nature of his education.[1] This was a true story and the boy did commit suicide later. He was however acutely sensitive and aware, and thus unique. The other boys who were already drawing airplanes and rocket ships probably underwent similar ignorance but at home and so they were already square and brown inside to fit in with their school.

The first years of our lives during our young childhood and in our infant and primary is the time when we are most affected by our environment. Our character is determined during these years when we are most under the influence of parents and teacher whom we readily believe. It was obviously a pity that the character of the boy was determined by influencing teachers. His individuality expressed in beautiful uncontrived drawings was crushed. Of course there is not a conspiring force which fights individuality in a deliberate attempt to suppress our character. The force is ignorance.

The teacher in the poem did not understand that the boy was different from the rest and wanted to stay different. She could not understand him or his drawings because she had suffered a similar education in her childhood. She was brown and square inside because she too had been told to draw pictures like all the other kids. And thus whole generations are square and brown inside. A whole generation is being educated into a squareness and brownness.

(Andrew, fifth year, aged sixteen)

'I am not free to write as I please about a subject even though I may had been told to explore it . . .'. Andrew reflects on how he wants a closer personal contact with the topic, and how he objects to the total separation between his own version, and received, academic versions of the facts — 'Thus a subject that I am genuinely interested in I am not allowed to write freely about . . .'. He sees the implications clearly: 'the repressing of our thoughts, is the repressing of our actions and, as a consequence of the moulding of our character . . .'. He seeks more help and encouragement in creating access between himself and the topic; specifically, he wants some of the freedom gained in his English studies to be extended to his History work, and he is particularly concerned that he should be able to concern himself with the issues in his own way — that is, not as either his English or his History teacher would necessarily 'expect' of him. His discussion of the 'Poem by a boy who committed suicide soon afterwards' enables him to highlight his own intense personal frustration about the particular homework, and the wider, public concern that he is developing about the way teaching and learning are organized. He suggests how the exceptional distress of the boy who wrote the poem can be taken to exemplify the treatment of 'whole generations' of people who are crushed

1. the poem was published in Peter Lomas's *True and False Experience* (1973), and had been the subject of class discussion.

and defeated by the blind momentum of education — 'Of course there is not a conspiring force . . . The force is ignorance . . .' The piece is sustained by strong feeling and clear argument. It marked the start of a lengthy phase of self-exploring for Andrew, which altered the course of his thinking and writing, from a somewhat depersonalized 'academic' model, to the kind of individually embodied thinking that he pleads to have space for in *A Sane Revolution*.

In the group from which these writing examples have been drawn, one prominent feature of writing at this stage was a taste for fluent, even over-long written discourse; thus, several highly interesting pieces have proved unsuitable for inclusion in this present chapter, for reasons of sheer length. The second example, in fact, is from a much longer piece which included reflections by Asta (whose writing features in Chapters Four and Six) on *The Caretaker, Brave New World* and two films. It was written as part of a CSE project, based on her reading of six books of her own choice. In this case she had chosen to explore themes of mental oppression, as treated in the texts and films. The film reviews were entirely self-chosen, for neither film had been shown at school. Having dwelled on the inhumane treatment of criminals, Asta turns to mental patients, as depicted in Loach's film:

Studies in Disintegration

. . . *Family life* shows two other methods of curing some mental illnesses. The girl Janice is placed into a mental hospital by her parents to be cured of her "illness". She is fortunately put under the care of a progressive psychiatrist who believes in group therapy, where the patients and the psychiatrist cure all the problems without any physical means. The treatment is just beginning to work, Janice now talks freely and is beginning to understand her own emotions, then, for administrative reasons the psychiatrist is sacked and the group is disbanded, patients being split up; discharged, or put in the care of a doctor who believes that drugs and e.s.t. (electric shock treatment) are the best cure. Janice is placed in a ward full of chronic mental patients and forced against her will to have an injection and have e.s.t. When the 'symptoms' of her illness have 'cleared' she is discharged and sent home to her parents. She works for a while in a chocolate factory and it can be seen that already she is lacking something in her independance. She has drugs for "use at home" which, with the help of her dominating mother, slowly destroy her. After a row between Janice's sister and her mother where the sister says that the illness is due to her mother, Janice has a relapse and returns to the mental hospital for another spell of drug and shock treatment. This time the symptoms do not disappear and Janice is completely turned into a cabbage. Her boyfriend, who is previously the only one to show her what life could be like, and tried to help her get away from her parents visits the hospital and takes her away. The hospital officials decide with the parents that Janice is incapable of looking after herself (which is probably true after the dehumanisation she has gone through) and force her back to hospital where she would probably remain.

The sad truth about the film is that it is far from being exaggerated — rather the opposite, and there are hundred of similar cases — many from very nice middle class homes. In some cases drug treatment and e.c.t. are effective, but there are many it does not good to. Had Janice been able to continue the group therapy she would almost certainly have been cured, but it is a slow expensive method of treatment and many psychologists and psychiatric treatment clinics using therapy have been closed down, mainly because the government are interested in cheap treatment that "cures" many patients quickly.

I know of a man who is being cured of overeating through corrective treatment, or rather, who has not been cured by it. A. reacted extremely violently after it but it has had no effect at all on this man. He had corrective treatment voluntarily because although group therapy was working, it was a very slow method.

In 'Family Life', Janice was lucky in that she was placed in a reasonable modern Mental Institution — with a private room. The majority of mental hospitals in Britain aren't a scratch on the one shown. There are filthy wards with gross overcrowding, in some cases (as newspapers have publicised) the staff are cruel and brutally restrain patients, and they may not receive any real treatment — let alone attention. They are either let loose in society hopelessly incapable of looking after themselves, or are shut away from society altogether with no real hope of getting cured.

One such case is an old lady who used to clean/babysit when we were very young. She is 'resident' in a hospital, one of five hospitals in our area. She has no friends or family, and she can only go out if she can state a destination, so we're the only people she knows, and many a time we've come home to find her sitting on the doorstep having been waiting all day just to say hello and have Mum give her a lift home. Although we all feel sorry for her we just can't bear having her around because she chain smokes, mutters and looks and smells so awful. It's pitiful really, we're the only ones who could do anything, but don't. The hospital can't cure her but it doesn't look after her at all well.

Society is in a horrible mess, but who's going to do anything about it? It'll probably get worse instead of better . . .

A recent letter from our ex-babysitter said:

'Dear Mrs. F.

Haven't seen you for a while. Now you are well I hope. Will call round one day next week. Love, J . . .'

(Asta, fifth year, aged sixteen)

In this review, Asta's critical attention is different in quality and direction from her 'identifying' pieces on such books as *Brave New World*, although she is drawing on these. Here, she is much more concerned with venturing out towards general points about what she sees as the social and political issues raised by the books she has read, and the films she has seen. There is no clear following of the stories here; her review mentions details simply as a vehicle for making her general points, mainly about a society which, she claims, treats its young with such insensitivity that ignored and unchallenged youth seeks respite in destruction, drugs and madness. She also uses her review of the films as a platform for protest against the practice of electrical and chemical therapy, and what seem to her to be other insensitive or ineffective treatments. Her case here tends to be both over-confident and over-simplified; it is likely that some of her indignant idealism has been incorporated — not too thoroughly here — from her mother, who was a therapist. But towards the end of her discussion she comes round to avowing that the most distressing thing about mental illness is that we still know so little about it and still have so few real cures; and that the link between individual and communal sickness must be faced. Writing about psychiatric patients she can see no easy solutions: 'They are either let loose in society hopelessly incapable of looking after themselves, or are shut away from society altogether with no real hope of getting cured . . .' — and she goes on to relate an example of how her own family has been unable to cope in even a minimal way with an appeal for help from a local hospital patient.

Asta's account ranged over two films, several book references and also some personal experiences. It proclaimed against social injustices suffered by the young and the mentally ill. As with other examples at this stage, it is easy to discern how the choice of general issues has arisen from the particular interests, problems and accidents of the writer's life. But there is a strong degree of impersonal concern too, and I would suggest that the assertions in Asta's writing stem from strongly generous feelings for the groups she defends, rather than being merely self-indulgent 'youthful' polemicizing.

The third example involves a brief account of a communal effort by the class and the year-group on which these chapters have been based:

The Publishing of UNDERGROUND

UNDERGROUND shows the difficulties of injecting Imagination into rational abstract beings . . . Whilst the imagination remains un-

thwarted, children will continue to learn and profit from experience . . .
UNDERGROUND has always taken the view that kids who from birth
are given full responsibility, will develop into true and whole individuals,
with a real self. Self-education is vital . . .

UNDERGROUND, No. 3

UNDERGROUND was the mildly provocative title of the year-group's
own, self-edited and self-produced journal. Issues of this journal appeared
regularly for two years, through the fifth and sixth years of the group.
The editorial Board included any pupils who were prepared to go to
UNDERGROUND planning meetings: but there was a regular core of about
six pupils. Being a genuinely 'underground' magazine, it was produced off
school premises and at private expense of a local youth centre, although a
more or less benevolently blind eye − at least in the early days − was
turned to its increasingly wide distribution throughout the school.

The first issue turned out to be the least controversial, in tone and
content. It was a celebratory issue, with a good number of pieces that
might have been highly acceptable, say, as a contribution in ordinary
English work; that is, it had a potential adult (teacher-and-parent)
audience in mind, as well as its main audience − the pupils of the school.
Some five to six thousand words long, carefully typed and cyclostyled,
UNDERGROUND was an impressive venture, which won general approving
comment around the school and in the staffroom. But a few firmly
expressed statements of disillusionment about examinations, comprehensive schooling, boring lessons and so on brought about a predictable
reaction against it among some groups of the staff; and informal pressure
was brought on the editors to improve its 'tone' although no clear guidelines were suggested (for example, advice about the law of libel might have
been appropriate).

The second issue was more intransigent ('If UNDERGROUND−1 was
happy, UNDERGROUND−2 is angry') but still contained some well-argued
articles on topics like 'A Community Atmosphere', 'Streaming and Setting'
and 'The Natural Artist in People', as well as (from an adult point of view)
less attractive ricochets about 'the system'. Pressures mounted among the
staff to have this issue and the whole enterprise suppressed; while at the
same time urgent preparations began for the formation of a school council,
a movement which UNDERGROUND−1 had devoted much of its issue to
advocating, in the light of a dispute among the fifth form about the
compulsory wearing of uniform, and the refusal of the Head and staff to
discuss this ruling with them. Subsequent issues of UNDERGROUND
developed a broadly 'anti-staff' attitude − though they showed in their
correspondence columns that they were being read by an increasingly
wide range of the school, and by adults both in and out of the school
who preferred to remain anonymous. The prevailing standard of its con-

tributions continued to remain high, in view of its growing sense of em-
battlement with the staff. There was, for instance, a series called 'Grass
Roots', which consisted of edited transcripts of taped interviews with local
people whom the editors felt to deserve attention, including 'an extremely
active and radical vicar, who has done a terrific amount of work for people
on a difficult local estate . .' The case for UNDERGROUND and for similar
enterprises was well put by one of the editors in UNDERGROUND−3, in
an article of 'The Importance of the Community Newspaper'.

UNDERGROUND is written by pupils in our school, meaning this,
that we can understand and often sympathise with the feelings and experiences of many school children. That sounds a bit arrogant but we
cannot be accused of that because we invite anybody to contribute
to the magazine. The few who now produce UNDERGROUND can never
represent all pupil feeling and thought in the school and we do not
pretend to. UNDERGROUND is directly related to your position in life
as a pupil at the school and the fact that the magazine is specifically
intended for you must promote an interest in and identification with
UNDERGROUND. This is the value of any community newspaper. Those
who write them are part of the community they write for and so, the
real problems and grievances of that community can be highlighted.
A newspaper of this kind can also help to unite the community and give
them more responsibility in their positions.

This long, well-documented article went on to attack newspapers which
were, in the writer's opinion, used, by minorities to manipulate control
over majorities for their own interest; and it concluded with a complaint
about its own position as an underground venture, having to work against
the pressure of official displeasure.

It has become obvious to me that the methods of communications
are not in the hands of the people but are used as methods to suppress
the real truth by the privileged classes. Although on a much smaller
scale our school is similarly structured. The microphone, bulletin,
typewriter, printing equipment, assemblies, etc., are all in the hands of
the teachers. Should this be so? If the school really *is* the pupils as we
are continually told then should not we be in charge of all these methods
of communication? UNDERGROUND are not allowed to produce the
magazine inside school although there is equipment on which it could
be done. That in itself is justification enough for any argument. The
antidotes are in the decentralized community newspapers, one of which
I am happy to say is in the hands of this school.

The tone of this article − it was typical of many others in the several
productions of UNDERGROUND − was simplistic, earnest, generous; and

the preoccupations were at least partly subversive. The best articles were well written and argued; the worst were sometimes as bad as the worst kinds of student journalism – vague, aimlessly aggressive and libellous. But UNDERGROUND became increasingly the voice of the pupils of the school, and especially of the year-group which provided the editorial Board. It provided an unmistakable indication that the pupils of that year particularly, had a growing sense of group and wider social awareness, which instead of dying away through lack of nurturing, grew strident, and even came to intimidate its seemingly uncaring parent-body.

The (varying) quality and direction of the UNDERGROUND articles raise questions about the kinds of decisions about teaching that need to be made, in order to foster this fourth stage, where commitment and appropriate causes are needed, for the full flourishing of learning. If we hold, for instance, that art discourse and the expressive arts are central to English studies, we are obliged to consider how this stage might be well fostered through, say, the study of literature. That UNDERGROUND had to be produced as an 'underground' magazine constituted, I felt, an important criticism of our approach to English studies in the school, as well as a criticism of other parts of the curriculum. We were half-way there, in that many of the articles in the first UNDERGROUND issue might well have come from any fifth-former's English work folder; but it had to be admitted that Andrew's criticism of his English course in 'A Sane Revolution' carried some weight. 'I could not feel free to put facts into an English essay . . .'. Andrew should have been made to feel unequivocally that form, content and direction could be self-chosen – including, of course, the recording of any 'facts' which has found to be significant. Political courage depends on a willingness to speak and intend truth, as we see it. Truly independent journalism has this quality, and the subversive powers of truthful information (something very different from calculated propaganda) cannot help but cause offence, as well as win approval. It is well known, for example, how ordinary working people in the past have shown considerable skill in literary and public discussion, whenever new contexts have required and enabled this. In *The Long Revolution* (1965) Professor Raymond Williams revealed how such true literacy has been energetically suppressed rather than encouraged in the past. In the early nineteenth Century, for instance, radical journals like Wade's *Black Book* sold 10,000 an issue, and Cobbett's Address to the *Journeymen and Labourers* sold 200,000 in two months. The dangers of such widespread reading were quickly recognized by the Government, which prosecuted editors and levied a heavy stamp tax on newspapers – in contrast to its policy with tracts of an 'improving' kind, which were given Government subsidies. Williams also records the massive sales of Tom Payne's *Rights of Man* – 200,000 copies between 1791 and 1793; and that Cobbett's *Register* was selling 40–60 thousand copies each week in 1817. Such publications had their own recognizable rhetoric; but they also had their own recognizable and highly individual wit, thrust of argument and informed awareness. It was, we may recognize, a kind of journalism that we could greatly do with today — popular, yet of distinct quality.

Without informed guidance, at this stage, the idealism of the young may fall into romantic iconoclasm, or fanaticism; or into relapse and inertia. Teachers cannot pretend to withdraw from the society, the cultural climate of the learning group, any more than they may merely seek to dominate it. They are needed to convey considerable personal (and eventually, public) authority, without being felt to be repressively 'in' authority. The teacher's task is, generally, to anticipate the real needs of the learning group; and to know that the one valid 'culture' to be referred to is that which grows eventually from the interacting of the teaching-learning group, in relation. There is special need for a clear cultural identity to grow among those in the learning group; and there can be special difficulties in promoting this, in a community which may — at least temporarily — have lost any strong sense of homogeneous patterns. In an unstreamed class of an urban comprehensive school, learners and teachers may come from widely different class backgrounds; may have experienced widely differing modes of upbringing; and may have learned varying and even contrasting moral and social patterns. Such a group may face great problems in enlisting the trust and confidence of each of its members. At best, each individual will flourish through the flourishing of the group. The individual needs the group; the group needs all its individuals.

But to argue for recognition of the group's identity is not to argue for abdication of the teacher's authority. Teachers who wish to encourage learners to realize a commitment to the particular conditions of their own times, will seek to strengthen their sense of place and belonging in their local world. They will also seek connections between that local awareness and commitment, and the insight of the most acute observers and thinkers in the world at large. Any honest effort at this task is likely to include an element of contest; the task of the young is to make claims on the world, and the duty of the adult is to allow space but not to yield until full growth has been fostered and until the young have demonstrated a fitness to inherit. (This point is made with classic persuasiveness in the final chapter of Donald Winnicott's *Playing and Reality*, 1971). The teacher who genuinely wants the learners to be independent, who welcomes a mental 'flexing of muscles' by the learner in preparation for the contests ahead, has to decide where to liberate, and where to offer discipline. When the energies of the young cause discomfort to an institution — as with the relatively harmless publication of UNDERGROUND teachers are bound to check out whether they are acting 'responsibly' in encouraging or discouraging such a venture. They know they have a commitment to living traditions; but they also recognize that the ways of the next generation will inevitably take a different shape from those of our own. And they will know from their own experience that a good deal of knowing and growing is bound up with being able to act, to make an impact on the world in some way. In a book that is devoted to a discussion on the relation between 'Knowledge' and 'Action', Roger Pateman has suggested that 'Not wanting to know is closely connected to feelings of powerlessness, themselves to be explained by the real powerlessness most people experience.' Our desire to know, in fact, grows hand in hand with our taking of responsibility: 'It is not knowledge which makes people feel free; it is more likely that struggling for freedom makes people want and need knowledge.' (*Language, Truth and Politics*, 1975). In this book is faced the problem of 'which should be first — the knowing or the opportunity to function?' with a directness that is lacking in much educational discussion on the subject. The Bullock Report, for instance, cautiously quotes a bland definition by UNESCO, in attempting to define literacy:

> A person is literate when he has acquired the essential knowledge and skills which enable him to engage in all those activities in which literacy is required for effective functioning in the group and community.
>
> (*A Language for Life*, 2.2, 1975)

But the difficulties that may be experienced by teacher and learner in seeking to prepare for those activities are glossed over in the Report — which was, after all, a Government publication. Many teachers would welcome realistic advice on the limits of political and social thought and action that might be admitted in schools, in order to foster that 'effective functioning in the group and community' which may properly be said to characterize full growth. At present the fourth, organizing, stage can claim only a precarious foothold in much of the teaching in the school curriculum. But we may acknowledge, meanwhile, that there are no short cuts to it; the creative-critical awareness from which the 'organizing' stage grows must be our first concern as teachers. Only through this can the learner move confidently into realms beyond art, while keeping essential contact with the creative-critical modes fostered through art-encounter. Nothing less than the freedom of the community is at stake here; Michael Polanyi has declared:

> We must somehow learn to understand and so to tolerate — not to destroy — the free society. It is the only political engine yet devised that frees us to move in the direction of continually richer and fuller

meanings, i.e. to expand limitlessly the firmament of value under which
we dwell and which alone makes the brief span of our mortal existence
truly meaningful for us through our pursuit of all those things that bear
upon eternity.

(Michael Polanyi, final sentence in *Meaning*, 1977)

CHAPTER EIGHT

Integrating

> We speak here of the ability to integrate and of the play back and forth between integration within the person, and his ability to integrate whatever it is he is doing in the world. To the extent that creativeness is constructive, synthesising, unifying, and integrative, to that extent does it depend in part on the inner integration of the person.
>
> (A. Maslow, *Towards a Psychology of Being*, 1968)

This final stage, termed the 'integrating' stage, is marked by the learner's growing involvement with the largest questions that may be raised in the quest for truth, knowing and meaning: what does my life mean? What meanings may we discover in, and confer on our world? What visions of living, of existence may be discovered? What unifying principles govern our existential being and relations?

It is held that while only a few individuals may come to develop a systematic interest in questions of religion, ethics, philosophy or advanced poetic and scientific speculation, the drive to come to terms with our own experience of such questions as are explored in these disciplines is natural and general. Man, it is long acknowledged, lives not by bread alone; beyond the drives for food, warmth and a mate is the urge to realize, to discover meaning. This is true of all but the most culturally impoverished communities (such impoverishment can, of course, afflict communities that enjoy material affluence and high technological achievement). And the search, however eruditely advanced within any particular discipline, must always involve a self-searching, must have the immediate context of an individual's experience in living. Camus called such a drive 'that nostalgia for unity' which we seek in our living; Lawrence, who declared in the face of uncomprehending criticism that he was, above all else, 'religious', wrote of relationship with a 'circumambient universe'; and Freud referred in a famous phrase to the 'oceanic feeling' — that experience of calm insight, mixed with heightened awareness and a sense of well-being, which comes when we are able to reconcile, to integrate the many drives, conflicts and tensions into some more comprehensive vision of our existing. From each individual — and from one culture to another — come many distinctions and varieties of emphasis; but the religious quest (in contrast to acceptance of any institutionalized religious credo or doctrine) may always be recognized by the present motive to *search*. 'What then', asks Merleau-Ponty in *Eye and Mind*, 'is . . . that dimension which lets Van Gogh say he must go "further on"? What is this fundamental of painting, perhaps of all culture?' The answer is implied throughout Merleau-Ponty's own writings; such a search looks to the possibilities of eventual, as yet unformed meanings, of a perfect communing between individual and world. But it embraces too the principle that incompleteness is a basic condition of our existing — a condition which gives the actual impetus to live creatively. In our learning as in our teaching then, these larger aims act as a basic implicit motive. 'What for? What, ultimately, *for*?', was Leavis's succinct form of the question, though he asked it without anxious concern that the faithful need props, since 'Wisdom we may call a higher plausibility, profoundly judicious and responsible. For in this realm of thought there is nothing certain or provable, no finality.' (*The Living Principle*). Those moments of realization, whose higher forms of expression are sometimes termed 'religious', are likely to come as the fruits of prolonged spiritual, mental and physical contemplation and struggle, to be reached usually in adult rather than pre-adult life; although there are earlier versions of such religious forms of belonging, as recorded for example in Wordsworth's poetry, or as explored critically in Rilke's *Duino Elegies*. None of these should be confused with that kind of relaxed well-being in creative play ('a ticking over of the unintegrated self') which Donald Winnicott describes in *Playing and Reality*. This, while being in itself a desirable state of being that is often accompanied by a sense of (untested) 'belonging' is, as Winnicott's own description implies, pleasurable because the effort and the risks of integrating have been relaxed. Such phases of repose are as vital as 'innocent sleep' in gaining strength for the creative venture, but they are not the venture itself.

Yet many writers — artists and philosophers such as Blake, Rilke, Buytendijk, Shakespeare, Buber, Wordsworth — have revealed how the roots of man's religious quest may be traced to the earliest human memories of connections and yearnings, in the symbiosis of mother and infant. The ante-natal experience of the child, indeed, is the source of our awakened drive towards meaning. In the womb our experience is of complete connection — there is no separation between ourselves and our 'mother-world'. The yearning in our lives to return to such a unity of communion may be seen not so much as a death-longing, as a desire for a state of perfectly loving connection with the world, with the universe.

That this is a child's as well as an adult's experience is revealed in a prose-poem of rare quality by Seamus Heaney. Several of Heaney's most interesting poems have dwelled on the child's capacity for wonder. In

'Personal Helicon' for instance (the final poem in his first volume, *Death of a Naturalist*) his own obsession as a boy with water-wells provides a perfect metaphor to describe the process of 'reflecting'. And in the collection of prose-poems called *Stations* (1975) he reveals increasingly intent preoccupations with the communicating of mutely intense experience. The opening piece of this volume is *Cauled* (from 'caul', the membrane that encloses the foetus in the womb):

> They thought he was lost. For years they talked about it until he found himself at the root of their kindly tongues, sitting like a big fieldmouse in the middle of the rig. Their voices were far-off now, searching something.
> Green air trawled over his arms and legs, the pods and stalks were a fuzz of lights. He caught a rod in each hand and jerked the whole tangle into life. Little tendrils unsprung, new veins lit in the shifting leaves, a caul of shadows stretched and netted round his head again. He sat listening, grateful as the calls encroached.
> They had found him at the first onset of sobbing.

Through this intimate, delicate defining of 'lodes of nodes' in inner feeling, is conveyed that early experience of one's separate-ness of being. We can no longer take the 'mother-world' for granted, but must learn to endure our separateness. Yet we can only achieve self-being through relationship, through developing the child's first instinct to connect: without this, we are left fearful, 'sobbing', like the mother-less child.

Profound and primary though this drive is (it could be seen as motivating *all* stages of growth), it can be discouraged by failure in earlier stages of growth, and by disregard for its own special character. It is a drive that is likely to be paid more lip-service in very general proposals for the curriculum, than in detailed lesson-plans. Through the routines of syllabus and examinations, teachers are tempted to prescribe on behalf of their pupils, to *impose* a world-view. Yet when teachers can admit that knowledge involves an individual and therefore unique act of knowing, they will wish to give room, as with earlier stages, for learners to take their own bearings here, in this final stage of understanding experience and preparing for further living. This is a stage, moreover, that is never entirely finished, since new makers continually create new meaning.

The distinction between encouraging and nurturing on the one hand, and attempting to impose on the other, can be blurred over by even the most enlightened educationists and thinkers, when their wisdom is transformed into orthodoxies. Even as liberating an educationist as Jerome Bruner, for instance, has recommended the teaching of a 'world view', in a way which seems to assume that there is a fixed canon of progressive faith, already established, and waiting only to be transmitted to the learner.

In a chapter where he outlined some influential proposals for an Integrated Studies course on 'Man: a Course of Study', he declared:

> The (world-view) section is concerned with man's drive to explain and represent his world. While it may concern itself with myth, with art, with primitive legend, it is only incidentally designed to provide the stories, the religious images, and the mythic account of man's origins. It would be more accurate to describe the subject as 'beginning philosophy' in both senses of that expression — philosophy at the beginning as well as philosophy for younger beginners.
>
> (Jerome Bruner, *Towards a Theory of Instruction*, 1966)

Thus the stories, religious images and myths become mere incidental illustrations for a logical framework to be provided by the teacher, rather than opportunities for learners to dwell within myth, art and legend, and ponder on these in the light of their own special conditions. Bruner's subsequent discussion of his proposals served only to reinforce the impression already given that there was here an entirely prescriptive version of 'world-view', albeit 'enlightened' in the sense of not being obviously committed to any established political or ethical creed. Yet no matter how rich, 'comprehensive' or plausible the 'world-view', such a prescriptive approach could only inhabit genuinely personal orientation, at this stage. It is crucial by now that the learner should be able to feel that while the teacher will make all possible knowledge available, and will give all possible tactful support to the learner's enquiries, there will be no attempt to press personal, or more general cultural preconceptions on the learner, for uncritical acceptance. In fact the learner now needs encouragement from the teacher to remain open, to test clichés of behaviour and outlook, not to accept inertly the labels of experts who may assume an uncritical acquiescence to their 'facts'. This is not to imply that learners have a licence to develop whatever they fancy in the form of outrageously eccentric or incommunicable 'world-views'; but to recall, rather, Polanyi's description of the tensions that need to be worked out between the individual learner and the outside world. 'All thought', he declared, 'is incarnate: it lives by the body and by the favour of society. But it is not *thought* unless it strives for truth, a striving which leaves it free to act on its own responsibility, with universal intent' (*Knowing and Being*). In this struggle for truth and resolution is contained what Polanyi has termed the 'ontological import' of tacit knowing.

Whether this movement must always be experienced as, or be born of a struggle is debatable. Harding's (1937) version of the movement towards insight was rather different, in that he envisaged a 'spectator-role', which allowed a 'detached evaluative relationship to experience' to grow. It was this emphasis on the *naturalness* of the movement which James Britton picked up, when he declared that 'It is typically human to be insistently preoccupied with this world representation, this retrospect and prospect a man constructs for himself.' Britton added that man could even be said to be 'more preoccupied with it than he is with the moment by moment interaction with environment that constitutes his immediate experience.' ('What's the Use?' in Cashdan and Grugeon (Eds) *Language and Education* 1972). Following Harding's 'spectator' analogy, Britton laid no emphasis on the conflict and stress that Polanyi's term 'striving' implies, in the movement towards integration. In a world which was ideally respectful of each learner's gaining of a 'world-view' it might seem appropriate to regard this stage as a natural and on the whole tension-free drawing together, an integrating of previous stages of growth-to-insight. Yet even then, in the best conditions imaginable, it is hard to see the psychic effort needed as a purely comfortable activity, any more than extra strenuous physical activity can be. To be so thoroughly engaged with what we see within, as well as what we see before us and around us – to be fully sensing, intuiting, feeling and thinking – must involve extra stress, at least during certain phases of the process. If the search for integration, for a true conscience ('with-awareness') is undertaken to help us fulfil life's demands, then the search requires more involvement of our full living being than the word 'spectating' might imply. We shall be involved, rather, in discovering, dwelling-in, and testing out the choice of roles that may be available for a given theatre of life, and adopting to ourselves whatever may be regarded as true, real and authentic – as opposed to false and compliant roles; we shall, in fact, be nearer to the audience-participators of the ancient dramas, our beings swayed by the rhythm of events, chorically responding to and potentially enacting the scenes, comic and tragic, as they unfold.

It is important that this fifth, integrating, stage should be seen to have its roots in the involvements and commitments that make up the fourth stage – that there should have been no 'cheap pass' to the beginnings of wisdom. Mary Horton's pungent satire on 'spectating', *The Song of the Spectators* broods on the dangers of detachment gained without the body's involvement:

> We are the lookers-on; we can spectate
> Street-holes and accidents with equal love.
> We have one rule: 'Do not participate
> But scan events always from one remove.'
>
> I'm told we stood six hours while darkness grew,
> To hear a nailed man with pity cry:
> 'Forgive them for they know not what they do.'
> Next day we came to watch another die . . .

We know that we, the onlookers, create
The spectacle, and too, we recognize
That we survive by being separate.
It is only the participant who dies.

But one day, with blank eyes, we will watch a bomb fall
That will eat its creators — good citizens all.
(Mary Horton, *Song of the Spectators*. In: Finn, F.E.S. (Ed) (1970).
Poems of the Sixties. London: John Murray)

When we repress our sympathetic responses, our human intelligence is diminished, giving access to blank destructiveness, to a lapse of full humanness. The true integrated conscience may only be born of the confrontation — sometimes involving a testing struggle — between myself as beholder and my experience of the world.

Mary Horton's polemical verses give a simple sketch of the dangers to others of our failing to take part in living. For a full account of the dangers to ourselves, we might recall Jane Austen's classic study of non-involvement, in *Persuasion*. Anne Elliott, persuaded against her own volition not to marry the man she loves, is presented as decling slowly into unwilling spinsterhood. To others she seems quiet, self-possessed and 'good', though no longer youthfully attractive. To herself she seems imprisoned in her own sensitive but too compliant nature. As the novel develops she becomes more acutely aware of her error, and of the wrong advice — wrong for its snobbish and acquisitive motives — given by her father and by the mother-guardian figure, Lady Russell. At first she is merely chastened by the gap that has grown between what she truly believes and how she has acted — '. . . like many other great moralists and preachers, she had been eloquent on a point in which her own conduct would ill bear examination.' From here, the true action of the novel comes to depend increasingly on action from within Anne herself, and happiness is secured when she eventually takes the chance given to indicate her feelings to Wentworth, who overhears her apparently general conversation with a friend on the subject of man's and woman's love. Having been teased for not allowing that men too can be faithful in love, Anne closes the debate with a statement from the heart:

'Oh!' cried Anne eagerly, 'I hope I do justice to all that is felt by you, and by those who resemble you. God forbid that I should undervalue the warm and faithful feelings of any of my fellow-creatures! I should deserve utter contempt if I dared to suppose that true attachment and constancy were known only by women. No, I believe you equal to every important exertion, and to every domestic forbearance, so long as — if I may be allowed the expression — so long as you have an object. I mean, while the woman you love lives, and lives for you. All the privilege I claim for my own sex (it is not a very enviable one; you need not covet it), is that of loving longest, when existence or hope is gone.'

She could not immediately have uttered another sentence; her heart was too full, her breath too much oppressed.

(Jane Austen, *Persuasion*, 1818)

In finding courage to reveal her feelings, Anne not only transcends her own previous 'maidenly' passiveness, but also enables Wentworth to realize an error in his own conduct; for though he had loved ardently, he had later become too cool to take any notice of her. Thus Anne's courage of heart brings about an integrating in the most obvious sense — a marriage between man and woman. The marriage represents too an integrating of principles — of unassertive patience with honest action; of direct, uncomplicated feeling with fine discrimination of judgement; of security in faith with the vulnerability of bodily life that is a condition of our existence (for they do not *quite* live happily ever after: we are told in the final sentence of the book that as a sailor's wife, she must live always 'with the dread of a future war'). It is worth recalling, too, that Jane Austen discarded a 'non-involved' ending to *Persuasion*, in favour of this final version which requires choice and action from both hero and heroine.

At some risk of seeming crudely diagrammatic, this true version of conscience that is achieved by Anne may be seen partly in Freud's famous terms, as the fruits of a contest between the id (basic, instinctual man), the ego (the personal 'I') and the super-ego (social conscience, as imprinted by custom and guidance from parent- and peer-figures). When there is no struggle, or when the struggle is unsuccessful, our being remains split-up in these three categories. Only individual, courageous acts of choice can then free the individual from false versions of existence, and move us into true self-being. The classic reference to exemplify independent vision and action on behalf of living is, of course, that of the Good Samaritan — a parable whose insights are echoed or translated in so many literary works. Artists since Homer have seen the growth to self-being as a lonely quest, needing the deepest resources of sympathetic ingenuity and courage — Bunyan's Pilgrim, Brontë's Jane Eyre, Tolstoy's Levin, Lawrence's Ursula, Shakespeare's Kent, Edgar and Cordelia come readily to mind, among many others. One celebrated particular instance — Twain's archetypally easy-going Huck Finn — is likely to be encountered by quite young readers; yet they will already know from their own experience of the gap that exists between true honour and 'doing what one is told'. Guided by enlightened teaching, they will have no great difficulty in appreciating the at first elusive connection between what they already know, and Twain's subtly particular treatment of Huck on the raft. Huck's harrowing struggle between 'social' conscience and 'real' conscience, before he confesses to being without the courage of a louse, in failing to betray Jim by handing him over as the property of 'Poor Miss Watson' is one of those critical moments in literature, where ethical insight is moved forward by art. Erich Fromm's term for the new state of self-insight reached by Huck was the 'intrinsic conscience' (in *Man for Himself*, 1947) – a state of integrating of being with experience that is reached entirely through individual effort towards full being.

Thus the fifth stage, where the learner works towards an integrated conscience, implies a role which is often attributed to the artist. The learner is moving towards a special kind of authority, based not on external position, but on experience, insight, self-trust and on bearing witness to the truth about self and world. In the search for self-knowing detachment is learned; the learner seeks out and contemplates hidden aspects of the self: feelings, aims, emotions, motivations, activities. This self-orientation is a culmination of previous stages, which enables a progress into wider realms of speculation. But such speculations will be merely an escape and a fraud, unless based on the primary need to achieve a firm integration of being and knowing in our own, local world. As Ian (whose work was studied in Chapter Three) saw it: 'Many people often go into discussions with each other of what life is all about, but how on earth will people ever find an answer, while people are giving off a false image of themselves.' If we should wish to take this fifth, integrating, stage seriously in planning secondary school English studies, then the form of literary and other expressive arts again come most naturally to mind, as offering the richest examples and patterns of integration. The value of art in this respect was recognized by Abraham Maslow (1968). In a chapter on 'Creativity in Self-actualizing People', he leads up to the remark quoted at the beginning of this chapter, by dwelling on the artist's capacity to 'bring together clashing colours, forms that fight each other, dissonances of all kinds, into a unity'. Such a reconciling of contradictions and opposites, suggests Maslow, is characteristic of *all* creative achievement – in the arts, in medicine and science, in parenthood: 'They are all integrators, able to bring separates and even opposites together into unity.'

A similar point about the artist's unifying achievement was made by Susanne Langer, where she dwelled in a chapter called 'Poesis' on the shapelessness of life's events.

The poet's business is to create the appearance of 'experience', the semblance of events lived and felt, and to organize them so that they constitute a purely and completely experienced reality, a piece of *virtual life*.

(Susanne Langer, *Feeling and Form*, 1953)

Setting aside some doubts already admitted about Professor Langer's reluctance here to credit the validity of art with more than 'appearance' or 'semblance' or 'virtual life', this passage reveals how the task of art is to endow form and meaning on the turbulence and fragmentary nature of experience. Such art may then act as a source to inspire the learner in his/her own search to shape a unified vision of life. And as an example, art can be an actual presence, something realized in the learner's own embodied vision of living. Thus the meeting with realized art may inspire further creative search in the learner-respondent, beyond a direct identification of the qualities of the art-form, and an application of its possible 'uses'.

This discussion of the integrating stage has tended to dwell on later, specifically adult aspects of becoming through learning. It should be readily acknowledged here, that the teacher of secondary school learners is likely to be more concerned with encouraging the healthy beginnings of this stage, rather than expecting thoroughly worked-out, well-integrated visualizations of life, for these can only take shape gradually and in the light of many kinds of experience. Among older school-learners, it is the willingness to 'risk the journey' that we should value – the willingness to take on for themselves the processes of learning as a personal responsibility, which will stay with them for life. Even though it may be accepted that nothing final will emerge at this stage, to have reached it at all implies the growth of a strong, well grounded sense of identity. Integrating represents a much more thorough response to life and to art-insight, than the kind of 'clever' or 'brilliant' work that can sometimes be mistaken for significant enterprise, on intensive academic courses in our schools and universities.

Some Examples
The first example is again taken from Andrew's work, and is composed of some passages from a very long piece of work that he submitted during the first year of his sixth-form course, after reading Kafka's short story *The Knock at the Manor Gate* (the story had been chosen as an accompaniment to work-in-progress on *King Lear*). Much of Andrew's writing around this time returned repeatedly – even against the grain of the lessons – to thoughts about his own individuality, and the problem of how he might be sure that he really *was* thinking for himself. For instance, in a piece of work at around the same time where he had engaged himself in attacking organized religion (a topic that had presented itself from A-level work on Peter Shaffer's *Royal Hunt of the Sun*) he revealed his earlier adherence to an evangelical Christian group, from which he had lately broken away: 'If you are told by others, and those who you hold in high regard especially, that they have found the way to eternal salvation or that they have found the secret of life – then this is religion against the individual. Any externalised concept of religion is an enslavement to the individual as it has,

consciously or unconsciously, a binding morality or life-style.' This particular piece broadened out into an attack on uncritical enthusiasms among students for thinkers and writers like Jung and Hesse, which, he felt had turned these men into cult-figures, and he went on: 'Even your English lessons are affected. The assertion that Lawrence is religious is a pressure on us to aspire to that pacific sweet veneer of Lawrence and his work. We are demanded to look at a grain of sand and in it see the world.'

Here, as in all his work around this time, he was submitting himself and all his familiar guidelines, including the English lessons, to radical inspection. In a letter of reply to a note of mine, which tried to clear up the point about Lawrence being a 'religious' writer, he remarked wryly on himself:

Thanks for writing – I needed some comeback on what I recently wrote to you . . . philosophers subordinate truth in order to justify what they are or what they would like to be. Thus I am trying to reach the state of individuality but I do not feel confident enough and so I try to resign myself to it in terms of rationalisations and philosophies. It is of no great wonder that one of the great individualist philosophers Max Stirner was a meek and long-suffering schoolteacher who lived under the shadow of his mother . . .

This line of quite severe self-criticism is furthered in his discussion of Kafka's short story, which opens with a sentence from the tale:

Knock at the Manor Gate
'Could I endure any other air than prison air now?'
'Unless you meet a boulder blocking your path the long and winding road has no interest.'
Right now I could rush to the television or put on a record or go and see how dinner is getting on – because they provide the prison air for me and just sitting here trying to write something real and honest to myself is air I can barely endure. So often I will not stand up to my own individuality but prostitute away my thoughts and imagination in idle discussion, television, records and newspapers. At present I feel that I am no more than the sum of my intellectual being, my whole life is run on a very intellectual, rationalised level. All my actions are analysed. Because of this most of the time I believe I am the epitomy of stability but occasionally, at times like this, I feel that the absolute stability is a sheen for a great sub-conscious instability. I feel no more than the sum of my intelligence – but there must be more! Where did Kafka find his mysterious images, where did Jung discover his dreams? Self-awareness has been the theme of English departmental philosophy for a long while but how really difficult this is. I used to skip through a few pages of Blake, nod my head, catch onto a few intellectual thoughts

and then believe myself to be worthy of my life. Now I can see through much dishonesty and now I hope I will be able to achieve real insight into myself, particularly into my subconscious mind that is beyond the intellect. I find it very difficult to find out the role my intellect must play, sometimes I say hell to everything rational and scientific while at other times I think I should be playing chess and doing mathematics because my mind has lapsed into intellectual apathy, to a point where I have stopped thinking things through or working things out. I used to like working out involved mathematics problems and found great satisfaction in unearthing the answer but then I went through a period when I thought that there was no use for mathematics, when 'art was the tree of life, science the tree of death' — I don't know whether mathematics is harmful and hinders my spiritual growth or whether it gives me the patience and work to help me.

Since being conscious of this grain of dishonesty the whole issue of self-awakening seems to have been sacrificed to my intellect. Today at school some friends were going over to the cafe and I would have liked to go but I said no for an unbelievable reason — I fancied that I was asserting a sense of individuality for myself. Again this was prison air and ridiculous to think that by staying alone at school that I would be advanced in my process of self-enlightenment. Perhaps the prison for me is my intellect — many people have found this to be true but they tend to disregard it too much — a balance can and must be achieved.

'Who am I?' I did this essay once before but avoided the main issue perhaps because of dishonesty, but more likely a subconscious urge not to discover what is there — I may not like it! The balance between consciousness and unconsciousness is very fine and I don't think there really is any division — I picture a railway tunnel in my head getting darker and darker as I move along. The subconscious moves in such a way that if one is told to look for yourself then there are many difficulties and it seems to me that this would be easier if it was a process of incidental discovery. Often I think my subconscious mind works against what is me. The very dark parts of the tunnel and the very light parts of the tunnel, that is the conscious mind that belongs to a world of idle chatter, idle business, time, impersonal work, vacant entertainment and abstractions and the deep unconscious mind that which Jung says we can never discover, both seem to work against what I feel is me. For example I am reading Jung's *Memories, Dreams, and Reflections* and so I have found the concept of dreams interesting and I also feel that dreaming is something I would like to do, and be mystified by. However as soon as I admit that, I feel that, my subconscious mind will give me interesting dreams or images that are not reality but conjured up for my own entertainment — thus I feel that my deep sub-conscious mind works against me. Very, very rarely do I dream but it so happens that when I am interested in the subject I can suddenly picture images in my head and dream dreams. It could be that I have become more aware of something that occurs all the time but I am very wary. I feel it is more likely that, as I said before, my subconscious mind sends these dreams and images to pander to my conscious whims. The dreamer, the mystic, the writer in imagery stands for strength and happiness, stand for something that I would like to be and so I try to become just that. Perhaps everyone is fooling themselves — sometimes I really feel this because the wowie zowie, trendy mystics speak in ridiculous abstractions as well as always seeming so superior. Even though they shudder at the intellectual often I feel that they are hyper-intellectuals who regard everyone else as mere mortals who don't know anything. That probably is a complete myth and I would be quite happy to be shown if it is otherwise . . .

It is impossible to discern truth from untruth all the time, most of the time its very hard. I am not convinced that dreams do hold any weight or are open to interpretations — why can so little mean so much? However Jung's dreams seem pretty convincing — especially in regard to the war. Nevertheless I feel the dream was a result of a thought and not the other way round. I believe the origin of the dream was a thought that the political situation in Europe might lead to war — whether this was a conscious, or unconscious thought — I do not know. I don't think this dream was the result of an extra-terrestrial will nor some willing premonition from the fathomless depths of unconsciousness. It was a picture of a thought that had already been. I think this is so with my own few and recent dreams which I can show after I have briefly described them.

While camping on Box Hill recently I dreamt that an escapee from Dartmoor prison come into our tent and stayed the night — however I have only a faint recollection of this and I cannot remember what he looked like or any details. I think this may have been the result of my interest with the personal imprisonment theme — could I endure other than prison air now? Thus the dream is simply a product of a few abstract thoughts and not some fantastic symbol of anything. My dreams of course are more easily bent to this theory because of their thinness and abstraction.

I have another recollection which I think occurred in a dream but I could not say — it is simply a massive womb like thing although that is imagined because I can only see a small part of it but it appears as though it probably stretches for a long way. To the right of what I can see is a very small face of whom I do not know. In fact I think it is like a pin man's head — all of the womb-like material is centered around this face and pulled in towards it. New life which this dream could signify is also a subject I have thought about in relation to the self-enlightenment subject . . . (a long account of a recent anxiety dream follows . . .)

Following my thoughts through on this I arrive at a tolstoyan attitude, particularly shown by Platon Karatayev in *War and Peace*, that this self-observation is an added complication to life that is unnecessary and can only bring unhappiness. Tolstoy's insistence is on simplicity and living life as we have it — dreams don't seem to have any real relation to life, my life. It seems a waste of time that we should worry about dreams and the sub-conscious mind when we have life now and can live it now — in every way we seem to make a complication of life — politics, money, mysticism and dreams, etc. etc. It's funny that I should arrive at that point of view after having talked of my dreams; but now I think I imagined that I had them because I had previously admitted the concept of dreams and their interpretation. Everything is fallacy but today's life — life, LIFE here and now — I wish I truly lived to that principle! Jung says that if people had understood their dreams then the first world war could have been avoided but that seems to be attempting a mountain climb when a molehill climb would do. Tolstoy, Jesus, Kropotkin never spoke of dreams but they had life and they lived it intensely. I am sure that there is a much more fundamental answer than dream interpretation to stop war. That does not meant to say it is useless, as Jung obviously profited from his dreams and their interpretation but they were vivid and precise and seemed destined for interpretation. For me dreams are nothing. The trouble is that I cannot find any balance, I either make dreams everything or nothing probably because they stand for an image which on the one hand I envy but on the other hand scorn. Dreams are dreams.

(Andrew, lower sixth year, aged seventeen)

Andrew conveys vividly here the actual, physical discomfort of having to wrestle with new concepts. Above all, he claims, he must endure the 'prison of the intellect' which has, he feels, held back the whole process of his self-awakening. In his exploring of conscious, sub-conscious and unconscious modes of experience, he makes some illuminating remarks about dreams, and the way in which the directions of the unconscious mind can seem as random to 'what I feel is me' as the accidental trivia of conscious responses, the 'world of idle chatter, idle business, time, impersonal work, vacant entertainment and abstractions . . .' He discusses the contrasting claims of 'mystic' and 'intellectual' and moves towards some quite carefully independent distinctions as his argument develops — as in his discussion of the special value of Jung's war-dream, where the thought had been able to work on the dream and thus provide a genuinely significant dream.

Despite his declared suspicions about the whole area of dreams and visions, he goes on to reveal some of his own dream experiences, which might, he thinks, properly be called thought-inspired. He shows a scrupulous concern for accurate reporting of his dreams, and carefully points out where he may be distorting the truth for his own purposes: 'My dreams of course are more easily bent to this theory because of their thinness and abstraction . . .'. After a fairly long descriptive excursion into his dreams (not included here) he finally turns to Tolstoy for a useful interim solution, that 'this self-observation is an added complication to life that is unnecessary and can only bring unhappiness . . .'. His writing has recorded yet another spirited, but as yet unresolved, struggle for him.

Andrew's broodings on the 'prison of the intellect' had preoccupied him for very many months, and it was around this time that he returned yet again for a final exploration (as far as his sixth-form career was concerned, at least) of the Jack London stories. When discussing *The Sea Wolf* he quoted the condemnation uttered by the brutal yet erudite sea-wolf Larsen against the 'refined (wet liberal) intellectual' Van Weyden: 'I do not sin, for I am true to the promptings of the life that is in me. I am sincere in my soul at least, and that is what you are not.' Reflecting on this, Andrew avowed a sense of confusion, in feeling that he was like both Larsen and Van Weyden, in admiring the ruthless life-urge in Larsen, but also respecting Van Weyden's doubts, and also admitting himself to living by 'others' philosophies', rather than individual promptings. Very often he would add to the end of a piece of work a remark like, 'I hope this outpouring of naive arrogance is of some use — please criticize heavily — I need to test my theories.' His writing was indeed moving all the time now beyond mere confusions, into a real confronting of incompatibles and opposites in his living. The Larsen-Van Weyden study enabled him, for instance, to declare a hope that he might integrate his 'Jack London' self in order to live with full vitality, rather than 'refine my life so that it offends no-one'.

Andrew recognized for himself the distances that he had to travel; yet he had in some ways already gone further than many older minds in working towards an individually-held vision. His writing at this stage was uneven, and sometimes very strained; but it shows a vigour and honesty which ought to prove valuable qualities in his adult enterprises.

The second example, by Myrtle (whose work was quoted in Chapter Four) is both briefer and less ambitious. Her poem, with its short prose preface, was written in response to a tense and unsuccessful lesson that she had endured on the problems of Northern Ireland — unsuccessful because I seemed only to have made the class wary and uneasy, at this first, too direct attempt to prompt them into recognizing that the issues involved the whole British and Irish community much more than we often cared to admit. Myrtle does not dwell on any details of the lesson in her piece (she had not enjoyed the directions taken, and also admitted in later discussion that she did not respond with any feeling that she could readily identify to television news coverage of the civil war in Northern Ireland, beyond 'a kind of numbness').

Sub-conscious

Jung said, 'The world into which we are born is beautiful and cruel'. That it is, nature is beautiful, the expressions of real happiness and joy on people's faces (not a very familiar sight): freedom, these make our world beautiful and make our lives worth living. The world is cruel too. A starving animal savagely attacking a child is an example of nature's cruelty. Authority can sometimes make the world a cruel and ugly place, by this I mean misused authority such as illustrated in the book '1984'. Man is cruel.

Jung then goes on to say that "man must sense that he lives in a world which in some respects is mysterious", this it is also. Nature is mysterious as well as man, both are unpredictable and I think this is one of the most mysterious aspects of our world. The feelings of good and evil cast a shadow of mystery over the world . . .

A man is dead unless he thinks. It is most important that he learns to think properly and not let them become deformed in any way. This is where the school's English lessons are so important. My English lessons at our school have been worth coming to. Often at my last school I would become bored with the teacher trying to drumb in how to describe an apple, a firework, etc., or going over for the umpteenth time the different tenses.

Going back to Jung, I often feel astonished, sad, fed up and joyful all at the same time as he does. I think if we are honest we all feel this way at times.

I often find it difficult to think when I come from a lesson as I have done today.

Silence,
nothing stirs,
And the cold air is
Biteing at my face.
I dare not move
Or breathe
Lest I break the spell
of nothingness

Floating down
Into the depths of the sea
I pass a grave,
Eternally cold;
I have no fear
And feel nothing

But the coldness
Clutching at my soul.

I pass through a world
Where people know no
Love or hate,
No on laughs or smiles
And I realise they
Aren't human,
But machines.

And I feel pain
It is the coldness
Wrenching out
My heart.

(Myrtle, fifth year, aged fifteen)

As an enthusiastic member of a local church, Myrtle quite often admitted into her writings a sense that she found her well-engrained Christian optimism difficult to reconcile with some of the grimmer facts of this world. Both her prose-piece and her poem reveal how her optimistic faith in a loving world has been disturbed by the lesson she refers to (and doubtless by other things too). Understandably she reaches out for support from Jung's 'theory of opposites' (based on some selected passages from *Memories, Dreams and Reflections* that had been studied in English during that term) in order to explain her sense of contradictoriness in existence; and out of simple good-heartedness, I suspect, she offers some lines in defence of her English lessons, on an occasion when they seem to have achieved very little for her beyond provoking a temporary loss of warm self-trust.

Yet both her prose-preface and her poem reach towards the deepest kind of thought, of psychic adventuring, that she can visualize; she must not only admit the shock sustained by some brutal facts, but must record the journey that the shock enforces. Temporarily cut-off from love or familiar friendships, but accepting an obligation to explore, rather than simply turn back to the familiar, she visualizes an Orpheus-like descent into a lifeless underworld, where 'I have no fear/And feel nothing/But the coldness/Clutching at my soul . . .' The exploration goes no further than this: it was not Myrtle's gift or method to probe with, say, Andrew's sustained deliberateness into the problems of existence. But it may be taken as authentic evidence of Myrtle's turning to contemplate with courage, on her own terms, the promptings of her own intuitions, even when painful and stark.

The third example is taken from a long piece of writing by Philip (whose work was quoted in Chapter Four), where he is summing up his thoughts on the two set books already studied on the A-level course. Prior to this essay he had written substantially on these books within all the earlier stages, and this piece was an unsolicited, personal attempt to 'put the term together', as he said:

from 'Reflections on two set books'

. . . In both books, *King Lear* and *Pincher Martin*, that we are reading at present there is a great deal of searching for identities and to a great extent this is like this world today because at one time or another each of us searches for some kind of identity to relate to.

Pincher Martin, himself, is perhaps the best example of someone searching for their identity but, within himself, he knows that he has left it too late and his constant struggling throughout the book emphasises this point. He is so scared and unsure of himself that he has to struggle — his life has been a struggle so he mustn't give up his struggling — it is his only hope for survival. Pincher has never before thought in search of his identity. For all he had cared there wasn't an identity for him to search for. He was just a number in the Navy and that is all he identified with. He had never thought that there was a reason for his life and that there was an identity to seek but when he was left, stranded in the sea this hidden search for his identity over-powered him and he was made to fend for himself. Never before had he been alone as he was now and because he didn't really know what he was capable of he had to try and search for his identity. Perhaps the only real truth that Pincher obtained from life was from those last dying moments. It was during this time that he realised he was a nobody and that his true identity could never really have been found in the Navy — his life hadn't meant anything and it had been wasted.

Pincher hadn't really achieved anything from life — he had been sub-consciously dead to himself throughout his life. The achievements he had reckoned with had been things like promotion and exam-passes. Spiritual and emotional achievements had never come into the reckoning for he had never tried to gain them and hence had never succeeded in doing so. My theory is that life is a kind of jig-saw puzzle and every now and again you strive to gain more, not necessary material but mental, each piece of the jig-saw is gradually put in it's allotted place. A useful, unwasted and satisfying life may have the whole picture full with all the pieces placed but some lives or pictures may be very empty and hardly any of the pieces will have been used.

The former jig-saw puzzle will be something like Pincher's for he has hardly gained anything from life and there are a great many segments of his life that still need to be filled in. The only pieces of the jig-saw that will have been filled in are those that Pincher struggled to secure at the end of his life at those last dying, struggling moments.

I know for certain that I won't be a "Pincher Man" when I die for even though, I hope, I have many years to come I am sure I know more about myself than Pincher ever would have known. In fact, although it may sound deceitful, even though I am very quiet a lot of this term has been spent thinking of myself and the way life is going and in fact many a time I have been near breaking point. I'm sure I would have passed this point by now if I hadn't carefully scanned the situation and then realised I had got a reason for life and a true identity to reach. I haven't found this identity yet, in fact I am going through a very confused and searching phase recently where I have been unusually tense and withdrawn but I find that writing and expressing myself on paper has helped a lot and breaks down these barriers that are holding me very easily. Perhaps Pincher would have found more about himself had he even attempted, but he didn't and hence the cold, harsh, un-real way in which he died symbolised the way he had lived and been driven into the cause of the way he died.

King Lear could also be likened to Pincher in that he never finds his true identity also. Lear, on the other hand, has heroically tried to do so though, although succeed he does not. During the book I find Lear to be a very restless, searching and confused man. I somehow feel that life doesn't come up to Lear's great expectations. Being a King, he feels that his life should be full of happiness but he doesn't want to make his happiness for himself. I agree that happiness should hold a great deal of our lives but I feel we *must* experience woe for us to feel so much for happiness. These emotions, good or bad, make up our lives and we must learn to take the rough with the smooth. Lear just won't face this and that is why he is so confused when his daughters turn against him. Lear's world is based greatly on material things — he thinks he can buy his daughter's love and respect by giving them parts of his Kingdom but he has "bought" their respect once too often and they pay him back for his foolishness by going against him. Lear should have realised that material gains aren't the only things in life for there are also the spiritual gains which Lear only realises when it is far too late . . .

My restlessness has been nearly banished although Pincher's never was. All I hope is that by the time my life expires I will have a satisfying outlook on life, I know we all go through certain phases in our lives when the reason for living or search for our identity might not look so bright but if that far reaching glimmer of light at the end of our seeming dark tunnel is still flickering there then we know that life is worth living.

(Philip, sixth year, aged sixteen)

'I know for certain that I won't be a "Pincher man" when I die . . .': the declaration here characterizes the tone and preoccupations as distinctly different from the concerns of earlier stages. He declares that he needs a valid and reliable identity, or outlook, which will enable him to stand separately from things he does not believe in: and he freely admits the difficulties of being an outsider to an acquisitive, materialistic, class-based social machine — not just having a different opinion, but *feeling* differently about these things; 'I haven't found this identity yet, in fact I am going through a very confused and searching phase recently where I have been unusually tense and withdrawn but I find that writing and expressing myself on paper has helped a lot . . .'. He moves on to consider some aspects of *King Lear*, in similar spirit. In a passage not quoted — where again, he is thinking much more clearly *beyond*, rather than about the book — he makes an astute comment on the Fool in *King Lear*:

> Perhaps the only person who comes near to finding their true self in 'Lear' is the Fool. The Fool finds himself in a perfect position to search for his identity . . . He has freedom of speech, unlike Kent or Gloucester who with just a slip of the tongue can be banished or blinded . . .

In the final lines, he sums up this point of progress through the 'seeming dark tunnel' of his experiences. Philip leaves the impression here that he is 'coming through' to something a good deal more important than just making it over the approaching and immediate hurdles of A-levels and University.

It is unsurprising that Philip's meditations on *Pincher Martin* and *King Lear* should bring him to such a considered rejection of acquisitiveness as an aim in living. Lear, above all, records the tragedy of loss of the Cordelia presence in human affairs — the harmonious chords of loving relationship, the binding cords of communal, ethical and religious commitment (the origin of the word 'religion' is, we recall, re-ligare, to bind; without the ties there can, paradoxically, be no transcending of self). *King Lear* is a tragedy for our own epoch, in that the most necessary struggle of all is towards fresh realization that love, if it exists, must be embodied in living being. Merleau-Ponty has pointed to the crucial effort of imagination that is needed, beyond materialism:

> The flesh is not matter, is not mind, is not substance. To designate it, we should need the old term 'element', in the sense it was used to speak of water, air, earth, and fire, that is . . . a sort of incarnate principle that brings a style of being . . . The flesh in this sense is an 'element' of being.
>
> (Maurice Merleau-Ponty, *The Visible and the Invisible*, 1968)

'A sort of incarnate principle' . . . 'a living principle': it is such a principle which comes to guide the learner's quest towards integrating. As with

Edmund Husserl's concept of 'intentionality', it embodies the power of conferring meaning on the world, and on our existence within the world.

But the concluding words to this book should be directed to art, which philosophy at best reflects and serves, as reason serves true thought. The integrity of art, and the integrating powers of art are achieved through the risks that individual men and women are prepared to take, in revealing what they truly feel. The artist's courage is a fully realized version of the ordinary human courage needed by us all, to take our true place in the world — as embodied in Anne Elliott, or in Huck Finn, or in Edgar, Kent, Cordelia and Lear himself, when he has fully taken the Fool into himself. Edgar speaks for them, and for us, when he advises at the end of the play to 'speak what we feel, not what we ought to say'. To speak out or to write in this spirit is in itself to enact that incarnate, or living principle.

Bibliography

ABBS, P. (1982). *English within the Arts. A Radical Alternative for English and the Arts in the Curriculum*. London: Hodder and Stoughton.

BEREITER, C. (1979). 'Development in Writing'. In: GREGG, L.W. and STEINBERG, E.R. (Eds), *Cognitive Processes in Writing*. Hillsdale, N.T.: Erlbaum.

BOLTON, N. (1982). 'The Lived World'. In: *Journal of Phenomenological Psychology*, Spring.

BOWLBY, J. (1980). *Attachment and Loss*, Vol. 3: *Loss, Sadness and Depression*. London: Hogarth.

BRECHT, B. (1965). *The Messingkauf Dialogues* (trans. Willett). London: Methuen.

BRITTON, J. (1970). *Language and Learning*. Harmondsworth: Penguin.

BRITTON, J. (1972). 'What's the Use?'. In: CASHDAN and GRUGEON (Eds), *Language and Education*. London: Open University/RKP.

BRITTON, J. (1975). (Ed) *The Development of Writing Abilities* (11–18). London: Macmillan.

BRUNER, J. (1962). *On Knowing – Essays for the Left Hand*. Cambridge, Mass.: Harvard University Press.

BRUNER, J. (1966). *Towards a Theory of Instruction*. Cambridge, Mass.: Harvard University Press.

BUBER, M. (1937). *I and Thou*. Edinburgh: Clark.

BUBER, M. (1955). *Between Man and Man*. Boston: Beacon Press.

BUYTENDIJK, F.J.J. (1968). 'Zur Phanomenologie der Begegnung'. Part trans. in GRENE, M. (1968). *Approaches to a Philosophical Biology*.

CALTHROP, K. (1971). *Reading Together: The Use of the Class Reader*. London: Heinemann Educational.

CALOUSTE GULBENKIAN FOUNDATION (1982). *The Arts in Schools. Principles, Practice and Provision*. London: Calouste Gulbenkian Foundation.

CAMUS, A. (1967). 'The Artist and his Time'. In: *Resistance, Rebellion and Death* (1967). London: Hamish Hamilton.

CASSIRER, E. (1944). *An Essay on Man: An Introduction to a Philosophy of Culture*. Yale University Press.

CASSIRER, E. (1946). *Language and Myth* (trans. S. Langer). New York: Dover.

CASSIRER, E. (1953, 1955, 1958). *The Philosophy of Symbolic Forms* (3 vols). Yale University Press.

COLLINGWOOD, R.G. (1939). *The Principles of Art*. Oxford: Oxford University Press.

COOK, C. (1914). *Peroc Playbook* No. 4. Cambridge: Cambridge University Press.

CREBER, P. (1965). *Sense and Sensitivity*. London: University of London Press. Revised edition (1982). Exeter: School of Education, University of Exeter.

CROCE, B. (1909). *Aesthetics as Science of Expression and General Linguistics*. London: Macmillan.

DIXON, J. (1979). (Ed) *Education 16–19: The Role of English and Communication*. London: Macmillan.
DIXON, J. and STRATTA, L. (1982). 'Argument: what does it mean to teachers of English?', *English in Education*, **16**, 1.
DOUGHTY, P. (1971). *Language in Use*. London: Arnold.
EGAN, K. (1979). *Educational Development*. Oxford: Oxford University Press.
FIRTH, J.R. (1930). 'Speech'. In: *The Tongues of Men and Speech*. (1964). Oxford: Oxford University Press.
FIRTH, J.R. (1937). *The Tongues of Men*. London: Watts.
FRANKL, V. (1962). *Man's Search for Meaning*. Boston: Beacon Press.
FREIRE, P. (1972). *Cultural Action for Freedom*. Harmondsworth: Penguin.
FROMM, E. (1965). *The Heart of Man*. London: RKP.
GOODMAN, P. (1973). *Speaking and Language: Defence of Poetry*. London: Wildwood House.
GREAT BRITAIN. DEPARTMENT OF EDUCATION AND SCIENCE (1979). *Aspects of Secondary Education in England*. London: HMSO.
GRENE, M. (1966). *The Knower and the Known*. London: Faber.
GRENE, M. (1968). *Approaches to a Philosophical Biology*. New York: Basic Books.
GRENE, M. (1969). (Ed) *Knowing and Being*. London: RKP.
GRENE, M. (1974). *The Understanding of Nature*. Boston: D. Reidel.
GUNTRIP, Harry (1968). *Schizoid Phenomena: Object Relations and the Self*. London: Tavistock.
GUSDORF, G. (1965). *Speaking (La Parole)*. Evanston: North Western University Press.
HARDING, D.W. (1937). 'The Role of the Onlooker', *Scrutiny*, VI, (3).
HARDING, D.W. (1963). *Experience into Words*. London: Chatto.
HARDING, D.W. (1980). 'The Process of Mourning', *Times Lit. Supp.*, 4 July, 1980, no. 4032.
HARRISON, B.T. (1979). 'The Learner as Writer: Stages of Growth', *Language for Learning*, I. 2. Exeter: University of Exeter.
HARRISON, B.T. (1980). *Poetry and the Language of Feeling*. Tract 27. Sussex: Gryphon Press.
HARRISON, B.T. (1983). (Ed) *English Studies, 11–18: An Arts-Based Approach*. London: Hodder and Stoughton.
HEANEY, S. (1975). *Stations*. Belfast: Ulsterman Publications.
HEIDEGGER, M. (1970). *Discourse on Thinking* (trans. ANDERSON/FREUD). New York: Harper and Row.
HEIDEGGER, M. (1971). *Poetry, Language, Thought* (trans. HOFSTADTER). New York: Harper and Row.
HEPWORTH, B. (1976). *Pictorial Autobiography*. St Ives, Cornwall: Hepworth Museum.
HOLBROOK, D. (1980). *English for Meaning*. Windsor: NFER.
HOPKINS, G.M. (1959). *The Journals and Papers*, HOUSE and STOREY (Eds). Oxford: Oxford University Press.
HOURD, M. (1972). *Relationship in Learning*. London: Heinemann Educational.
HUGHES, T. (1967). *Poetry in the Making*. London: Faber.
JAMES, W. (1899). *Talks to Teachers on Psychology and to Students on some of Life's Ideals*. London: Longmans, Green and Co.
JONES, R. (1968). *Fantasy and Feeling in Education*. London: University of London Press.
JUNG, C.J. (1933). *Modern Man in Search of a Soul*. London: RKP.
JUNG, C.J. (1956). *Symbols of Transformation*. London: RKP.
JUNG, C.J. (1963). *Memories, Dreams, Reflections*. London: Collins and RKP.

KLEE, P. (1924). 'Jena Lecture'. In: GROHMANN, W., *Paul Klee* (Second ed., 1957). London: Lund Humphries.
LANGER, S. (1953). *Feeling and Form*. London: RKP
LANGER, S. (1957). *Philosophy in a New Key* (Second ed). Cambridge, Mass.: Harvard University Press.
LANGER, S. (1974). *Mind: An Essay on Human Feeling*. Baltimore: John Hopkins University Press.
LAWRENCE, D.H. (1923). *Psychology and the Unconscious*. London: Secker and Warburg.
LAWRENCE, D.H. (1936). 'Introduction to his Paintings'. In: *Phoenix*. London: Heinemann.
LAWRENCE, D.H. (1936). 'Morality and the Novel'. In: *Phoenix*. London: Heinemann.
LEAVIS, F.R. (1932). *How to teach Reading: A Primer for Ezra Pound*. Cambridge: Gordon Fraser, Minority Press.
LEAVIS, F.R. (1975). *The Living Principle*. London: Chatto and Windus.
LEAVIS, F.R. (1976). *Thought, Words and Creativity*. London: Chatto and Windus.
LEAVIS, F.R. and THOMPSON, D. (1933). *Culture and Environment*. London: Chatto and Windus.
LEAVIS, Q.D. (1981). 'The Englishness of the English Novel', *New Universities Quarterly*, Summer 1981.
LEWIN, H. (1974). 'Touch'. In: FEINBERG, B. (Ed) *Poets to the People*. London: Allen and Unwin.
LEWIS, M.M. (1963). *Language, Thought and Personality in Infancy and Childhood*. London: Harrap.
LOMAS, P. (1973). *True and False Experience*. London: Allen Lane.
LOMAS, P. (1981). *The Case for a Personal Psychotherapy*. Oxford: Oxford University Press.
MACMURRAY, J. (1957). *The Self as Agent*. London: Faber.
MACMURRAY, J. (1961). *Persons in Relation*. London: Faber.
MACMURRAY, J. (1962). *Reason and Emotion* (Second edition). London: Faber.
MASLOW, A. (1968) *Towards a Psychology of Being*. New York: Van Nostrand Rheinhold.
MERLEAU-PONTY, M. (1962). *The Phenomenology of Perception*. London: RKP.
MERLEAU-PONTY, M. (1964). *Signs*. Evanston: North Western University Press.
MERLEAU-PONTY, M. (1968). *The Visible and the Invisible*. Evanston: North Western University Press.
MERLEAU-PONTY, M. (1974). 'Eye and Mind'. In: O'NEILL (Ed) *Phenomenology, Language and Society*. London: Heinemann.
MILNER, M. (1971). *On Not Being Able to Paint* (Second ed). London: Heinemann.
O'MALLEY, R. (1981). 'Plain Texts', *The Use of English*, 32, 2.
ORTEGA Y GASSET (1968). *The Dehumanization of Art*. Princeton: Princeton University Press.
ORTEGA Y GASSET (1972). *Meditations on Hunting*. New York: Scribner's (Charles) Sons.
PATEMAN, R. (1975). *Language, Truth and Politics*. Devon: Russell Press.
PEEL, M. (1975). *Seeing to the Heart*. London: Hart-Davis.
POLANYI, M. (1958). *Personal Knowledge: Towards a Post-Critical Philosophy*. London: RKP.
POLANYI, M. (1967). *The Tacit Dimension*. London: RKP.
POLANYI, M. (1969). Essay in: GRENE, M. (Ed) *Knowing and Being*. London: RKP.
POLANYI, M. (1975). *Meaning*. Chicago: University of Chicago Press.

POTTER, S. (1966). *Our Language* (Revised ed). Harmondsworth: Penguin.
PURVES, A. (1972). *How Porcupines Make Love: Notes on a Response-Centred Curriculum*. Xerox Corp., University of California.
PURVES, A. (1973). (Ed) *Literature Education in Ten Countries: an Empirical Study*. New York: Wiley.
QUILLER-COUCH, A. (1916). *On the Art of Writing*. Cambridge: Cambridge University Press.
READ, H. (1955). *Ikon and Idea. The Function of Art in the Development of Human Consciousness*. London: Faber.
READ, H. (1960). *The Form of Things Unknown: Essays Towards an Aesthetic Philosophy*. London: Faber.
RENOIR, J. (1962). *My Father*. London: Fontana.
RICHARDS, I.A. (1926). *Principles of Literary Criticism* (Second ed). London: RKP.
RICOEUR, P. (1978). *The Rule of Metaphor*. London: RKP.
ROSEN, C. and H. (1973). *The Language of Primary School Children*. Harmondsworth: Penguin.
SAMPSON. G. (1921). *English for the English* (reprinted 1975). Cambridge: Cambridge University Press.
SAPIR, E. (1949). 'Language', In: MANDELBAUM (Ed). *Selected Writings of Edward Sapir*. Berkeley: University of California Press.
SAPIR, E. (1956). *Culture, Language and Personality*. Berkeley: University of California Press.
SCHOOLS COUNCIL. (1979). *English in the Eighties: a programme of support for teachers* (Working Paper 62). London: Evans Methuen Educational.
SMITH, GOODMAN and MEREDITH. (1976). *Language and Thinking in Schools*. New York: Holt, Rinehart and Winston.
SOLZHENITSYN, A. (1970). 'One Word of Truth' – *The Nobel Speech on Literature*. London: Bodley Head.
STURT, G. (1923). *The Wheelwright's Shop*. Cambridge: Cambridge University Press.
THOMAS, H. (1935). *As it was, and World Without End*. London: Heinemann.
THOMPSON, D. (1974). 'Non-Streaming *did* make a Difference', *Forum*, 16, 2.
TOLSTOY, L. (1862). 'The School at Yasnaya Polyana' in *Tolstoy on Education* (trans. WIENER, 1967). Chicago: University of Chicago Press.
TOLSTOY, L. (1865). *Anna Karenin*. (trans. ROSEMARY EDMONDS) Harmondsworth: Penguin.
VAN GOGH, V. (1882). 'Letter' In: *Dear Theo: The Autobiography of Vincent Van Gogh* (1973). London: Cassell.
VYGOTSKY, L.F. (1962). *Thought and Language* (trans. from Russian text, pub. 1934). Cambridge, Mass.: M.I.T. Press.
WALEY, A. (1939). *Three Ways of Thought in Ancient China*. London: Allen and Unwin.
WALSH, W. (1959). *The Uses of Imagination*. London: Chatto.
WHITEHEAD, A.N. (1929). *Process and Reality*. London: Macmillan.
WHITEHEAD, A.N. (1950). *The Aims of Education* (new ed). London: Williams and Norgate.
WHITEHEAD, F.S. (1966). *The Disappearing Dais*. London: Chatto and Windus.
WHITEHEAD, F.S. (1970). *Creative Experiment*. London: Chatto and Windus.
WHITEHEAD, F.S. (1977) (Ed) *Children and their Books*. London: Macmillan.
WILKINSON, A., (Ed) (1980). *Assessing Language Development*. Oxford: Oxford University Press.
WILLIAMS, R. (1958). *Culture and Society*. London: Chatto and Windus.
WILLIAMS, R. (1965). *The Long Revolution*. London: Chatto and Windus.

WILSON, J.D. (1916). *Poetry and the Child* English Association Pamphlet no. 34.
    Oxford: Oxford University Press.
WINNICOTT, D. (1971). *Playing and Reality*. London: Tavistock.
WITKIN, R. (1974). *The Intelligence of Feeling*. London: Heinemann Educational.
WOLF, T. (1978). *Reading Reconsidered*. Berkeley: University of California Press.